# DAUGHTERS OF DURGA

# DAUGHTERS OF DURGA

Dowries, Gender Violence
and Family in Australia

Manjula Datta O'Connor

MELBOURNE
UNIVERSITY
PRESS

MELBOURNE UNIVERSITY PRESS
An imprint of Melbourne University Publishing Limited
Level 1, 715 Swanston Street, Carlton, Victoria 3053, Australia
mup-contact@unimelb.edu.au
www.mup.com.au

First published 2022
Text © Manjula Datta O'Connor, 2022
Design and typography © Melbourne University Publishing Limited, 2022

This book is copyright. Apart from any use permitted under the *Copyright Act 1968* and subsequent amendments, no part may be reproduced, stored in a retrieval system or transmitted by any means or process whatsoever without the prior written permission of the publishers.

Every attempt has been made to locate the copyright holders for material quoted in this book. Any person or organisation that may have been overlooked or misattributed may contact the publisher.

Text design and typesetting by Megan Ellis
Cover design by Nada Backovic
Cover image by © Ninassart
Printed in Australia by McPherson's Printing Group

 A catalogue record for this book is available from the National Library of Australia

9780522878257 (paperback)
9780522879155 (paperback, signed)
9780522878264 (ebook)

# Contents

Introduction     1

1. Women of India     11
2. The Happy Family     25
3. The Costs of a Hierarchical Society     38
4. A Daughter is Only Ever a Guest in the Father's Home     61
5. The Malady (Dowry Deaths)     85
6. Societal Fear Paralyses Social Change     97
7. Wish You Were a Son     118
8. Caste and Honour Killings     127
9. Huge Cost of Mental Illness     145
10. Migration, Family and Suicide     162
11. Education is the Key to Equality     177
12. The Burden on Men of Indian Society     196
13. Actions Against Dowry Abuse in Australia     212
14. The Way Forward: *Manusmriti* Reimagined     223

Acknowledgments     231
Notes     237
Bibliography     253
Index     283

# Introduction

In the past decade, some Indian women in Australia have been dying in ways that have left the Australian-Indian community shocked and searching for answers. Of a cluster of suicides in a small area of Melbourne—seven of them in total—more than half had contacted police for family violence.[1]

One woman per week is killed in Australia by a current or former intimate partner. Our Watch, the peak Australian body charged with prevention of the deadly problem, labels family violence a serious problem in Australia.[2]

It touches all segments of society, and never fails to shock. It is worse when it affects the people we know. We can no longer deny it. It threatens to disrupt our peace of mind.

One of the leading community members said, 'we are blindsided, we did not see it coming'. Previous reports of murder-suicides reported in 2012 to 2016 were once again under focus in 2022, when Raj Sharma was charged with the murder of his wife Poonam Sharma and their six-year-old daughter Vanessa.[3] A series of murders, then, of women and children in Victoria by the men they loved and who were meant to love them. Why were women and children dying in domestic violence episodes? The Indian community was in shock.[4]

Why the profound silence around mental health, and family violence?

We get by without thinking about it.

My work as a psychiatrist to women of mainly Indian and South Asian heritage had already given me some of these answers, and writing this book crystallised my thoughts.

Indian and South Asian women share many experiences with women across the world, but their lives are also different in significant and unique ways. It is in these differences that answers and solutions can be found. Answers and solutions that will make the lives of this group better. Answers and solutions that will keep them alive.

Exposure to industrialisation and modernisation is changing India, and with it, the lives of Indian women. They are better educated than their mothers, and wealthier. But sociologists and academics are curious: will modernisation benefit the status of Indian women? Will they continue to be the subjects of traditional societal gender roles of modesty and submission, or will we see a change in women's position in the family and society?[5] Is the new Indian woman going to be brave and claim her power, like the Goddess Durga, or will she follow the ideal of the submissive, pleasing wife modelled on Sita—the consort of Lord Rama of the epic Ramayana?[6]

Goddess Durga (literally 'the Fort' in Sanskrit) is the mother-protector of the Hindu Universe, the goddess of power. Durga is multi-limbed, and rides atop a lion or tiger so that she may always be ready to battle evil from any direction. Men pray to her. In the great battle of Mahabharat, Lord Krishna urges Arjuna to pray to Durga before the war. Women hope to imbibe her power.[7]

But Sita's submissiveness and modesty is the ideal of Indian womanhood: a wife, who uncomplainingly administers to the needs of her husband, and bows down to his will. Sita is the consort of Lord Rama in Valmiki's *Ramayana*. Written more than two thousand years ago, it is one of the most significant and influential narratives that has shaped Indian culture.

Professor Amartya Sen's book *The Argumentative Indian* influenced me profoundly. In bringing India's missing women into the light—a result of systemic elimination of females in utero and in infancy—it illuminated the lives of those women of India, and Indian women in Australia, who suffer abuse. In its pages, I understood the suffering of Indian women from the cradle to the grave, living as a burden to their families from conception to widowhood.

Life without bearing a child, preferably a son, is incomplete for many women in South Asia. This event brings joy, power, gifts and status. Perhaps even an aspiration that she will one day become a powerful mother-in-law and have the authority to inflict onto her daughter-in-law the abuse and violence she herself suffered. Deniz Kandiyoti, a Turkish writer, identified this patriarchal bargain in 1988: women suffer at the hands of the patriarchy, yet pray to have sons and will give them preferential treatment over daughters in the hope they will get power back from their association with their son. If she is widowed, she will once again become a burden to her son and his family. As a woman, she will not have the resources to live alone. And, even if she managed to, she would find herself in a dangerous situation.[8] Living alone as a single or widowed woman is a serious safety risk for many in India.

More than twelve years ago, I began my work supporting victim-survivors of domestic family violence in Australia. The most hard-hitting stories kept coming—transnational abuse, dowry exploitation, economic exploitation, domestic servitude, and sexual exploitation. How could these things be stopped? To answer this question, I had to find answers to many others. What makes women travel to Australia? What are the roles of globalisation, culture, migration, acculturation stress, the pressures of moving into a new country? My passion to find answers was sustained by the parents of victim-survivors, many of whom had travelled from India to Australia to support their daughters and were themselves often suffering from extreme distress, insomnia, clinical depression and anxiety triggered by the pain of what their daughter had been through. Marriage is an essential, defining moment in many women's lives, but it's not always a happy one, be it in India or elsewhere in the world—including Australia.

I was luckier.

I am a child of a middle-class, educated family. We had no affiliations to caste. I grew up knowing that we as children could bring female or male classmates and friends to our home, or if I was to choose a partner for myself, it would not be a big problem for my family. Many of my girlfriends' families were the same. So, when I fell in love with a man well outside of my family's caste and religion, an Australian man of Irish-English descent,[9] my parents and family did not put up any barriers.

When I came to Australia in the early 1970s as a young wife, I had some idea that Australia would be very different to India. But I did not know how different.

I loved this country from the day I arrived. Almost the first thing I noticed was the freedom from a persistent fear felt by every woman in India—that of being called 'characterless' or a 'loose woman' if she spoke to a member of the opposite sex. At medical school in India—a supposedly modern and progressive institution—I'd had a male friend who was a year senior to me. I found his company intellectually stimulating and would often go to have a conversation with him. One day he told me, 'People say you are shameless,' in a tone of voice that was both protective and censuring of me. I had no idea that such things were being said, and this only added to my deep-seated feeling of oppression. The modern education of intelligent young women and men was not bringing in the fresh breeze of new ideas or new freedoms for Indian women. I stopped talking to him.

As a small child, I always felt uncomfortable when I went to play with my friend next door. Her father would make us sit in his lap and I can recall feeling his erection and not knowing what it was but becoming very anxious. After this happened a couple of times, I stopped going to her house. Around this time, a middle-aged man grabbed me and took me to a fire-escape staircase and shut the door. I felt fear—something evil was going to happen. I was not sure what it was, but I knew I had to escape from him. Quick thinking at the age of five, I said, 'I can hear my mother, she is calling me.' He opened the door and let me go.

Harassment and assault, and even rape were ever-present dangers for a young girl growing up in India. The societal pressure was not on men to change, but on young women to always prove and protect their 'honour' in the face of men's behaviour. In public spaces, particularly, extreme caution was needed. In the first two years of going to medical school, I had to travel there by bus. I would always attempt to grab the seat labelled 'women only', but every other woman would want that seat too, looking to avoid the gratuitous staring, touching and rubbing we were subjected to. There was some public discussion about this behaviour—dubbed 'eve-teasing', which both minimised and mischaracterised what was occurring—but even now, it's still ever-present. In 2012, a physiotherapy student, Nirbhaya, was gang-raped by five men in South Delhi, in a moving bus at night. The driver stopped the bus to rape her as well. Not even having a male friend with her protected her from what they wanted to do. She later died from her injuries. According to the BBC report, these were 'ordinary, apparently normal and certainly unremarkable men'. The case drew worldwide attention. One man, a bystander who had nothing to do with the case, told a BBC reporter that she should not have fought back. These accusations—also made by women doing the work of patriarchy—inhibit and constrict the lives of girls and women all over India, and bring shame and dishonour to the woman's family. Boys and men have no such constraints. They are free to explore the world and speak to whomever they wish. They may gamble and drink. Their behaviour brings no shame or dishonour. And the patriarchal system remains firmly in place: favouring males, enforcing unequal treatment, and ensuring women's lives remain secondary to those of men.

In Australia, that women talked to men or vice versa was simply not noteworthy. There was no concept of shame and dishonour for the family, only accountability to oneself.

But it also dawned on me that Australia has its own deep work to do regarding racism and colonisation.[10] Family violence is still present. In Australia it touches 1 in 4 women, and 1 in 13 men suffer partner abuse.[11] One woman per week is killed by an intimate partner.

Violence against women is a wicked global problem, not confined to any class, religion, and country. The question is what tools or tactics are used, by whom, and in what context.

Over time, I was to learn the tools of the "trade" of domestic violence used by men and their families against South Asian—including Indian—immigrant women, as well as what could be possible solutions.

In my role helping victim-survivors, I was reaping the fruits of the hard work done towards the end of the nineteenth century and at the beginning of the twentieth century by women's and feminist movements of both India and Australia. In pre-independence India, many women led social reform movements. Sarojini Naidu and Kamala Devi Chattopadhyay were among the first women to participate in the freedom struggle. Then there were others, like Dr Muthulakshmi Reddy (1886–1968), the first woman House Surgeon of Maternity Hospital in Madras Constituency; Amrit Kaur (1889–1964), the first woman to head WHO and Minister in India; and Purnima Sinha (1927–2015), a physicist who built her own X-ray machine from recycled war materials in Calcutta. Numerous other women, such as Savitribai Phule (1831–1897), Tarabai Shinde (1850–1910), and Ramabai Ranade (1863–1924), spoke up for disadvantaged women. Women leaders also proved to be catalysts for female participation in political processes, influential enough to get Indian women the vote in new India in 1947.[12] These women defied the patriarchal silence and paved the way for millions of Indian women to find their voices, myself included. Simultaneously in Australia, Edith Cowan, Mary Lee, Rose Scott, Vida Goldstein, and many others were fighting for women's rights. Their pioneering work led to the age of sexual consent being raised to sixteen and equal inheritance laws. In 1902, Australia became one of the first countries in the world to give women the right to vote in federal elections, and the first country in the world in which women could stand for national parliament (except, in both instances, for those who were 'aboriginal natives' of Australia, Africa, Asia and the Pacific Islands).

With the passage of time, life changes, and a new partner, I started to examine my position as an immigrant in Australia. I acquired a deeply analytical attitude to my continuous study of Western versus Eastern cultures, and of Indian versus Australian culture. I learnt of the enormous strengths that lie within both cultures and their values. Simultaneously, I learnt of their weaknesses and harmful cultural practices.

Migration, I recognised, added yet another layer of complexity to the life of South Asian women and men. There are many challenges to be faced—changing gender roles, greater freedoms, loss of family, new language, and more. How do these add to vulnerabilities like family violence and mental health issues?[13] Many of these issues are dealt with in this book.

After more than a quarter century in Australia, I reconnected with my heritage through teaching at Dev Sanskriti Vishwavidyalaya, a university in Haridwar where students come from all over India to learn a mix of Eastern and Western subjects. The university is 'devoted to the preservation and propagation of the Indian Culture … that could combine the precepts of practical knowledge (*shiksha*) and spiritual education (*vidya*) to create truly enlightened individuals'[14]. The university has a program that welcomes foreign tutors and lecturers willing to donate teaching time in return for board and lodging. I would go to the university twice a year for six weeks at a time and enjoy the calm and quiet; its gates leave the busy cacophony of cars and trucks outside. The residential quarters are surrounded by gardens and a temple. There are many buildings for the senior academic staff, lecture halls, a library, and a student hostel with separate areas for men and women.

I connected with these students, women and men of all socio-economic backgrounds, and I learnt to speak Hindi properly. I taught Western subjects of psychiatry, mental illness, diagnoses, neurochemistry, medication, and cognitive behavioural therapy, while the students taught me yoga and meditation. I often met with the dean and with the vice-chancellor, Professor Surya Prasad Mishra, to discuss the concept of combining Eastern and Western treatments for patients suffering mental illness. And those patients who attended the university's clinic received both types of treatments to achieve the maximum benefit—meditation, prayer, and their intense belief in their faith, sometimes coupled with appropriate medications. Through working with children of nomads who were in primary school at a local NGO Divya Prem Sewa Mission in Hardiwar, I learnt about the lives and resilience of some of the poorest people. I also met victims of domestic violence. Their experiences reinforced the truisms stated in *The Argumentative Indian*.

Finding solutions to the many problems faced by Indian women, whether in India or Australia, couldn't be done without fully learning the life cycle of the Indian woman. This book is the culmination of fifty years of thinking. It is a distillation of analysis and thoughts about my culture in comparison with other Asian and Western cultures. It wonders how to harness the strengths that existed in ancient knowledge and combine them with the modern evolving India and the science-based culture of the West to shape the destiny of the modern, mobile Indian woman, whether in India or in Australia.

It is an attempt to support modern-day activists and advocates in line with the vision shared by Prime Minister Nehru in the most famous speech in the history of modern India, delivered to the people of India on the day of independence from the British Raj, the 15th of August 1947:

Long years ago we made a tryst with destiny, and now the time comes when we shall redeem our pledge, not wholly or in full measure, but very substantially.

At the stroke of the midnight hour, when the world sleeps, India will awake to life and freedom. A moment comes, which comes but rarely in history, when we step out from the old to the new, when an age ends, and when the soul of a nation, long suppressed, finds utterance.[15]

The question this book seeks to answer is this: how can we enhance the living conditions of women such that both halves of a heterosexual relationship, woman and man, are recognised as equal and essential for each other's survival? Lord Shiva and the Goddess Parvati in Hinduism are always depicted as a man and a woman together, and Parvati is referred to as *ardhangini*—a Sanskrit word for a woman, which means the other half of the man. According to the sacred Hindu text Satapatha Brahmana, 'The wife is verily the half of the husband. Man is only half, not complete until he marries.'[16] How can we effect change so that society, families and individuals do not see daughters as a handicap, but rather as individuals who add strength? Where daughters and sons are equally valued, and parents do not have to wish their daughters were sons?

This book is a synthesis of my education, cross-cultural experiences, research, deep clinical observations, and community-based work. It is built on the foundational experiences of my family life, inspired by India's thinkers and leaders, and most of all by the vibrant women of India and Australia. It gives expression to my inner thoughts and breaks the enforced silence of those women who are unable to exercise free will, who feel trapped, who are unable to see options and possibilities; it is for those who are traumatised, depressed, anxious, or suicidal; it is for those who are forced into domestic servitude or who have had their visa sponsorship withdrawn and been deported. It is for those for whom change did not come quickly enough—the women who took their lives or were killed by those who were meant to love and protect them. Those seven women in one small area of Melbourne. The many, many others.

Domestic family violence is an enormous and complex issue to explore. This book has a tight scope. It is about the lives of migrant victim-survivors of domestic abuse as they presented to my clinical psychiatric practice. It does not purport to be a comprehensive treatise on the role of caste and gender in domestic violence as it is found in India; rather, it investigates some parts of the women's heritage (which I share), and its role in their problem, and solutions. These women reveal to me that while victims of abuse suffer, they are not passive; they have strengths, and they use them to survive the unspeakable abuses caused by this crime called family domestic violence.

It is a privilege to be a psychiatrist. Every day I learn about humanity from the vantage point of an insider. Though I listen to unimaginable stories of trauma and abuse suffered by my patients, usually inflicted by other humans, my patients have also taught me about human resilience and strengths and the myriad ways in which they find inner power to survive.

In recent years, spurred on by the rape of Nirbhaya in India in 2012, the concept of female 'shakti', or power of women derived from goddesses of India, has been mobilised to challenge oppression and violence suffered by women.[17] The title of this book is inspired by that movement, but it represents stories of all women. It depicts women who, as survivors of domestic or other forms of violence, have shown themselves to be strong like Goddess Durga; with power, they have shown themselves to be not passive recipients of violence. The book shows how these women can produce a meaningful change. The mythology is Hindu in origin, but the book *Daughters of Durga* represents the power of all women, no matter what segment of society they come from.

# 1
# WOMEN OF INDIA

When my father developed cancer of the liver in the year 2000, I took leave from my practice in Melbourne. I wanted to do all I could to help and to be with him in Delhi in his last months. It was painful to watch him lose weight each day, to go from a strong, healthy, once-powerful man to this thin 84-year-old in distress and pain. I decided to turn that period into something worthwhile, and I asked him to tell me his life story.

My father spoke to me about his father. In the early 1900s, my grandfather lived on the North-West Frontier of Pakistan in a province called Dera Ismail Khan, where the family attended their local temple regularly and were devout followers. They did not have a lot of money, and when my grandfather's older brother died of a heart attack they couldn't afford to pay for his funeral. They asked the priest to help them and do the cremation free of charge. He would not. This enraged my grandfather, and he had his brother cremated in the woods with no rituals. The family renounced the temples and idol worshipping, and adopted a newly formed social-religious movement—the Arya Samaj, which translates as Society of Nobles. Founded in 1875, in British times, by revered thinker and ascetic scholar Swami Dayananda Sarasvati, Arya Samaj is a modern Hindu movement inclined towards programs of social reform and away from superstition. It is based on the wisdom of ancient Hindu scriptures, the Vedas, written 3000–4000 years ago in the ancient and highly evolved language of Sanskrit, known as the mother of all languages. Vedas are known to Hindus as the 'revealed truth' spoken by God to ancestors.

The Arya Samaj opposes caste-based discrimination. It does not believe in the abhorrent concept of a caste system, and the 'untouchability' of the so-called lowest caste, Dalits (originally Sudras), or in child marriage, which was widespread when outlawed in 1929.[1] It believes in the empowerment of women. These are the values of my family, and the values I grew up with.

Mahatma Gandhi, who paralysed the British Raj by mobilising nation-wide peaceful spiritual protests (called Satyagraha), was also a follower. He believed in and respected women's abilities and pushed for women's equality in the early 1900s. The same values were reinforced by his protégé Jawaharlal Nehru, who was the popular leader of the Indian National Congress during the struggle for independence from Britain and, later, prime minister of India, from 1947 to 1964.

We children adored Prime Minister Nehru. I can recall listening to his Independence Day speeches every year on the 15th of August. They were always stirring and, with the tricolour flag swirling on top of the Red Fort, we felt very patriotic and proud of our country. India was on the march to becoming a modern country. He inspired us children, me and my younger sister and brother. He envisaged the women of India to be modern and fearless. There would be no dowry and no female feticide in the land of Nehru. Women would be educated, leaders, equal to men and equally valued. But this support for women was not Westernised: it was firmly based on ancient Indian cultural practice.

Gender relations are largely power-based in societies globally—largely patriarchal systems devised by men.[2] But in India, women were educated and mixed with educated men, according to ancient Indian traditions dating back more than 3000 years.[3] In the Rig-Veda period (1000–1500 BC), women in India enjoyed an unprecedented position of strength and respect, described beautifully in the eloquent poems of the time. The Vedas were written in Sanskrit by a number of unknown writers, including, many believe, more than twenty women. Of Goddess Saraswati:

> Thou art the goddess of letters ... Thou, beautiful goddess, art knowledge of devotion, great knowledge, mystic knowledge, and spiritual knowledge, which confers eternal liberation. Thou are the science of reasoning, the three Vedas, the arts and sciences: thou art moral and political science.[4]

The national character of modern Indian womanhood is strongly influenced by its educated women: religiously equal, politically savvy, fearless warriors and queens, poetesses and ones who were allowed to choose their own partners in a ceremony called *swamvaar* depicted in poems of Rig-Vedas, the dramatic stories in *Puranas*, the tales of *Mahabharata*. The Upanishads—part of the Vedas—contain accounts of learned women, including that of Gargi, an eminent philosopher who debated her male peers in the King's court.[5] Early evidence of literature by women can be seen in Therigatha—Buddhist verses written in India over a 300-year period from sixth-century BC to third-century BC. Its seventy-three poems and 525 verses were written by early women practitioners of Buddhism from all walks of life—they were royalty, sex workers, wives, courtesans, mothers, widows, and so on.

But the rise of women was not acceptable to Manu, the great legislator of the first century CE. In his ancient legal text, the *Manusmriti*, which told of duties, rights, laws, conduct and virtues, and formed the basis of Hindu law, he wrote the decline of the Indian woman. Manu shrank her world to one of a dependent creature—dependent on father as a daughter, on husband as a wife, and on the son as a widow. As Clarisse Bader describes: 'Manu minutely detailed the duties of man to the gods, but as far as woman, what a fall!'[6] He at once demonises women and Dalits and solidifies the hierarchy of the caste system and the patriarchy, elevating men and the highest caste, the Brahmins. Today's customs of son preference have not changed in more than a thousand years.

One may forgive the *Manusmriti* as being a document of its time, when the whole world was patriarchal.[7] In the contemporaneous West, the rise of patriarchy and privileging of 'masculine' characteristics—such as strength, dominance, and bravery—accompanied by a devaluing of social attributes that were seen to define womanhood, such as being submissive, emotional, nurturing, and vulnerable, began early. In the second century, Christian theologians spread the notion that female inferiority was a result of sin, depicting Eve as seductive and subordinate and inferior to Adam.[8] Women came out of the Middle Ages and fared somewhat better under the Age of Enlightenment from the eighteenth century. However, there were limited challenges to those notions in India.

Indian women under the rule of the Mughal Empire, and later Britain, were largely unable to benefit from their own ancient tradition of fearlessness, nor from the expansion of knowledge and science. They were not able to vote until 1947, when India achieved independence from Britain.

There are, of course, exceptions.

For part of the Mughals' 300-year rule, a woman played an unprecedented role in running the empire. Emperor Jahangir's reign, from 1605 to 1627, was a time of unprecedented prosperity, commerce, and vast national and international trading. It was an impressive period of stability and art, and Jahangir's wife, the Empress Nur Jahan (translated as 'light of universe'), was the most powerful woman in seventeenth-century India.

Nur didn't belong to a royal family. Her family—wealthy noblemen—had fled Persia to settle in India. She was married off but widowed at a young age, then taken into the Emperor Jahangir's harem (he already had nineteen wives), where she ascended to winning his heart and becoming his favourite queen. In that male-dominated world of kings and wars and battles, Nur Jahan proved herself to be a remarkable leader and an astute politician. As Jahangir became physically weak due to alcohol and opium use, he relied on her, allowing her to rule the Empire alongside him. She made decisions to protect his subjects, hunted, and attended court meetings where only men were allowed. She also wrote poetry, designed clothing, built gardens, and issued her own imperial orders and coins. The coins showed both her and the Emperor's names. She was a patron of the arts and played polo as a sport with other women.[9]

This is an uncommon story of a powerful female figure in patriarchal times, when women were playthings and part of rich men's harems. Strong women were ignored by history or judged as manipulators, opportunists, or murderers.

The more typical treatment of women of that period was that of Jahangir's father Akbar—the third Mughal King of India. Akbar, who reigned from 1556 to 1605, was a successful king who implemented a modern administration, encouraged cultural development and increased trade with Europe. But the women of his court—daughters, wives, concubines—stayed behind the walls of harem, and he called them 'the veiled ones'.

During this period, the system of 'purdah' was introduced by the Rajput and Muslim communities. Women were to remain behind a curtain and keep themselves covered. Their faces were to be veiled, especially in the presence of male family members. The purdah system, which was prevalent among the royal families, nobles, and the merchant class prior to the Muslim empire, began to have an influence upon ordinary families.

Through the East India Company, Britain gained control over much of India from the 1750s. By 1890, about 6000 British officials ruled 250 million Indians. The British espoused the myth that they were enlightened rulers, and that the modernisation of India couldn't have happened without them.[10]

Yet India invented the concept of zero; it was the land of Vedas and Shastras written in Sanskrit, which is one of three ancient documented languages that arose from a common root language now referred to as Proto-Indo-European language, some 3000 years before the British arrival. Ancient texts explored medicine, surgery, the art of governance, yoga for mind and body, mathematics, and astronomy. India would have also come organically to science and the modernisation of women. It did not need the British Raj to do so.

The British introduced various legal reforms to enhance the status of women—while writing out of the history books the key role played by Indian modernists and reformers, including Raja Ram Mohan Roy and other enlightened Indians such as Pandit Vidyasagar. These laws included forbidding sati (in which a widow immolates herself on her husband's funeral pyre), female infanticide and child marriage; they raised the age of consent, allowed widows to remarry, and improved women's inheritance rights.

But the impact of British colonial rule for women was not purely progressive. It was also harmful to Indian women.

Hindu law was flexible, based on custom, able to be interpreted in line with prevailing opinion, and embodied a vast diversity of approaches according to cultural, regional and caste differences.[11] Most law was unwritten, except that of the Brahmins, the highest caste. For example, the *Manusmriti* was written by the Brahmins, for the Brahmins. According to scholars Liddle and Joshi, 'Its rules mostly applied to high caste women who were subject to the strictest legal constraints on their activities in order to preserve the purity of caste. For instance, most high caste women could not own immovable family property, could marry only once even if widowed in infancy and were not allowed divorce. Lower caste women had no customary prohibition on divorce or remarriage, and owning property.' But the British, accustomed to the British laws being written down and applied uniformly, interpreted the *Manusmriti* laws as a universal code for everyone in India, making the once-flexible system into a rigid system that became unfair to all women of India.[12]

At that stage, Nayar communities of Kerala had a matriarchal system, lower castes allowed relationships between pubertal women and men without cohabiting, and women generally lived with their parents and owned property. The patriarchal and Christian British rule could not accept the concept of women being in charge of property and the family line, and their subsequent 'onslaught against Nayar organisation of sexuality and inheritance destroyed the structure of the matrilineal family, removed the women's sexual rights, abolished collective ownership of property and dispossessed the women from their inheritance.'[13]

Indian women began to fight back.

The Rajput warrior queen, the Rani of Jhansi, led her army against the British in the 1850s.[14] The Rani was trained in warfare by her widowed father who had brought her up in unconventional ways. She is said to have been outspoken and confident. A swordfighter. She assembled an army of rebels, including women, and fought the British Army valiantly for two weeks, with her four-year-old adopted son Damodar Rao tied to her back. She died on 17 June 1857. 'The dauntless bravery of the Ranee [sic] was a subject of great conversation, in the soldiers' camp,' a British army surgeon reminisced.[15]

From the beginning of the 1900s, women of India began organising themselves into an anti-British force to be reckoned with. This could not have happened had they been an entirely enslaved or oppressed lot in pre-British India. Or perhaps they drew on their cultural history. After all, India is the land of powerful goddesses—Laxmi, the goddess of wealth; Sarasvati, the goddess of education; Durga, the goddess of power; and Parvati, the goddess who stood next to her powerful husband Lord Shiva and was *ardhangini*—meaning 'half his body'—these women have been part of the psyche of Indian women since time immemorial.[16]

In 1943, in Singapore, the nationalist Subhas Chandra Bose created the Rani Jhansi Regiment (RJR), an all-women corps of soldiers. They were approximately 5000 in number, drawn from the Indian diaspora in Burma, Malaya and Singapore, where racism and patriarchal and imperial attitudes were rife. The women were seen to be lower in social status than men, and many who joined from the rubber estates in Malaya 'lived and worked under conditions that approached slavery. Sexual abuse by the mainly white estate managers was a common occurrence. The Rani of Jhansi Regiment offered an environment where the young women found themselves respected and free of the social stigma of 'coolie' status. Now with their heads held high, they experienced a level of egalitarianism in the company of their Rani comrades that they had not known before.'[17]

The women, recognising that it was patriarchy re-enforced by colonialism that oppressed them, joined the men to oust the British Empire, fighting under the Indian National Army in the Second World War and allied with Japan.

Sarojini Naidu, poet and activist, and Kamla Nehru, freedom fighter and wife of the future Prime Minister, along with many other women, participated in Gandhi's Satyagraha, the passive political resistance organised by Mahatma Gandhi and which gave momentum to *Swaraj* self-rule. Fighting with peace, they went to jail and fasted like their male counterparts.[18] As Jawaharlal Nehru wrote: 'Most of us menfolk were in prison. And then a remarkable thing happened. Our women came to the front and took charge of the struggle. Women had always been there of course but now there was an avalanche of them, which took not only the British government but their own menfolk by surprise.'[19]

Indian women played a decisive role in the 1947 downfall of the British Raj. Their actions challenged the stereotypes of Indian women—they showed themselves to be complex and resilient, not simply the subjugated creatures the British had supposed. They came out in dozens, women of every class, and caste, educational status, to participate in Satyagraha.[20]

The women also recognised that the patriarchal family structure itself was oppressive, and made demands to improve family life for women through 'the Hindu Code'.[21] A thinker and a freedom fighter, Dalit leader Dr BR Ambedkar, wrote India's constitution and incorporated women's ideals into legislation.[22] The Hindu Code, as it was called, advocated monogamy, inter-caste and inter-religion marriage, divorce, widow remarriage, and equal inheritance. The Hindu Code laid a framework for gender equality in India. It would usher in the modern era.

Many women in this time of movement against the British Raj went on to become leaders in free India and globally, inspiring younger generations of Indian women. To name but a couple Sarojini Naidu, educated in the 1840s, became the first woman President of the Indian National Congress in 1929, and first governor of Uttar Pradesh, and Kamaladevi Vijaya Lakshmi Pandit, sister of Jawaharlal Nehru and an activist in pre-independent India, went on to have distinguished diplomatic career. She was the first woman to hold the post of President of UN General Assembly in 1953.

But there are many ways in which their fight, the many pioneering women's aspirations, Swami Dayananda's dream, Nehru's and Gandhi's ambitions, and Dr Ambedkar's aspirations for India have not come to fruition. The 1974 Status of Women Commission report, 'Towards Equality', brought to attention women's low and diminishing status in Indian society. Women continued to have an inferior status in many areas—political, economic, and social. The Indian women activists alerted the nation to rampant crimes against women, including dowry abuse, dowry murders, sex selective abortions and rapes.

In India, the son preference that has prevailed since the times of *Manusmriti* risks the lives of Indian girls and young women. Despite laws to ban sex selective abortions and persistent social education campaigns in India such as Beti Bachao Beti Padao (Protect Your Daughter, Educate Your Daughter), the practice continues, and has travelled globally with the Indian diaspora.[23] In Canada, South Asian second-generation mothers who already had two girls were two times more likely to have an abortion waiting for a male child to be conceived. This led to an increase of male births in this group, with a ratio of 280 boys to 100 girls. Australian mothers from India had boys at a rate of about 104 to 100 for their first child (the natural ratio), but for their second child, almost 122 boys were born to every 100 girls.[24]

Why is there an obsession with having sons? There are many answers to this question, including economic, religious and social norms that favour sons. One of the social norms is that parents expect sons to provide financial and emotional support in their old age (more on that later); but perhaps the most important one lies in India's patrilocal culture, whereby daughters have to give up their biological family upon marriage, relocate to their husband and in-laws' home, and serve their new family.

Countless women I've treated during my work have spoken about what happened if they tried to contact their parents as new brides. They were told: 'You cannot speak to your mother or sister for more than a few minutes, you belong to this family now.' They were beaten and belittled. I once treated a young man who came of his own accord after having perpetrated violence against his wife for talking to her parents. He loved his new wife and did not want to lose her. I asked him how it would feel to him if he had to leave his family altogether and go to live with his wife's parents. There was visible disgust on his face as he said, 'I cannot even imagine. It is too hard.' I pressed him. He said, 'I would feel very uncomfortable.' He recognised the loss of power associated with living in someone else's family home. Since the time of *Manusmriti*, which states that a girl must live with her parents if she cannot find a suitable groom, Indian society has not stopped to think about the plight of the woman who is asked to lose contact with her biological family, fit in with a strange family she barely knows, treat her in-laws as her own parents and meet their demands of domestic servitude. The son, on the other hand, gets to stay home with his parents and bring a wife home. In addition, he gains dowry gifts, gold, and cash. His wife is asked to look after his parents and family, she is expected to produce children and especially sons to carry on the name of the family. In this system, who would not want a son?

To date, no country has achieved equality between men and women. The Global Gender Gap Index was introduced by the World Economic Forum in 2006 as a framework for capturing gender equality across nations, tracking progress annually. The index laid out measurable criteria around four areas: health, education, economy and politics.[25] The top ten countries on the 2020 Global Gender Gap Index include Iceland, Scandinavian nations, Nicaragua, New Zealand, Ireland, Spain, Rwanda and Germany. On average, they have closed only 68 per cent of the gap. Australia slipped from the thirty-ninth position in 2018 (out of 149 nations) to the forty-fourth in 2020 (out of 153 nations). India, too, fell from 108th in 2018 to 112th in 2020, while New Zealand maintained its spot at seventh. In Australia, educational access for girls is at number one in the world; however, although Australian women first stood for election in 1903, it took forty years for the first woman to be elected to parliament—one of the longest gaps across the world. Even now, Australia just makes it into the top fifty countries for political representation of women.[26] (India is nineteenth on this measure, and 114th for educational access.) Violence against women in Australia remains high, at one in three women being directly affected over the course of their lifetime. On average, one woman is killed each week in Australia, and one in two women have experienced sexual harassment or violence.[27]

I could not contain my shock when just last year, a GP friend in Melbourne told me that a mother had come into their clinic wanting labial surgery for her twelve-year-old daughter. She wanted her daughter to fit into a certain idea of genital beauty. Women across the world are subjected to such pressures. In the West, the obsession with appearance is all pervasive and, if taken to the extreme, is damaging if not deadly. The worst example is evident in the high rates of anorexia nervosa in Australia, where 1 in 200 women will suffer from the eating disorder. (One in 11 sufferers is male, though this ratio is on the increase.) Twenty per cent of people diagnosed with anorexia nervosa will die of self-imposed starvation.[28] India's modern women have also succumbed to this pressure, and the rate of anorexia nervosa—previously a relatively unknown condition in Asia—in the past two decades is becoming a greater concern to psychiatrists of India, especially in affluent areas such as Delhi.[29] It used to be an adolescent problem, but now it starts earlier, sometimes even in primary school. Orthodontic braces being worn on teeth purely for cosmetic reasons is another uncomfortable, very expensive trend. Beauty ideals differ across countries and generations; for example, plastic surgery to enhance breast size is common across Western countries, but in Brazil, smaller breasts and round bottoms are preferred. The beauty pressures on Indian women are influenced by invading forces over millennia; Aryans with lighter skins fuelled obsession with white skin, reinforced by both class divides and the white colonial rulers. South Asian women are pressured to whiten their skin, even as their counterparts in the West are tanning their bodies.[30]

What price must women pay to look the 'right' way? The influences are powerful, and unconsciously imbibed, driven by advertising and social media. This is culture largely dominated by a masculine sensibility. The women of India, Australia and the world are awake to this, but everyone must work harder, and speak louder, to condemn the oppressive nature of societal expectations.[31]

Indian women in India suicide at a rate more than twice that of Australian women.[32] In Australia, young First Nations peoples experience four times greater risk of suicide than other Australians. Different risk factors are at play. Colonisation and the resultant lack of cultural continuity, lower social connectedness and support from communities are some factors associated with greater risk for Indigenous peoples.[33] In India, women are more restricted and less educated than men; they do not have the same access to information, are not as often employed as men, and not as often employed in high level positions; they have less income and less superannuation/retirement income.[34] All these things lower a woman's power within the family, and unequal power, combined with entrapment, are key contributors to family violence; which, in turn, is associated with higher suicide rates and homicides, as well as a significant dollar cost to society. As immigrant women in Australia, they are subject to isolation from family support networks and family violence, making it a dangerous combination.[35]

Globally, domestic violence costs twenty-five times more than war and terrorism.[36] Government support for programs to enhance women's empowerment is not enough and gender equality is a concept that will not gain traction easily.[37] The government and NGO sectors need to engage men and boys, much more than they are currently doing.[38]

When I arrived as an Indian migrant in Australia in the early 1970s, I could not help but compare the two countries. Once, they were united as Gondwanaland, but they are far and separate now. Although Australia is an ancient land with an Indigenous culture more than 50 000 years old, white settler culture was implanted just over two hundred years ago. India's civilisation and culture, initially settled 65 000 years ago by out-of-Africa migration, gradually evolved into a complex society more than five thousand years ago and has continued largely uninterrupted.[39] And together, the ancient Vedas, religion, traditions and the laws of *Manusmriti* have led to the evolution of a highly complex societal and family structure, one that creaks and groans with age and needs oiling with new ideas and customs.

# 2
# THE HAPPY FAMILY

RC Dutt's classic *The Civilization of India,* written in 1900, provided a powerful rebuttal of colonialist James Mills' portrayal of Hindu culture's degenerate treatment of women in the family. With painstaking translation of the Vedas, Dutt demonstrated that women were intellectual companions of their husbands and affectionate helpers in the 'Vedic golden age' of India. They were deemed capable of high culture and religious discourse.[1]

There was a decline in the status of women after that; however, cultures are not static.

So let us imagine the ideal image of a modern-day typical Australian-Indian family, in the mind of a migrant Indian, and the relationships between the husband, wife, and their two young adult children. In the family kitchen, the father is singing a happy song as he cooks breakfast for everyone, and his wife is a smiling, loving, demure, stay-at-home mother. His two children are gifted and beautiful; both the daughter and son attend university. The daughter is a studious type and gets the highest marks in all her assignments, while the son is an award-winning athlete. They are obedient and well behaved. They make their parents happy by living up to their expectations. The father fulfils his duty and provides for them.

The ideal Indian man is a perfect father-provider. He praises his children and gives them gifts. He also makes decisions for the family. He is a benevolent patriarch—meaning that he is the male head of a family, the household—the one who makes all important decisions. A benevolent patriarch is someone who makes well-meaning decisions, cares for his family, deeply loves them and wants the best for them. He also sees himself as the main provider for the family.

Indian and South Asian homes are largely headed by benevolent patriarchs. The children and the wife are fully cognisant of his love for them, they appreciate his hard work, and they respectfully accept his authority. The son gets to win the scholarships and go outside the home to study or play sport, to explore the bigger world. The daughter will dutifully study at home. The gender norms will be reinforced—he learns how to be a man and a provider like his father, and she will learn how to follow in her mother's footsteps as the submissive wife.

In this system, the concept of mutual obligation is completely rational. Roles in this family are clearly defined. The patriarch provides financial support, guidance and love to all members of the family. They, in turn, are obliged to live by society's rules which are also his rules; the family is governed by their society.

Therefore, in South Asian families, Western notions of equality and individualism are not encouraged. Their close family ties cannot withstand such subversive notions that support individuals to think independently and aim for a totally different way of thinking. This helps to maintain stability for South Asian families and societies. But at what cost? And who bears the cost? The family, the individual or the society? Or is it all three?

My father was a benevolent patriarch. He was highly educated with a double degree—a first-class Masters in economics and a degree in law, from the time of the British Raj (the period of British rule on the Indian subcontinent between 1858 and 1947). After moving to India as a refugee from Pakistan, he found a good job in the new government and rose to the top. He cared deeply for all of us—my mother, me, and my siblings, but also the entire extended family—aunts, uncles, cousins, my grandparents—who in turn saw him as a role model and sought him out for advice. He made all the important decisions and my mother deferred to his judgement.[2]

It worked—except for when it didn't.

Let us consider a situation where he was challenged in some way. Over our schooling, for example. Although my father and mother wanted us to go to a private school, it would be expensive, prohibitively so. My mother would have to work. She had trained as a schoolteacher during the British Raj, which was rare for a woman to have done. In the 1950s, there was a nationwide shortage of schoolteachers, and my mother was offered a job at the prestigious Delhi Public School. My mother was eager to start teaching: she would feel valued, she would use her training, it would bring much-needed income into the family, and we children would receive a free education at the school. It was a neat solution.

My mother discussed her exciting job offer with her husband, as most people would find normal—a married couple discussing major decisions. But was this a discussion between equals? Did he try to understand her reasoning? Did he explore the pros and cons of her job offer? My father said no. He told her it was more important for her to stay home and look after us. She tried very hard to convince him, but he had the last say. She was deeply disappointed. She had tried to modernise our family and emancipate herself, and she had failed.

We all ended up going to a small private school for part of our schooling and later to a public secondary school.

One can only imagine why he denied her 'permission' to work at the school. At one level, he was being protective of his children—she would be away from home and busy with her commitments, so perhaps he imagined we would feel abandoned or uncared for, or to fall into predatory hands. But that was unlikely, given we would be at the school with our mother. So was it about the threat to his masculine role of earning the income and providing? Would he no longer feel like the head of the household? After all, these traditional rules and roles had been established by his culture thousands of years ago.

Over the years, my father inevitably had to cope with other challenges to his self-image. How did he handle this? In situations both important and unimportant, he would become dogmatic, shout, and scare the living daylights out of us as young children and even as adults. He was retired from his senior government post at the young age of fifty-four, as mandated by the government. Unaccustomed to being irrelevant or uninfluential, he took over the food shopping for the kitchen. Previously, kitchen work had rarely concerned him. This experience is echoed by Yuchen Han of China; after retirement, his father became the 'Minister of the kitchen', and there was some 'gender reversal of kitchen work'.[3] My father would bring home huge amounts of food. My mother would have to find time to cook it all or it would go bad. Soon he discovered that this new habit was not sufficient for his needs; he found himself a bigger project. He partnered with a builder and built a commercial-cum-residential building at the site of our four-bedroom family home. It brought material luxuries, and it brought problems. The builder's secret plan to gazump the property was discovered by my father just in time.

Like many men of his era, he could not retire, look weak, or have no power. He lived the role of the ideal man, by the masculinity 'script' handed to him by society and modelled by his father.[4]

Globally, women are idealised as submissive, passive, and sensitive. Anything else is masculine and abhorrent[5]. The ideal Indian woman is no exception. She is often smiling, and never angry, in the image of Sita of Ramayana. But does that reflect how she truly feels? Let us examine the time-honoured rules she has to obey. She must be sweet, smile, and respect her husband at all times. She cannot criticise him or his decisions. He can speak loudly but she must not. She must be a devoted and adoring mother at all times.

What if she wanted to change her life? Can modernity and traditionalism co-exist? Can she be a modern working woman, educated and worldly, and at the same time be devoted to her family and a traditional housewife? After all, about a third of Indian women are in paid employment.[6] How do they manage it?

The societally-enforced role for Indian women is as strong as ever, as has been revealed in numerous sociological studies. Philosopher Bina Gupta explores how the Indian family system—its kinship ties, obligations, and sense of reciprocal duties—are still maintained in modern times.[7] She reveals that the modern, educated, working Indian woman still places greater value on her children and the extended family than on her job. Of course, this may not be an indication of women's subordination or oppression, it simply could be about values—an indication that these women value relationships over the social and financial capital obtained through capitalism. The question is about choice. Does the society, or indeed the family, allow women independent choices, or are these 'values' the result of enforced oppression, control and submissiveness?

In a focus group study of Indian women conducted in Melbourne, questions regarding an ideal family were answered in similar terms.[8] The women felt comfortable going to work and making big decisions there, while at home they found a good deal of satisfaction in making day-to-day family-oriented decisions while their husbands made the major decisions, including around finances. These women had adapted to a Western lifestyle, but simultaneously adhered to the essential ideology of Indian culture, Hindu religion, and social and philosophical traditions.

Synonyms of the word 'traditional' include 'old', 'out-dated', 'past', 'ancient', and 'unchanging'. But there is another view, Gupta suggests: that tradition represents the crystallisation of thought and action which has survived a considerable period of time, and signifies stability and an unchanging social order.[9]

Perhaps this shows a way forward of sorts.

My father was convinced the decision he made about my mother's job offer was in the best interest of his family. And sixty years later, my mother still regrets not having been able to take the job and finds it difficult to understand why he would crush her dreams. She had to seek his permission to become modern and it was refused. The things it meant to her—being independent, goal-oriented, assertive, confident, using her education, being exposed to new ideas, to new friends and making decisions—were never realised.

My father was a highly modern man, and used his Western education when at work, yet he could not allow this sort of flexibility into his home. Perhaps the contrast between the tradition of patriarchy, which offered stability and control over the future, and the rapidly changing modern world was too much for him.

As we sat talking on one of my visits to my mother's tidy, well-furnished penthouse apartment in South Delhi, my mother and I reminisced over the incredible strength of my father and the decisions he made over their married years. Some good, some bad. She said my father was offered a post by the United Nations to work in Afghanistan as their financial advisor in 1960s. She was keen for him to take the post, though we children would have to go to a boarding school, most likely in the UK. He refused the job. He was worried about the family separating; he did not want his children to go to boarding school. He wanted a UN post in the UK or the United States where we could have been together. But that was not on the table, and he stayed working in Delhi. My mother wondered how it might have been different for her if she was respected for her opinion and if her education had been valued—if she had been treated as an equal in her marriage. But she never imagined she could contradict her husband, who she had believed was an all-knowing and powerful man, revered by society and by the extended family.

My mother had internalised her oppressed and submissive status in the marriage; it was compartmentalised and held deeply in her subconscious mind. She was only able to give herself permission to examine her hidden traumas seventeen years after her husband's death, while listening to her daughter talk about her work with victims of domestic violence.

The theory of social change states that change can occur through contact with new ideas, but only if the internal mindset is ready to adopt the change. Would she have examined this trauma had my father still been alive? I don't know. Maybe he might have been ready for change, as well. He had been listening to his children and grandchildren adopt new ideas, live in far-off lands, marry into foreign cultures. He had been accepting of some very modern processes occurring in his children's lives.

He was an intelligent man and, like many men, he accepted that life is ever-changing. He would often say, 'Eighty years is a very long time to live, anything can happen, things do change.' He had seen his life change drastically after the India-Pakistan Partition—when he was uprooted from a stable, well-off existence to an uncertain, unsafe and poor life in the new India, where, over time, things changed again and he found safety, certainty and economic security. He knew that change is the only thing that is certain in this uncertain world.

Most Indian men, whether they live in India or Australia, live up to the scripted role imposed on them by society, also known as the 'man box'[10]—to be a provider, to make all the important decisions, and to be seen to be the one who is the head of the family. They treat their wives and children with benevolence and kindness, never dreaming of raising their fists to them, though they may limit them in other ways.

But after listening to families in distress in my work—hundreds of female victims and dozens of male perpetrators—I have thought more about this generalised respect for family life in India, and in expat communities around the world. I've thought about the significant minority of families where the head of the family is not benevolent or kind. Where there is domestic violence, or the beginnings of it. Where the family is distorted in favour of the patriarch and the senior matriarch who panders to the patriarchy. And again, the question of who bears the cost of traditional ideas about gender roles comes to mind.

Another question: can a patriarch be benevolent? Is all control coercive? Or does well-meaning control—the type that is usually accepted by traditional society, and part of normal family life—not count as coercive?

Normalised control was acceptable in my family because it did not have malevolent intent. By and large, my father did not interfere with the freedom and sense of agency of the women in the family. However, his control took away my mother's agency, rendered her less powerful, less able to make decisions. She did not complain, just as Sita would not have. She normalised it in her mind.

The line between so-called 'benevolent' control and coercive control is very thin.

Not long ago in Melbourne, a young woman called Preeti contacted me in a state of distress and fear. She had been married for a couple of years—an arranged marriage in India to a non-resident groom. A year later, she'd followed her husband to Australia on a partner visa. She was new to Australian life; she had no contacts in the country, no biological family. She came with the mindset of an Indian wife—that her husband was her family and her future life. She imagined he would support her. She thought he would help her to understand Australian culture, its beaches, the shops. But he made no effort to do this. Instead, his attention was directed to his family and his mother who lived in India. Despite the distance, he would ring her daily and she would often talk to him about how to conduct his marital relationship. Perhaps he was uncertain as how to perform his role as a husband. His mother provided him with that direction, and it turned out to be misdirection.

When we met, Preeti was highly distraught and tearful, and had conflicting emotions. She was a victim of severe violence, but she also feared losing her marriage. She had left her parental home for her husband's home with the deep cultural assumption that it would be forever. She had, like many others before her, obtained an intervention order against her husband only reluctantly, when the violence became something she could no longer ignore.

Her husband had hurt her four times since she arrived in Australia—the last time had occurred the previous week, and it had been severe. I asked her about the circumstances around his violence. The problems arose, she told me, after she had dared to offer an opinion to him and his mother. His mother had come to live with them in Australia for three months. It was wintertime and Preeti's mother-in-law was cold at night. Preeti had suggested she would be better off with two warmer and thicker doonas instead of one.

Her mother-in-law replied: 'You are suggesting I take up two doonas of inferior quality?'

Her husband shouted at his wife: 'No one asked for your opinion.'

When Preeti offered a counterargument in her defence, she was hit with a closed fist and told to shut her mouth. By using violence against his wife, Preeti's husband was following his mother's directions. Preeti needed to be kept in her box, to play the role of the submissive wife and daughter-in-law who has no opinions. She could not be allowed to become too modern.

Let us consider again the cultural practice of daughters having to give up their own family upon marriage and move to serve the groom's family. Preeti, in spite of her natural intelligence, had been trained by society into knowing that her own family was not her real family. Her husband was her real family, and when she was abandoned by him, she was like an orphan. She belonged to no family, and that was frightening.

John, a young man from Kerala living in Australia, came to see me after he was rudely awakened from his behaviour towards his wife, Mary. He was following in his father's footsteps: providing well for his family and drinking heavily. As his father had done to his mother, John would regularly insult his wife, put her down, criticise her, and slap and push her. At the same time, he was no longer the family's sole provider. His wife, who was a doctor, was outperforming him. He was not able to live up to the scripted role of the husband. His grip was slipping. One day he became violent over a small argument about food. Why had she not cooked what he wanted to eat that day? She was tired, she told him, and he slapped her hard. As she answered back, he attempted to strangle her. He let go of her as she started to choke. The police came. He was charged. Something changed in him. He felt shame and disgust at himself. He'd shocked himself. He enrolled in a Men's Behaviour Change Program (MBCP).[11] At the same time, he started treatment with me, which included medications and therapy. Over the next six months, John awoke from his ignorance. He had not realised that he was repeating the patterns of his father. He had never seen his father show respect to his mother. As a young man, he had felt sorry for his mother and supported her. He remembered feeling disgust for his father and his drinking. But after marriage, he imitated his father. And this script was enforced by a society that made him the superior and more powerful partner in his marriage. Was his drinking genetically influenced or learnt? Did he drink because of his depressive illness? Or was alcohol making him depressed? How much power did society have over his violent behaviour?

When he came to see me, he was showing signs of a major depressive illness. He stopped drinking all together. He learnt the meaning of power in marriage and the abuse of that power, what controlling behaviour looks like, and saw that he was driven to demonstrate to his wife, on a daily basis, that he was superior to her in every way. His criticisms, humiliations, and the ways he demeaned her were designed to show his superiority—because inside, he was feeling anything but superior. He was threatened by his wife's success. He had felt insecure and unsure as she started to climb up the ladder of success, while his progress dwindled—his drinking had left him less competent in his professional world of IT.

John made full use of therapy and the MBCP, complied with medication, and, through this, he changed. He started to own his uncomfortable anxiety. He worked through the trauma of being an abused child, and of feeling fear and disgust towards his father. He grieved the loss of fatherly love, and understood how he had repeated this dynamic for his daughter. It was pleasing to watch him grow emotionally, as he went from a violent, drunk, aggressive, controlling, condescending man to a devoted and supportive husband and father, a caring man, an activist who supported women's rights and his own wife's professional success.

Mary, meanwhile, went through a minor depressive illness that gradually resolved as John's behaviour improved. With support from her GP and Maternal and Child Health Nurse, she recovered. She continued to work and got a prestigious job at a research institute.

While John was being abusive, Mary found herself unable to leave her husband. This is not unusual. For example, lack of financial resources, not having a job or having limited income, is a limiting factor. Lack of support—and even blame—from family, friends and professionals can stop women from leaving abusive relationships. Isolation and distance from families for migrant women is a strong factor for many. Most Indian women believe that marriage is forever and that their real home is their husband's. The fear of being alone and feeling abandoned, as well as the stigma of being a divorced woman in South Asian culture, keeps them in unhappy and even abusive marriages. In a study that I was part of, the women participants said divorce was not an option for Indian women: 'Divorced women are considered less respectful and are isolated.' 'For a woman it is like even if this man is physically abusing me, I can't divorce him because what would people think of me, I'm going to lose friends, my place at work.'[12]

Fear of judgement for breaking societal norms enforces entrapment in abusive marriages.

Preeti, with the question of staying with her husband taken out of her hands, took medication to help her control her intense anxiety, fear, panic attacks, and sleeplessness. In addition, we did eight sessions of trauma therapy that helped her to make sense of the abuse perpetrated against her.[13] What Preeti went through was not just personal violence from her husband and mother-in-law, but a societal problem where the value and voices of women do not equal those of a man, and where a mother-in-law is bribed by society to maintain the strength of the patriarchy and male dominance, which she does by encouraging her daughter-in-law's suppression and isolation, sometimes inciting violence against her.[14]

Preeti, like my mother, had internalised her devaluation. She started to recognise that she had imbibed those values and that they were holding her back from enjoying her life as a single woman. Initially, she could not imagine that she could make a life for herself alone in Australia without a husband; that she had enough education and personal strength to get a job, take financial control, make friends, and, with only a little bit of help from the state's domestic violence services, find housing. The Australian immigration department allowed her to continue living here as a permanent resident without her husband's sponsorship, and she went back to study to become an early childhood teacher. Therapy allowed her to unleash her strength, and she used all her resources to take control of her life and started to live happily for the first time ever as a woman with free will.

The question is how to make society as a whole move towards Preeti's and John's realisations. As Johan Galtung, Norwegian founder of the discipline of peace and conflict studies, said, 'When one husband beats his wife, there is a clear case of personal violence, but when one million husbands keep one million wives in ignorance, there is structural violence.'[15]

John explored this concept in therapy with me and in the MBCP; he examined the roles played by the cultures and systems that work together to suppress women and give men a sense of entitlement to perpetrate violence. A strong and immediate police and judicial response helped to shake him up. And Australian society as a whole is recognising that domestic violence is not acceptable, and that gender equality is necessary.[16] John and his wife now have a happy marriage; and he is the main carer of their young daughter, while Mary works full time and is the primary breadwinner. He does not feel constrained by switching roles or daunted by those who criticise him for not being the head of the household. John had to learn, explore, and think through the meaning and significance of the caring role, and to see the value in it. He likes to cook and manage the home, and he is thriving. His daughter is thriving as she has two devoted parents—no more fear, no rancour, no violence. His wife is thriving, climbing the ladder of success with his unconditional love and support. They discuss and share all decisions. They are now a happy family. But it has been a tough passage out of India.

# 3
# THE COSTS OF A HIERARCHICAL SOCIETY

It was the most precious moment of my life. It was pouring rain; the month was July, 1964. The monsoon season in Delhi had begun after a long, hot summer. The rain falling on dry earth makes the most beautiful smell—a promise of life once again.

I had received a letter: an invitation to appear for an interview for admission to the Maulana Azad Medical College. My father and mother were very pleased. All our dreams were being realised; not just mine, but theirs as well.

My dad said, 'Let me drive you to the college, the bus will be uncomfortable for you.'

The college was ten kilometres away from our home in Kalkaji, south of Delhi. Kalkaji was a refugee suburb; everyone there had been a resident of Pakistan and arrived in India penniless and homeless after the Partition. The Indian Government had given land to my father for a nominal amount in lieu of properties and assets left behind in Pakistan. Every parent in the suburb dreamt of their child becoming an engineer or a doctor.

It was a big moment, indeed. But I refused a lift from my father. I wanted this to be my victory. But my father, always a patriarch and used to prevailing, would not let me go alone. He wanted to enjoy the moment too. After a brief argument I had to give in.

As I was invited into the interview, the director of the college asked my father if he would like to come in. He was pleased to be invited and sat and listened to my answers.

The first question was: why do you want to study at this college? I told the director that I had been admitted to Lady Harding College as well, but I did not wish to study at an all-girls college. I wanted to have a broader education and view of life, and a mixed-gender college would give me a better opportunity to achieve that.

It was a brave answer for a young woman of India, where talk of the opposite sex could earn you the label of a 'loose character' or 'characterless', the biggest dishonour possible. This had crossed my mind, but I was not deterred.

I had felt suffocated by narrow cultural gender norms all my life in India. Why could women not travel freely in India? Why could we not talk to boys and men freely? Why were we always being told to dress this way or that? Why could men walk late at night but not women?

I was accepted into the Maulana Azad Medical College.

My medical course, which was five years long, was shortened to four and half years with a further six months of a compulsory internship. The government needed doctors quickly.

We were free of colonial masters and no longer felt inferior to any race. The young students in my class felt hip and modern; the future was in our hands. After graduating, the entire class decided to travel across India and hired a whole train that could sleep about a hundred new interns. I was desperate to go with my classmates.

But my father put a stop to it. I shouted, I fought with him, I put counterarguments to him, but he said no. That was that. I still do not know his reasons, but I imagine the potential for premarital sex and an unwanted pregnancy is what would have been at the back of his mind. But he would not state it openly. I could have reassured him had he been straight with me, because that was the last thing I wanted for myself. The lack of open discussion about sex in India remains an impediment to young people maturing, yet sexuality was, and is, the subtext in many social interactions and decisions to control women.[1]

I had dreams of becoming a gynaecologist and obstetrician and helping women. But events unfolded that changed the trajectory of my life. A year after I graduated, I met an Australian travelling through the city, Evan. A few days later he left the country. After six months of travel to the UK he returned to India. We had missed each other and the next thing we knew we were married, with my parents' blessings. He was an intelligent and loving person, respectful of me, who held the promise of an exciting new venture.

In medical college, notwithstanding the societal pressures, a group of us women had a group of male friends, and they all frequently came home to visit my family and have a meal with us. It was not unnatural that I would bring home a foreign friend to meet my parents. Evan came home and had dinner with us. My family were intrigued and welcomed him. My mother spoke to him very nicely and later said to me in Hindi, 'I cannot understand his Australian accent. He speaks very fast. How do you understand him.' 'I don't know,' I said. 'I just do.' My mother cooked traditional Indian fare and he used a knife and fork to eat her mutton cutlet. My mother said in Hindi, 'He seems to use his knife and fork as if it is an extension of his fingers.' In our house, food was mostly eaten with hands, liquid food with a spoon. When visitors came, forks were put out but used only by young people. Evan was friendly and warm to my parents as they were to him, and he loved the vegetarian food my mother had cooked. I saw that my father enjoyed chatting with him. They talked about the world and international politics, about Australia. One of my uncles (a family friend) who met him later had been to Australia in the 1960s to buy wool for his company, and he spoke fondly about the friendly people of Australia, their great quality sheep and wool, the solid economy. Everyone seemed to be enjoying learning about Australia. No one in my family knew that Australia had a dark-skinned Aboriginal population—that came as a major surprise to us all.

Evan treated me with enormous respect and care. It was wonderful to listen to stories of his travels and experiences. We spoke about family values, Western versus Eastern. He seemed open-minded. I was used to dogmatic ways of thinking and the inflexibility that goes with that. We could discuss his rebellion against his parents, where he'd travelled halfway across the globe without informing them, or seeking their permission or their financial support. As an Indian child that would be unthinkable. It was liberating, and exciting. We would talk about Western philosophy, sexual relations between men and women, politics, travel. It opened a window in my mind. It *was* possible to do what you considered ethical and appropriate without being constrained by thoughts of what people would say—the one refrain that holds most of us back from being free in India.

But an international love-marriage in India in the 1970s! It was a rare occurrence. Why did my parents not object? What let my benevolent patriarch of a father support such a thing? How could he have refused to allow my mother to work but let me marry across nationalities and live across an ocean? Luckily, my father was far from simple.

I later learned that when he was in his early twenties, my father had a girlfriend in a town on the North-West Frontier. It is a scandalous story. Apparently, my father used his ten-year-old nephew (my cousin is now in his eighties) to be his messenger boy, taking letters back and forth. But for some unknown reason he did not marry this woman. Perhaps he knew the pain of thwarted love and that is why he let us marry. Or perhaps it is in my genes to go against tradition and forge a new path.

My mother did not object, either. Most likely, she took the lead from my father's acceptance of my decision. Later, she told me that she cried for years, missing me, but that they had respected my judgement in letting me marry a foreigner.

I now reflect on my choice to marry a white Caucasian from a land I hardly knew anything about. How could I leave my family and all that was familiar and gamble with something and someone so totally unknown?

I now recognise it came from the same place that led me to a co-ed college. Evan met my deep desire to move away from India's view of women, to broaden my horizons, to feel excited by new challenges. It was wonderful to explore the world together. My future mother-in-law sent me *Australian Women's Weekly* magazines as soon as she knew we were getting married. That was so touching. She wanted me to know how women of Australia lived. At the time, I remember thinking that the dreams of Australian women were not much different to those of Indian women: the magazines were full of articles on caring for homes, children, beauty, fashion, weddings. Australian women seemed elegant and free.

But arriving in Australia in the 1970s was, in some ways, disappointing. It was not the same as India, perhaps, but patriarchal culture was still strong and male domination in medicine was profound. I was surprised when I started work in a maternity hospital in Victoria: all the consultant and resident doctors were men. It seemed strange to me that men were dealing with the problems of women; surely female doctors could understand them better? In India, 100 per cent of obstetricians and gynaecologists are women. My application for a registrar position in an Australian hospital in 1974 was rejected: 90 per cent of specialists were men. One day I wore trousers to the hospital.

'This is the new dress code?' my senior male consultant said. I did not wear trousers again to work for the next two years, until I decided to challenge his opinion of what I should wear. At the same time my mother-in-law, June, gave me *The Female Eunuch* by Germaine Greer. She was an avid reader and my best ally. She knew that I should learn about patriarchy in Australia and should not be exposed to racism or oppression. June lamented her lack of formal education, having married into a farming family in the 1920s. She'd suffered at the hands of her snobbish English mother-in-law who treated her with disrespect, and who refused to meet me as I was 'a brown Indian'. Evan's support and respect was unwavering and freeing.

Although common in India in modern times, medical education for women was a relatively rare phenomenon in the 1970s. It gave women uncommon respect, and an unusual ability to exercise some choices. It was an era when young women of certain sections of society were daring to express choice in relation to their life partner. In my class at medical school, most of us married the partner of our choice. After all, education is a liberating force. Education gives us a better knowledge of the world, an awareness of ideas, respectability—both in our eyes and the eyes of others—as well as empowerment, the power to earn an income, and control of one's future. It gives us the dignity of relief from poverty.

But this is not the norm in India. My marriage was as far from the Indian experience as it could be, both in how I met my husband, and how we married. What enabled us as young women was a lack of rigid adherence to caste and religion. Many married out of caste, or from a different part of the country with different language—one classmate originally from Delhi married a classmate from Gujarat;. Some married out of religion: Hindu to Muslim, Sindhi to Christian. We did not consider it an issue worthy of discussion, possibly because we had absorbed the messages that depicted us a secular country.[2]

Despite being educated and holding high-powered positions—despite becoming astronauts, doctors and IT engineers—most women in India (90 per cent) still prefer arranged marriage, which has come to be seen as the most respectable route.[3] First- and second-generation Indian migrants in the UK, Australia, and the USA also retain the custom.

The parents and families of young women want to arrange the best possible match for them. A woman's life partner is chosen based on class, caste, social position, earning capacity, and levels of education. The hunt for a good, reputable, high-status groom is widespread—each family looks far and wide, abroad and at home—and begins early. The groom must be older than the bride and be seen to have more power in societal terms—higher income, better education, and higher family status—than the bride and her family. The practice of marrying 'up' in this way is also called hypergamy.[4] Some brides are married off at eighteen or earlier while others wait until they complete their tertiary education. By and large, young women and men are not encouraged to find their own life partner. It is considered too important a task to be left to young foolhardy people. Older, wiser heads must prevail. And it is more respectable to have an arranged marriage; the stigma of 'loose woman' must not be allowed to stick to the daughters of the family.

The families emphasise the value of arranged marriages compared to Western-style love marriages. Love is not seen as strong enough to hold a marriage together. In an arranged marriage, there are shared interests and similar goals in life. In the 1970s we did not hear about divorce in India. But in Australia, the divorce rate had been rising since the 1960s. Almost 44 per cent of marriages ended in divorce, facilitated by the introduction of the *Family Law Act 1975*, which came into operation in January 1976 and allowed no-fault divorce.[5] Rapid changes in Western culture in the 20th century—allowing for more individual freedom, sexual revolution and self-actualisation—both in Australia and across the globe assisted the increase.[6] About

5 to 7 per cent of marriages in India and Indian migrant communities will end in divorce, compared with nearly 41 per cent of Australian marriages. But are the partners in an arranged marriage together because they are in a happy relationship, or is it the fear of being divorced that means women do not leave the relationship? This is a question that is being asked often in Indian media now that the divorce rates are starting to rise rapidly in metropolitan cities.[7]

One recent summer, I visited my mother's home in New Delhi. I got talking to a man who was working in her house as a painter. He was in his late forties or early fifties, although he looked older. He was a 'daily wage' labourer and worked for himself. These casual workers wait on street corners and at shopping centres until someone comes by looking to hire them for building or household jobs. Painting is one such job, and he had been picked by the builder who was fixing up my mother's property. I was intrigued by this seemingly emotionless, blank-faced man who was working so hard. He was there to do a job and his humanity was of no interest to the builder who hired him. Living in Australia and feeling somewhat distant to my country of birth, and coming from a family for whom caste was an insignificant issue, I have developed a need to talk to anyone who is from a different background or caste, whether in Australia or in India.

I asked him about his life, his home and children. He said with sadness that he had just lost his wife. He had been very selfish, he told me. He had five daughters but he wanted a son, so he kept pressuring her to have more children and each time it was a girl. She died giving birth to their sixth child.

He felt guilty, as he realised for the first time that he actually needed her as a companion not just as a child-breeder or, more accurately, a son-breeder. He said he was working very hard to provide a dowry for his two youngest daughters. The older three were already married and he had provided a dowry for all three. All his life he had worked hard so he could provide dowries for his daughters. His home was a broken-down tin and brick building in a nearby shanty town. The painter had not enough money to improve his living situation or to have adequate food, but society and his pride dictated that he must provide dowries to the men who will marry his daughters. He was looking for grooms for his youngest two daughters. The grooms would have to be Brahmins and be paid a 'good, respectable' dowry. I asked him why the grooms would have to be Brahmins. 'We are upper class and I do not wish her to marry someone in a lower class,' he said.

In this meeting with the painter, two of the biggest problems faced by victims of domestic violence were revealed: caste and dowry. We as Indian society must face them moving forward. Let us begin with dowry.

## DOWRY

Dowry was first recorded in Athens in sixth-century BC, where it was 10 per cent of the father's wealth. In the years 969–1250, Jews gave 150–1500 dinars when 800 dinars could maintain a family for thirty years. In urban Tuscany during the years 1420–1436, the bride's family would offer 1507 lire—six times the annual wage of a skilled worker. In Delhi, from 1920 to 1984, the bride's family would spend four times the annual male income.[8] The practice of dowry in Western Europe has ended. But in many parts of the world, like South Asia including India, Africa and China, it has continued.

The original point of dowry in India (and elsewhere) was to support the bride in her new life. It was a pre-mortem inheritance in lieu of the family inheritance that was to go to the sons under India's skewed inheritance laws. But the exploitation of the bride and her family was and is rife, and dowry is far too often a cause of harassment, mental illness, and violence, including the scourge of 'dowry deaths'.[9] It is a social evil and, as such, the Indian Government outlawed it in 1961. However, between 1960 and 1995, 93 per cent of marriages still involved dowry. (In rural India, between 1960 and 2008, dowry was paid in 95 per cent of marriages.)[10] Not only that, the dowry price has kept increasing since 1949. A recent study confirms that dowries are almost universal and that the laws against it have been entirely ineffective.[11] Many theories have been advanced as to why the dowry is still intact and why the dowry price continues to rise.

A Bangladesh study by Sarah White suggests that dowry is given to bolster men's economic position and social status. It helps sustain the economic system of a country.[12] Receiving dowry also re-enforces masculine gender norms of being the provider.

Previously only an upper caste or Brahmin or kshatriya practice, dowry came to be an all caste/class phenomenon. It has replaced the symbolic exchange of gifts between families of the groom and the bride to something different and much bigger. It has now become gifts for the groom and his family, who in the process acquire higher standards of material life, status, and security, with negative consequences to women's status, including their survival.[13]

Another theory posits that dowries have risen in line with the increasing education and earnings of grooms—higher educated and higher earning grooms command higher dowries, signalling their ability to be better providers, and more grooms have become high earners.[14]

Marriage is a marketplace where there is competition over good quality grooms, who are relatively scarce. The ideal groom must be older, but he can marry a younger woman of any age bracket, and he therefore has many more options than women do. The bride is further handicapped by the rigid expectation that she must 'marry up'. This increases demand for educated and well-earning grooms and leads to the choice of foreign-based grooms.[15] Australian or Western non-resident Indians (NRI) grooms are a particularly attractive lure for parents, as their situation implies a higher level of education. One woman's father, when asked why he married off his daughter to a

NRI husband, told me 'there aren't good grooms left in India'. The scarcity of good, educated grooms leads to higher dowry amounts. Several studies support the idea that increases in the educational attainment and abilities of men—and even women—are related to large increases in dowry.[16]

In India, marriages are mostly arranged, occur within the same caste and usually within known groups, and 80 per cent occur within neighbouring localities. Parents feel safer marrying their daughters within their Jati—a subset of a caste—and sending them off to places that are not too distant. In Australia, I find the same pattern in some migrants arriving from India—parents prefer arranging marriage within the same Jati and, in doing so, overlook other key attributes. I saw a woman with tertiary education—a degree in IT—who was married off to a man who had failed Year 10. They lived within 100 kilometres of each other in two small towns in India. No dowry was given. Why? Her education was the dowry. He wanted to migrate to Australia, and her education was the passport to her getting an international student visa; he would travel as her dependent. This did not reduce his sense of entitlement to control her working hours, her friendships, and so on. Marriages within caste groups, such as this one, maintain 'purity of caste', fortify male privilege, and increase husbands' power and sense of entitlement outside and in the home.[17]

However, while dowry is ubiquitous, it is not always recognised as such.

'No one gives or takes dowry now,' an Australian-based Indian lawyer said to me not so long ago.

What he said made me wonder if he, and many others, did not quite understand what is meant by dowry.

'Is it true,' I asked him, 'that the bride's parents pay for the significant part of the wedding ceremony that often goes for three to four days?'

'Yes,' he replied.

'Is it true that the bride's family have to give her expensive gifts like sarees, clothes, jewellery?'

He agreed that was true.

'Is it true that, according to Indian tradition, the mother-in-law, considered the matriarch of the family, usually takes the expensive jewels for safe-keeping?'

'Yes,' he said.

'Is it true that the majority of times mothers-in-law do not hand the jewellery back to their daughters-in-law when a marriage ends?'

He reluctantly agreed.

All of this is dowry.

Every gift given during wedding celebrations is dowry. Even the expense of the wedding is part of dowry. Indian marriages typically go for three to four days; they are extravagant, extremely expensive, and overwhelmingly paid for by the bride's parents.

That marriage is the defining moment of Indian life is best captured by the following phrase: 'Probably, no other people have endeavoured to idealize the institution of marriage as the Hindus have done. Even in the patriarchal society of the Rig Vedic Hindus, marriage was considered as a sacramental union.'[18]

By and large, a modern North Indian Hindu or Sikh wedding—whether in India or Australia—usually consists of six separate celebrations. In an arranged marriage, the 'boy' and 'girl' meet for the first time in the presence of their immediate families at the first celebration.[19] Though there are hundreds of regional communities with distinctive customs and traditions, usually this is called the Rokka ceremony. This is where the bride's and the groom's family have agreed to the arranged marriage—*rokka* literally means 'stop' or 'stop looking'. Usually, the Rokka ceremony occurs within hours or days of the two people meeting each other. There is a colloquial saying in India: *'aaj mangain, kal viya'*, meaning 'engaged today, married tomorrow', and that typically describes an arranged marriage.

Rokka is held with a small number of family members from both sides. The bride's family gives gifts to the groom—a gold chain, cash, and sweets. The cost of the gifts and ceremony is borne by the bride's parents. The bride usually does not get anything from the groom's side; sometimes she may get a gold chain.

The engagement ceremony is next. The bride's family pays for an extravagant event with food, entertainment, and music. Here the groom's whole extended family and friends are invited, along with the bride's family and friends. There can be hundreds of guests. In addition, the bride's family buys gifts for the groom and his family—his mother and father, sisters, brothers, their partners, uncles, aunts, grandparents, nieces and nephews. They are usually expensive gifts—a gold watch or bangle, a diamond ring for the groom, clothes for the groom and his immediate and extended family. In addition, money is given to the groom and his family, and this can be anything up to AUD$50 000. Some is given in cash to impress the guests, and to display the bride's wealth, which is linked to the social status of the groom. The rest can be transferred through a bank. The bride will receive gold jewellery and expensive clothes from her parents. The groom gives her an engagement ring and perhaps one set of gold necklaces. The bride's mother-in-law and father-in-law usually send a list of people who should be given cash gifts, clothes, and/or gold.

The cost of the engagement ceremony is borne by the bride's parents and can run into several hundred thousand rupees or more. If the bride's family is seen to be falling short, according to the groom or his mother or father or sister or whoever, the new daughter-in-law is subjected to sarcasm after the marriage, criticism of her and her family, and unfavourable comparisons with someone who might have brought a lot of gifts. The comparisons may not be direct. A mother-in-law might say to her new daughter-in-law something like, 'The neighbour's daughter-in-law brought a beautiful big car to her new in-laws' home' or 'She gave her mother-in-law a huge diamond set of necklace and earrings.'

The third ceremony is called Sangeet, and again the cost is borne by the bride's parents. This musical evening is usually held three to four days before the wedding. There is dancing, food, and the henna ceremony. Usually, this event is meant for the bride's family and friends, but in modern times the groom and his family and friends join in. Again, it is usually an expensive function with upwards of a hundred guests; the bride has to have a new and expensive gold-embroidered dress and jewellery for this event.

The fourth ceremony is dowry giving, and many people wrongly believe that dowry is restricted to what happens here. Typically, it comprises a display of the gifts given by bride's parents for all relatives and friends to see—cars, air conditioners, furniture, bed linen, televisions, refrigerators, washing machines and anything else demanded by the groom and his family. In addition, gold jewellery is given to the mother-in-law, father-in-law, sisters, brothers and their partners. The gifts are displayed in a room or announced to the community. This has been termed 'groom-price'.[20] The bride's expensive new wardrobe is displayed, and gold necklaces, pendants and diamond earrings are given to her by her family. This is bridal-wealth, or *stree–dhan*, in Indian law. The dowry includes the groom-price and bride-wealth, is borne entirely by the bride's parents, and can run into tens of thousands of dollars.

Dowry calculations should also include the cost of the actual wedding ceremony, which is the fifth ceremony. It is an elaborate tradition. The 'Baraat' is the wedding procession, which starts at the groom's house and arrives at the wedding venue. The groom might be on horseback, harking back to the days of the kings, or in a car with a long entourage of relatives, extended family, friends, and sometimes his entire village. It is not uncommon for upwards of two hundred guests, even a thousand guests, to attend. In the olden days, the venue was the bride's home; now it is usually a five-star hotel. The groom is dressed in an expensive gold-brocaded tunic or sherwani costing up to AU$1000; this is paid for by the bride's parents, as are his mother's and father's clothes. He has paid to hire a brass band, who play as the entourage stops at doorstep of the wedding venue. All the time, the groom's entourage dances in front of his horse or car. The bride is sitting inside with her family and friends. She does not get to see her groom arriving.

The next step is 'Milni', or 'meeting'. Male elders of the bride's family receive those of the groom in a ceremonial fashion upon arrival, and hand them packets of cash, gold, and gifts. The female relatives of the bride then greet their counterparts—especially the groom's mother and aunts, who are also given cash, gifts, and gold.

The actual ceremony follows, and the couple takes vows.

Many Australian-Indian grooms or NRI grooms (non-resident Indians living abroad) demand big dowries and that the wedding be held in the poshest hotels so they can show off their high social status. The unconscious bias of the bride's parents always works in favour of those grooms who live abroad. And the grooms, who are aware of their unearned exalted status, know that migration abroad affords them an even higher status. There is little regard for how much the bride's parents have to pay.

It costs between 1000 and 10 000 rupees ($20–$200) per plate in a posh hotel in India. Multiply that two hundred times, or a thousand times, and the cost may be anything from $4000 to $200 000 for the wedding function alone.[21] Not every groom and his family demands or expects cash or gold; not every wedding is extended to the full five days of celebrations. However, many do, and many are.

Dowry ends up increasing the value of boys and diminishing the value of girls.

At the wedding ceremony, the bride and groom are tied to each other via trinkets dangling from bangles or a knot in their scarfs. They untie each other's scarfs and bangles in the presence of relatives. This is Kangna Kholna (Sanskrit for 'opening up bangles').

The bride then sits down, and members of her new family come to introduce themselves to her one by one.[22] It is at this stage the mother-in-law (who from here on the bride would address as 'mother') quietly tells her daughter-in-law to give over her gold and diamond jewellery for safekeeping. I have heard this from numerous victims of dowry abuse. The new daughter-in-law is hesitant and may feel wary of handing over her expensive jewels to someone barely known to her. But there is unspoken pressure, sometimes oppressive, if she refuses. A first refusal by a patient of mine earned her the label 'difficult, she is not to be trusted', and it set the scene for future domestic violence. For others who did hand over their jewels, when the marriage broke up the mother-in-law denied she had ever taken them or lied that 'the daughter-in-law already has taken them back'. An arranged marriage takes a lot of trust, and this trust is easily breached.

The last ceremony is the post-wedding function called the Reception, where the bride and groom come out to the world as a married couple. This is the only event that is completely hosted by the groom's family, and is attended by his family and friends with some of the bride's family and friends invited.

The entire process of a wedding is managed by the families. Marriage is a marriage of two families. Because the elaborate cultural tradition is considered sacred and permanent, the parents of daughters feel safe in handing her over to an unknown family, along with her dowry—groom-price and bridal-wealth. Even weddings of second- or third-generation migrants follow the same path.

Compare all of this with an average Australian Western-style marriage and wedding. The partners find each other, and after a period of engagement, a date for the wedding is set. Sometimes there is an engagement party too. Bridesmaids and groomsmen are chosen by the couple and their garments are usually paid for by the individual. Before the wedding, the bride takes her girlfriends out and the groom takes his male friends out. This is followed by the wedding ceremony and honeymoon. The role of the family is minimal, though this was not always so; in Western societies, the bride's family too gave dowry and paid for the wedding. With greater equality and education of women, the custom of dowry dwindled to token gifts in the form of trousseau, meaning a wedding dress and some gifts; and then that too finally disappeared. These days, 73 per cent of couples cohabit before marriage. They marry later and they pay for their own wedding, or split the costs between themselves and their families.[23] The average age of an Australian bride is twenty-nine; for Indian women it's twenty-two.[24] A survey of more than five hundred Australian brides in 2018 found the average wedding cost to be $51245 and the annual income at the time was between $55432 and $72800.[25] The divorce rate is high; the threshold of marital unhappiness required to trigger a divorce has declined over time. The daughter-in-law does not go to her husband's family to live.

Indian parents dedicate enormous resources towards the groom and his parents, hoping their daughter will get a wondrous life and wealth in return for their huge investment; especially when she is married off to an ex-pat Indian living in a first-world country like Australia.

The investment is based on a fragile dream, one that can shatter easily.

Recently, I heard from a friend that a member of the long-established Australian–Indian community exclaimed with pride that he had not taken any dowry for his son's wedding. He forgot to say that the entire wedding expense was borne by the bride's family, including accommodation and air fares for the groom's family attending the wedding from interstate and overseas. This exposes his cultural blind spot. Dowry is not just what is received in the dowry-giving ceremony. This Indian bride and groom were brought up in Australia, yet neither the groom nor the bride objected to the extravagant cost borne by her family; nor did they offer to discuss a fair distribution of expenses. (Research shows that the big wedding event may signal the social status of the bride's family as well as the groom's—the result, though, is that the bride's family may well be left bankrupted.)[26]

My mother married my father before the Partition in united India, in 1946. The wedding was held in Karachi. Life for my mother, her sisters, and her parents was comfortable then. Her parents spent freely on her education, her teacher training, boarding fees, expensive clothes, books. When it came to my mother's marriage, her grandfather spent lavishly on her wedding, bestowing expensive gifts, including a huge amount of gold jewellery, on my father's family. (My father refused the gifts.) Apparently, the cost of the marriage hardly made a dint in my great-grandfather's wealth. He reportedly used to eat with gold utensils.

No one in my mother's family felt economic stress over her dowry. But raising dowry for her two sisters in post-Partition India in the 1950s and 1960s was different.

I once asked my aunts: what did they receive in dowry?

'The country was recovering from colonial occupation,' my older aunt said. 'We were refugees from Pakistan having arrived just a few years earlier. Everyone was attempting to restart their life, money was scarce. My husband's family did not ask for anything. They were happy to have me as part of the family. But still my parents gave more than they could afford. They gave me expensive sarees, gold jewellery and gifts for the groom's family.'

My younger aunt said: 'My brothers worked very hard, and saved everything so they could pay for my marriage.' They paid for sarees and gold which were for her use. Her husband-to-be did not want any gifts for himself. My grandparents, my father, and his two brothers paid for the wedding day and a small engagement ceremony. It was nonetheless an expensive affair and the family's hard-earned money was depleted. Yet societal obligations dictated their actions; they were obliged to hold a wedding function and give dowry gifts that were beyond their means. They did not complain, they simply did it.

The need to pay for the bride's wedding was initially internalised only in the high castes: Brahmins and the kings; in lower castes it was not required. I asked my aunts why their brothers and parents spent all their hard-earned money on the wedding when cash was so scarce and they needed money to set themselves up in India. Why not hold a simple ceremony in a temple? My aunt said that it was not much; they did whatever little they could. She recognised life was tough for her parents and brothers all sharing the same home, but she would not dare to tell them to give her nothing. Women had no voice in their marriage matters. It was how it was done, and no one would ever think of questioning social customs that had gone on for centuries.

But had they?

An Iranian scholar, Bīrūnī, Muḥammad ibn Aḥmad, who travelled to India with King Mahmoud in the eleventh century, lived in the country for thirteen years and wrote extensively about its traditions. Regarding marriage laws, he noted no dowry as it is today:

> No gift is settled between them. The man gives only a present to the wife, as he thinks fit, and a marriage gift in advance, which he has no right to claim back, but the wife may give it back to him of her own will.

A daughter inherits one-fourth the share that her brothers will. Her part of the inheritance was to be spent on her until the time of her marriage, and any leftover given to her as dowry at the time of marriage.[27] Dowry was income; a daughter's income from her father's estate. Not a gift to the groom.

Professor Veena Talwar Oldenburg, through painstaking research of pre-colonial times, presents ground-breaking work.[28] Her thesis is that dowry as an ancient custom in the Punjab was not onerous on the bride's family. It was primarily a women-led practice that honoured the bride, enabling her to establish her status and have recourse in an emergency; something she could use in hard times, like jewellery, and which remained her property within the marriage. Women of her extended family would start saving small amounts from the time the girl child was born. This shared the burden, and no one was impoverished as a result. Dowry as a practice was confined only to the Brahmins and upper classes. In pre-colonial times, Oldenburg tells us, women participated in local economies and were co-partners in landholding arrangements with kings and rulers. Taxes would be paid in good seasons, and not when there was drought. It was a flexible regime. In the 1850s, British attempts to control the economy and extract income from the land led to parcels of land being distributed— but only to men, and only to be worked on by male labour. With the ownership of land, the imposition of onerous land taxes followed; taxes that were inflexible to droughts and poverty, to be paid twice a year at fixed dates. This led to the 'masculinising of the economy': a preference for male labour and worsening of gender inequality.[29]

This set up the context in which men and boys had a higher value, and facilitated power differences between men and women. A son-in-law was always exalted in the Indian tradition, and the new arrangement increased his value. This meant that dowry could be demanded, and it became an economic transaction that served to support the groom's family in times of drought and hardship, rather than to support the bride. Men started to make demands on the bride's family. Girls and women became economic burdens. India's patrilocal culture, where the bride relocates to her husband and in-laws' home after marriage, made her vulnerable. Dowry was no longer a way of showing appreciation for a daughter-bride; it was a feared essential obligation. It became the means of ready resources to pay taxes and the like. This historical context sheds light on the current trend of Australian-Indian men going back to India to get married, expecting dowry as means of paying off their student loans or other debts, starting a new business, or buying a house. It is a practice that is used as a tool of coercive control and abuse. Its upward trajectory after independence is fuelled by consumerist economics. Confirming this evidence, poorer Indian states like Bihar and Uttar Pradesh show higher rates of dowry murders compared with richer states like Tamil Nadu. The theory is that as economic development increases to a high level, modern formal institutions like the law and police replace traditional family-based informal institutions, such as restriction on women's paid work.[30]

When I got married in 1971, my father was a government employee and had a reasonable income as the deputy secretary of a department. He spent his income on household needs like the telephone (in the house since 1960) and a car with a driver (since 1955). There were no savings left over. My father would have spent about 10 000 rupees ($200) on my wedding, and that would have been his salary for three months. (In today's money, Rs 424 000 or AUD$8400.) Fortunately, he did not give cash or big gifts to Evan or his family. They had little knowledge of Indian customs, and would have been bewildered if he had.

But my family gave me nine expensive sarees and gold jewellery, things I did not need and rarely used. I don't know where my father got the spare cash—most likely he borrowed it from the bank. In addition, he had already spent money on my upbringing, education, books, and boarding house costs. I remember always feeling worried for my parents' financial situation—running a big house, the cost of raising four children, and so on. Why have a wedding that cost so much of his income? Why did no one ever question it? I was never asked if I wanted any of it. The tradition took over. This is exactly why the girl child is a poor economic investment, and that is why greedy parents act unconscionably and get rid of girl babies and keep their sons.

The man painting my mother's house told me he was preparing to put away one to two lakhs (between $2000 and $4000) each for his daughters' dowries. His daily wage was about 500 rupees, around $10. Although this was an enormous amount for the painter, it is a tiny dowry compared to the average.

The imperative to save for the dowries didn't appear to trouble him. His desperate need for a son was understandable, too. If he has to give so much dowry, then he should also reap some benefit. A son would bring a daughter-in-law to the family. She would come bearing cash, gold, household gifts, a car and whitegoods. She would work as a housemaid and earn a wage as well. A son would also carry his name forward—it is commonly said in India that the family must continue its *vansh,* its lineage.

In this system, having a daughter means he has also the pain of losing her. When the painter found the right husbands for his daughters, his daughters would go to their new husbands' families. So it was obvious—who wouldn't want a son? Who wouldn't put pressure on his wife to keep having babies until she produced a son? Who wouldn't have an ultrasound during the pregnancy to see if it is a boy or a girl, and get rid of the baby if it is a girl?

The pressure of giving dowry is justified in parents' minds because the family inheritance will go to sons and dowry to daughters. Can modern laws, and equal inheritance for boys and girls in family wealth and property, help? Introduced in 2005 in India, this had the opposite effect to gender equality.[31] The backlash occurred in the form of increased female feticide, with families fearing that property inherited by women could fall into the hands of her in-laws.[32] Australia has gender equality laws, however similar issues are faced by the Australian South Asian community. The notion that a daughter is only ever a guest in her father's home, and that her only rightful home is that of her husband, underlies much of the malady. And sisters do not demand their share. Threats of violence, and fear of their male relatives, prevent women from fighting for their inheritance rights. The custom of dowries is maintained, and inequality continues.

The painter had his own unconscious image of what it is to be a man. He must have a son and he must pay exorbitant dowries for his daughters. And he could impose his wishes on his wife. But after meeting him, I was left with the impression that his power to control her life left had him with an acute emptiness. He had surprised himself at the loss and grief he felt, having not appreciated his wife prior to her death. Had he consulted her as an equal partner he could have enjoyed his daughters, his grandchildren and his wife in his old age. The painter looked depressed, older than his years.

Self-pride is important, and a strong identity is important. But what if it is based on a house of cards and its maintenance costs dearly—maybe, as in the case of the painter's wife, life itself? What costs is our society willing to pay?

# 4

# A DAUGHTER IS ONLY EVER A GUEST IN THE FATHER'S HOME

Marriage is based on trust.

When I moved to Australia with my husband, we went to my parents-in-law's farm near Dimboola, straight from Delhi. It was the most beautiful time of my life. I felt deeply loved by my gorgeous mother-in-law June and by my shy but sensitive and intelligent father-in-law Patrick. My mother-in-law became a second mother. She showed me how to cook Australian style; roast lamb or lamb chops with three veg for dinner became my favourite food. I was impressed by the dozens and dozens of eggs in the refrigerator as there were numerous chickens on the farm. I was introduced to the extended family and the neighbours from nearby farms. I was enveloped in homely warmth, and I did not miss my family in Delhi. My parents were happy when they heard how loving my in-laws were. Every parent's nightmare is the fear of their daughter relocating to her in-laws' home far away, not knowing what her fate will be. How will she be treated by her in-laws and new husband? The man painting my mother's house would be worried about this too, as he saved for his daughters' dowries. My mother and father had also been worried.

In going to Evan's family, I was echoing India's patrilocal culture, where the bride goes to live with her husband's family.

Traditionally, a new bride arrives at the groom's house, and his mother and relatives extend an elaborate welcome to her. In the ritual of 'Griha Pravesh' (Sankskrit for *home entry;* 'Pani vaarna' for Sikhs), her mother-in-law offers a traditional prayer as she puts her foot inside for the first time. The bride is then made to kick a vessel full of rice and grains with her right foot. This symbolises her bringing prosperity into the house. She no longer belongs to her own family, but to her husband's family. Sometimes the bride's name is changed at this juncture, signifying a start to a new life, leaving her old life behind.

All parents hope for the warmest of welcomes for their daughter into her new family. But some hope in vain.

Here is the story of one of my patients, Ina E. At the Rokka ceremony, Ina's husband-to-be and his parents gained her parents' confidence by saying, 'We do not want anything.' (A common phrase to bypass the laws against dowry.). 'We really love your daughter. Please just make sure the wedding is a very posh event, in the best possible hotel.'

Despite spending a fortune on her wedding—in the vicinity of AUD$120 000—Ina said her parents felt quite relaxed. About five hundred guests were invited to a five-star hotel in Delhi over four days of extravagant functions. Most guests belonged to the groom's side. The wedding arrangements were in place and hotels had been paid for, when, just one day before the wedding ceremony, the groom's mother told the bride's parents she would like cash for a Mercedes car.

Ina said, 'They already had been given dowry—for example, all household items, furnishings, linen, whitegoods such as a refrigerator, TV, air conditioner.'

Ina's future mother-in-law accepted a refrigerator when she already had a refrigerator in the house. None of the household items were going to be shipped to Australia, where the bride and groom would live. They were to be left at the groom's parents' house on the outskirts of Delhi.

A while after the wedding, Ina went to Australia on a tourist visa to spend time with her new husband. She is one of many Indian women to marry an NRI—a non-resident Indian man. And that she didn't join him immediately after the wedding is common too.

Domestic violence began soon after Ina's arrival. Her husband asked her to ask her father to send money. She refused, saying: 'My father has already spent around $120 000. I cannot ask him anymore. I will earn money here and give you that money.'

He said, 'No, it must come from your father.' Then he asked her to ask her father to transfer the title of an apartment in his name. She refused again. After abusing her, and calling her and her family names, he began to shout at her, to push and shove her. This happened daily for a while. He then moved out of the house, abandoning her in a strange city with no support system, and a tourist visa. She had only just applied for permanent residency. She was homeless, with no job, and no government support; domestic violence victims on temporary visas do not qualify for it. If women in this situation do not have a job, they will have no housing or food.[1] Ina's husband refused to pay her maintenance. She was lucky to have parents who could send her money from India until she found a job. Luckily, she also got her permanent residency visa—after two years of anxiety, panic attacks, and flashbacks of violence.

Another story: this time of Laushika, a young, educated woman whose retired, widowed mother sold her family home to pay for her daughter's wedding to an Australian-Indian man. She gave a cash dowry of $40 000 to the groom, and gold jewellery and gifts for the whole family. A grand wedding over three days cost her $60 000. But that was not enough for the groom. He knew that his mother-in-law had some savings left over from the sale of her home. When his new wife arrived in Australia, he demanded more money. 'There is nothing more left to give,' she responded, daring to refuse him. He started to call her vulgar names, to humiliate her, to deprive her of food. He told her she was ugly, that her skin was 'too dark', that she and her family were lower class. Her mother-in-law added, 'The going rate for a marriage to an Australian-Indian groom is $75 000 cash.'

She is now an abandoned bride. He withdrew sponsorship for her partner visa. She is living in Australia, wondering if she will be deported back to India, or whether the Australian Government will give her permanent residency based on her experience of emotional abuse and dowry extortion. Her mother in India is devastated. She now lives in rented accommodation, and has only her small amount of savings to support her in her old age, there being no government pension in India. Her mother had dreamed that her daughter would live a happy life in Australia, but the only person to benefit was the groom.

Not all mothers-in-law exert coercive pressure on their daughter-in-law at the time of the wedding to give her all her gold and diamond jewellery for "safe-keeping". Many do. Most often the young women comply, as Ina did. If she dares to refuse her mother-in-law? 'She is too cunning, not trustworthy and will not fit into the family.' Such criticisms are common.

A husband who hardly knows his wife, and is usually extremely close to his mother, easily becomes suspicious of his new wife's motives. The bonding between the new couple is disrupted. And if the mother-in-law continues to criticise the quality or number of gifts brought to the family, the new husband can be incited to abuse and violence towards his new wife. This can lead to depression and suicidal behaviour, as well as to complex post-traumatic stress disorder, which Ina experienced.[2] She was on a tourist visa and then a bridging visa. She remained on the bridging visa, with an uncertain future in Australia and no Centrelink support income, for nearly two years. Her mental condition improved to some extent after she found a small job, but her nightmares and anxiety, her sense of hopelessness, and fear of the future remained until she received permanent residency. Her dowry could not be reclaimed in Australia because it was given in India. But regardless of where he lived, her husband got to enjoy the benefits of the dowry: he did not have to support his parents; he did not have to find the money to buy them a car.

There are a plethora of cultural assumptions and unconscious biases behind every aspect of marriage in India. Take the case of an arranged marriage between an Indian woman and an Australian-Indian NRI in India. This young woman, Shivani, was twenty-four when she heard that her parents were looking to arrange her marriage and had just graduated with a degree in biochemistry. She told me she was excited. The idea of an Australian-Indian migrant who had been living in Australia for the past decade after arriving as an international student conjured up several subconscious and conscious assumptions and images in Shivani's mind. The images, in order of importance, were: NRIs are highly educated, modern, sophisticated, and wealthy; they live in big houses, have fantastic cars, and make great partners and providers. Her unconscious bias towards this man was that he was the ideal husband package. She looked forward to her wedding, which was an expensive ceremony that stretched over three days.

She overlooked the common knowledge that in recent years, many NRIs have gone to India to get married and, after a brief honeymoon, disappeared with their wife's dowry. Shivani's parents did not carry out any checks on the potential groom. They fell victim to their unconscious bias, and they accepted the superior status of this NRI.

Bit by bit, her groom and his mother revealed their true selves. The groom's mother said she expected the bride's father to honour their exalted social status as migrant Indians. The bride's father should hold the wedding ceremony in a five-star hotel in Delhi and should pay all the expenses for the five hundred guests. They also wanted gifts and gold jewellery.

The bride's father—unwilling to change his mind (or unable to change his mind; after all, his assumption was unconscious)—did not investigate or question his assumptions or 'bias' about their higher social status as migrant Australian-Indians and submissively agreed to their demands, even if it meant having to sell the investment property kept for his retirement. He spent about $120 000 on the wedding.

Shivani arrived in Australia on a spousal visa. She then encountered bias against her as the daughter-in-law of the family; though it was conscious rather than unconscious, and it was conspicuous. Her husband asked her to wash the dishes that had accumulated over the past few days, and iron the clothes that had been washed but sat in the laundry.

She was to take care of her mother-in-law's physical needs. Her father-in-law had heart problems. She had to cook and clean for them. Her husband never entered the kitchen; it was not his job, because he was the son.

Shivani was an educated woman and had been brought up in a privileged environment by her parents. She felt humiliated, inferior, and she talked back to her husband. He criticised her and her parents. She criticised him and his parents.

He slapped her. 'How dare you talk back to me? Have you got no manners or no respect for your elders?'

Her university education had given her enough confidence to stand up for herself. Her parents had given her support and love, never treating her as any less deserving than her brother during her childhood years. She found enough strength to speak up to her husband again, risking another slap.

The education of women is a two-edged sword in some communities. Research shows that where there is a family or community background of strong female employment as a result of education, the educated-employed woman does not face the threat of violence. But in communities where education levels are lower, and fewer women work, the greater education of a wife is seen as a threat. In Shivani's new husband's family, the new bride's sister-in-law was educated and working. But her mother-in-law was educated only to Year 10. Her husband was less educated than her, working in Australia as a chef.

So much had been assumed in Shivani's marriage—who he would be as an NRI; who she would be as a wife. He had imbibed the cultural bias against women who challenge traditional gender norms, who challenge their husband's or in-laws' right to control their behaviour. He wanted to control her for being intelligent and outspoken. She has not expected this to occur to her in Australia. A neighbour called the police after an episode in which he split her head open, leaving her bleeding profusely. Shivani was taken to the hospital, then to a refuge. She was referred by a domestic violence service provider to me for treatment of panic attacks and post-traumatic stress disorder. She described terrifying flashbacks of abuse and violence. During trauma therapy sessions, she said her parents in India were pressuring her to go back to her husband. But over time, she found resilience, resisted them, forged a new identity, chose a new path to study, and started work at a bank.

Another young woman, Yesha, also had an arranged marriage in India. Because she had previously suffered a severe head injury in a car accident and had scars on her body, her parents had to pay a huge amount of dowry (nearly $1 million) to her Australian-Indian husband as a compensation for taking on 'damaged goods'. It was his third marriage, but he was not regarded as damaged goods by her family. He was a man; that was enough. He had no barriers to exercising his power, and he abused his enormous power over her. He tried to control her every move. *Don't go out alone, wear this dress, wear this jewellery, you cannot work in a childcare centre.* He wanted to project a certain image of their social standing, and what his wife looked like and what she did was part of this. He was determined to shape her social image. But for Yesha, it was not a comfortable situation. She found it all fake, and often refused to comply. Once he told her to wear a revealing dress. She refused because she was brought up to be 'decent'. He pushed her down the stairs. This happened many times. Once he choked her until she fainted. He hit her until she could bear it no longer and she called the police. Yesha suffered a severe depressive illness and post-traumatic stress disorder. She was unable to sleep, had nightmares of being hit and pushed. She could not eat properly and became anaemic. Her isolation from her own family made it worse. To maintain his control, her husband wouldn't allow her to make social connections in Australia. He would only allow her to come to Australia on a tourist visa (for nearly nine months), and later on a partner visa. He threatened to withdraw sponsorship for her partner visa if she did not comply with his wishes. He would give her $75 a fortnight to spend on herself. Like other newly arrived immigrant women on temporary visas, Yesha experienced the harm created by multiple layers of disadvantages that made her vulnerable to violence.[3] No contact with family, no friends in Australia, no knowledge of helpful resources—all these things put her at risk.

What happens to women who do not give dowry?

Durga was subjected to abuse and violence from the day she arrived in Australia on a spousal visa more than five years ago. While living with her husband and his parents, she was emotionally abused, criticised, physically beaten by her husband, and excluded from the family. Her mother-in-law forced her to sleep in the guest bedroom downstairs while her husband slept with his parents upstairs. She was isolated and bullied. The reason? Her father—an influential and educated man in India—chose to follow the law and refused to give dowry.

In an arranged marriage, the couple do not usually know each other prior to getting married. Nor do the families. Traditionally, parents control the process of looking for a match, whether through advertising in the newspapers or on a matrimonial website. Sometimes an intermediary brings an offer of a potential son-in-law or daughter-in-law to those looking. A marriage can be arranged in a matter of days.

The bride's parents will make enquires and endeavour to discover the bona fides of the potential son-in-law before they put their trust on him. But if he lives in a foreign country and has limited family in India, this is often overlooked. In any case, it is hard to make inquires that will give the proof they are seeking. And NRI grooms are highly sought after, regarded as men of principle, achievement, intelligence, and wealth. They are seen to be trustworthy, not as men who would cheat or run away with their wife's dowry. Their permanent residency in Australia, a first world country with all that implies, gives them instant respect. They seem to offer the parents of daughters the best chance of providing her with a good life, and parents willingly entrust their daughters' lives to men they often know little about in a country far away.

The Australian immigration system supports the power of the potential groom: the vulnerable bride must provide him with every bit of information about herself, but he, as the sponsor, does not have to reveal anything about himself. He may have been married before, may have a criminal record, or may not have the educational degrees or income he claims to have. He may also withdraw sponsorship for her application for permanent residency at whim. The system enhances the power of the groom over the bride. It needs to be equalised by the Australian Government.

The bride's parents tend to believe that people will tell the truth in such a serious matter; however, the groom has no incentive to admit his deficiencies, flaws, and failings. In his desire to maintain his dominant position in the marriage, he does not tell his new wife about the difficulties he may be facing—for example, previous debts, student loans, or criminal activity. This starts a married life based on lies, which the bride discovers to her distress and shame.

As the trend is shifting to marriages being arranged through matrimonial websites, this only increases the potential for misleading information being supplied, and a transnational marriage makes the element of trust even more necessary.

Grooms disappearing with dowries add a further layer to emotional trauma. 'We trusted him,' said Rani, who married her husband in India. 'He looked like a decent person. He spoke to my father in an extremely respectful way. My father was impressed by him. I am an educated woman—to tertiary level—and thought I was marrying a similarly highly-educated man, but I later found out he lied about his education. He had not even finished high school.'

Rani's jewellery was taken by her mother-in-law: she did not want to hand it over but was pressured to do so. Rani's family gave $25 000 in cash gifts to the groom and his extended family. Her father spent $25 000 on the wedding, as demanded by the groom. As soon as Rani was married, her husband left India and her mother-in-law verbally abused her, deprived her of food and excluded her.

Her husband, now in the United States, would barely speak to her on the phone. Her husband disconnected his phone, and mutual contacts who had arranged the marriage refused to give any information.

Rani now suffers from severe mental health conditions—post-traumatic stress disorder and depressive illness. She has not been able to return to her high-flying corporate position as an advertising executive. Her husband did not return the furniture given by her family, and the thousands of dollars' worth of gold and gifts given to the relatives of the groom have never been acknowledged or returned.

I have met hundreds of victims of dowry abuse and hundreds of parents who have had jewellery, cash and household goods stolen from their daughters who have been abandoned by their husband. Dozens of victims of broken marriages have told me of Australian-Indian grooms demanding lavish weddings in lieu of dowry payments, and that their family were pressured into spending all their savings on just the one celebration. Later, they were taunted for not giving enough gifts to the groom's family, or cash or household gifts.[4] Dozens have told me that oppressive dowry demands can go on for years.

They all say, 'We trusted him.'

Honesty and a lack of corruption are important factors in any society. They hold society together. They improve commerce, making countries richer. It is no surprise that where there is most corruption, there is a serious imbalance in power and wealth, impacting on the health and happiness of those within the society.

This lack of happiness is echoed on the family level too, in the corruption of the system of arranged marriages.

Dowry increases a man's value, whether he is a criminal or not.

The dowry system allows grooms and their families to steal in broad daylight, in full view of all. No one suspects anything foul when demands are made for cash or furniture or gold in the name of family status and honour. In any other circumstance, someone demanding money and oversized gifts in a coercive manner would be considered a criminal. But dowry is an institution that excuses such behaviours because it is being committed by the groom, or by his mother or his father, all of whom have a God-like status. The criminals roam free and the law does not catch up. And those who we might consider 'real' criminals, such as those involved in drug dealing—though the distinction is barely warranted—are also taking full advantage of unsuspecting parents and the dowry system to deceive and defraud.

The Indian National Council of Women's report on NRI marriages states: 'In the eagerness not to let go of such lucrative marriage offers, the families totally ignore even the common cautions that are observed in traditional matchmaking.'[5] This is how criminals get through the normal checks that parents would apply to male strangers they meet for the first time. It is how the normal caution parents would exercise about the safety of their daughter and their entire life savings is ignored.

Why do some parents not treat such people with the suspicion they deserve? Is it because marriage is more important than the individual person? And, if so, why is marriage the only respectable avenue of life?

An answer came from the Indian community of Victoria, Australia. A community participatory theatre *Natak Vihar* (Sanskrit for *theatre space*) was created in 2016 with the Indian and the broader South Asian community. Its purpose was to understand the drivers of family violence, raise awareness, break silence and, most of all, to seek solutions to it.[6] The community interaction during one play brought up many issues around the foundational questions in the culture of arranged marriage. The most significant is that a daughter is only ever a guest in her father's home. Her rightful home will be her husband's home. In *Manusmriti*: 'In childhood she should remain under the control of her father, in youth under that of her husband, and on the husband's death under that of her sons; the woman should never have recourse to independence.'[7] Our audience told us that 'families start to get tensed up when the daughter is getting to the marriageable age'. This has serious consequences on the psyche of the whole society, driven by the need to arrange the best possible marriage for a daughter as soon as is practical.[8]

Growing up in India, I myself was not immune from Manu's teachings. That I would get married one day and leave my parents' home was a given. Though subconscious, the thought was strong. However, my father, the ultimate patriarch, fortunately never pressured me to get married when I finished medical school. Just last year, my aunt told me this story. Some friends had approached her with a marriage proposal for me. She brought it to my mother and father in my absence. She tells me that my father exploded at her. 'She has just finished studying. Do not bring proposals.'

We were always aware of the pejorative term for grooms who relied on their wife's family income or lived in her family home—*ghar jawaii*, meaning home-based son-in-law. They were objects of derision and laughter, ridiculed by society. Unacceptable. Why? Because this behaviour weakens the patriarchal dominance. No one laughs at grooms who extort gifts, cash, and gold. Why should that be so? Dowry and dowry demands enhance and reflect the power of the groom over that of the bride. Dowry strengthens patriarchy and devalues women.[9]

Society ensures the system does not change.[10]

Women doing the work of patriarchy ensure the system does not change.

Sujatha's mother-in-law illustrates how it is done. She demanded Sujatha give in to her husband and comply with his abusive demands—be it cooking in the middle of the night or sex when he was intoxicated. She was told not to backchat. She coerced Sujatha into handing over her jewellery to her, and her hard-earned income to her husband. Sujatha was an educated woman; she knew her rights. She was starting to feel oppressed, and she objected to his behaviour. He hit and attacked her on multiple occasions. Her mother-in-law openly supported her abusive son by criticising Sujatha's 'dominating' attitude and backchatting. She herself had been a victim in the not-too-distant past.

Why was she facilitating violence? What was the advantage to her? Kandiyoti's thesis helps us understand. She was enjoying the power over her daughter-in-law; power handed to her by her son.

She was doing the work of patriarchy in return for power. She was maintaining the system that perpetuates male dominance and abuse.

Her father was a wealthy businessman visiting from North India, to support his abused daughter. He told me that he hadn't been concerned about getting his daughter married quickly. But according to her grandmother, she was too old at thirty. 'She must be married off. What is wrong with you?' Sujatha's grandmother told her son. 'Everyone in the neighbourhood is talking about it. Get her married.' He felt compelled to do so. But they could not find good grooms in India, he said. Sujatha was a successful manager in India. She had her own car, a great office, and was respected at work. She was in no hurry to get married. But an offer of an Australian-Indian groom was too good to refuse. They were married; a dowry of $40 000 was given in cash, a similar amount spent on the wedding, and more on gifts for the new in-laws along with Sujatha's gold jewellery.

It all went bad in Australia after her arrival. She found out her husband worked part-time due to a heavy drinking problem but wanted to buy a posh house in the Adelaide Hills. He demanded she ask her father to send him money to buy the house, but she refused. She was a strong woman and she was offended. She spoke loudly and told him off for drinking too much. Incensed, he hit her, then hit himself and called the police to say that he was the victim of violence. Sujatha was charged, a restraining order was issued against her, and she was thrown out of the house in the middle of the night in a city in which she knew no one.

Sujatha got her permanent residency visa, but has not been able to reclaim her extensive dowry. Sujatha and her father often spoke about the immense pressure he felt from the women in his family to marry off his lovely daughter. Sujatha said, 'I was in heaven in India. I had a great life. I did not need to come to Australia.'

The custom that a daughter must relocate to her husband's home is noted in the ancient Sanskrit scriptures of *Manusmriti*. It has been as harmful as girl children being married off.

Sujatha's case also highlights the transnational nature of the crime of dowry abuse. Men who are criminal exploit the bride, knowing that no law can catch up with them. Dowry was given in India, but the crime happened in Australia. The man ensured that all transactions occurred in cash or were transferred into his brother's

Indian bank account. Australian courts cannot catch up with him. Extradition orders have been issued by the Indian courts, but he has not returned to face justice.

Returning to Rani: what if her parents had not found this man to marry their daughter? Her age—thirty-eight—worried them so much. By Indian standards she was very old for a single woman, and they were desperate to see their daughter become respectable in society by being married. A man can be any age and single and there is no judgement. But not a woman. Indian culture disadvantages single women and privileges single men, and this criminal and his family took full advantage of this cultural bias. Rani's parents would never have wanted to put her in harm's way, but their unconscious thoughts and biases were powerful. Societal pressure and years of conditioning and training become attitudes that drive our actions without full conscious control. We think we are making logical, rational decisions, but we are driven by what we have soaked up from our environment. Our unconscious brains can be managed by conscious rational thought, but in far too many cases, rational thinking does not override the unconscious bias for women—they must marry, marry early, and marry up the social ladder, and who better than an NRI groom? He ticks all the boxes, earning him greater privileges and a greater sense of entitlement than the local grooms.

Within a week, Rani started to recognise that she had been lied to and cheated. She was educated, not lacking in the self-confidence to settle down or the ability to express herself. Her husband had banked on her lack of knowledge about how many Indians abroad live in poverty—struggling to just survive, let alone become wealthy. There is a common misperception in the minds of Indian parents that money is easy to come by in countries like Australia, Europe, the UK, and the United States, and that their daughters will live in luxury. This lie is perpetuated by those who are too embarrassed or ashamed to admit that they are not as successful as the mythical ubiquitous, wealthy, successful expat Indian. The man that became Rani's husband purposefully exploited this misperception, and trapped Rani's parents into paying him a huge dowry. Adding to the bargain, it was expected that Rani would follow the tradition of the 'ideal' Indian wife—like Sita, the submissive wife of Lord Rama Ramayana—diffident, submissive, and putting up with everything to adjust into his family, including sacrificing her individuality and her voice.[11] But she didn't. Rani started to ask questions. Where did he get his degrees? What was his job? And why did he go missing for days without informing her? He met her questions with hostility and told her to shut her mouth.

This is often the impetus for violence—when the new wife realises that she cannot trust her husband and starts asking questions, in situations where the groom has been withholding information from her and her parents about his social position or his visa status. (He may only have a temporary visa while pretending to have permanent residency, for example.) The husband becomes incensed because his authority and control are challenged. He must be trusted implicitly and not questioned. His sense of entitlement demands this—ever since he was a child, he has been told that he is the sun that shines in his parents' lives. He is successful and smart, the prince who will inherit his father's fortunes. The fear of not living up to this idealised image is a trap for many men, leading them to lie and exaggerate their achievements—something that is easier to do when living abroad, as an NRI. He is the one who will bring a bride home, and he will get dowry. His bride will be there to serve him and his family, just as his mother served his father and his family. He has seen his father seated while his mother hovers over him, looking after his every wish. Unconsciously, he feels entitled to have a bride, to have her trust, to have her money and her parent's money, and to have the money of his own parents over and above his sisters. And the shame, the fear of societal judgement if he is not a wealthy or successful migrant, may fuel his greed and sense of entitlement. What a situation to send a young woman into.

## DISCARDABLE BRIDES

The Western/Australian concept of marriage and the Indian concept of marriage appear to be entirely different on the surface. However, both systems are based on patriarchal structures, with gender-based inequalities. In the Western system, individuals appear to be empowered by making their own choices. The choice of life partner and marriage begins with an initial lustful encounter. It is love between the partners, primarily romantic, sensual love, or individual affection that begins the journey. It can be argued that lust is not a good basis for making informed decisions about a life mate; that the overestimation of romantic love leads to disillusionment and break up of marriage.[12] In the Eastern/Indian system, the heads of the families (sometimes along with the prospective groom/bride) make a considered decision that will fulfil the demands of loyalty to the family and society. The marriage is between the two families, with dowry as an investment, and it is forever. Love hopefully grows after the marriage.[13] In this system, brides are not discardable. But in modern times, benefited by huge migration, the system enables deceit and abandonment. The system of sponsorship of visa by the NRI partner—usually a husband—perpetuates inequalities that are pre-existent within the institution of marriage. These inequalities are exacerbated by economics and foreign policies. The groom's family is able to command greater resources, knowledge of state institutions, and legal mechanisms. The bride, who is legally dependent on the sponsorship of the groom, is disempowered. She is easily discardable.[14]

Change is needed.

Imagine the heartbreak for the whole family when the bride is abandoned, either through breach of trust or domestic violence. In a society where women are defined by their marital status, divorce is unsurprisingly not something that women want for themselves. Many women end up doing everything within their power to keep their marriage together. I have seen that happen in Australia in many traditional ethnic communities, including Indian. Women will put up with physical violence, rape within marriage, emotional abuse or financial abuse, dowry extortion or demands, but not call the police for fear of marital breakdown and the stigma of divorce.

Rekha, a 38-year-old early childhood teacher who was married to an Australian-Indian engineer for fifteen years, begged her husband to not break up the marriage. She cried and she cajoled, but he had no intention of re-uniting with his wife. He simply sent her an email. He blamed her depression. She had received treatment for depressive illness because of his violence, financial abuse, and exploitation. She had started suffering severe pain in her elbows and shoulder because of arthritis. 'He made me pay the majority of the household bills, mortgage, while contributing very little to the household finances, in spite of being the higher income earner,' she told me. She was distraught. She had been exploited and deceived by him. She was going to be homeless. She could not afford to buy him out. Her family in India were not supportive of her separation. She was lonely and isolated. She would not join the Temple for fear of being judged. Had she left him early on in the marriage, perhaps she would have been in more control of her own life: she might have pursued better education. But she had left it so long, and felt broken.

NRI marriages carry great risk of abandonment—many brides are simply left behind in India and never invited to the foreign residence. By some estimates, 50 000 women have been deserted by their NRI husbands in this way.[15] The Indian government received 6094 complaints from distressed women between 2014 and 2019.[16] The Indian National Commission of Women chairperson Rekha Sharma, speaking in 2019, put the number of complaints at 4700 in the last ten years.[17] Of these, 1105 referred to NRI husbands living in the US, 378 in Australia, and 326 in Canada.

This number represents a very small portion of actual numbers.

In my own clinic, from the years 2012 to 2020, I saw more than 600 women abandoned by their husbands within Australia (and more than that are living back in India). That is just one clinic in Melbourne. It does not include other organisations and services helping women in Victoria and across the rest of Australia. More and more domestic service providers are seeing or perhaps recognising dowry-related abuse and abandonment. The second-largest group seeking help in Australia from the national domestic violence support call centre 1800RESPECT is Indian women.[18] Some of my patients were already permanent residents; some were students with no rights or pathway to permanent residency; some were here on inadequate student visas. The most vulnerable were the partners of international students and skilled migrants. Some were being sent back to India or going back of their own accord. The picture is highly complex, and the exact numbers are difficult to find.

A Supreme Court petition filed in India by eight abandoned brides of NRI husbands notes the number to be 40 000.[19] Another estimate comes from the NRI wing of the Punjab Government, which estimates 30 000 legal cases are pending in Punjab alone.[20] These are newly married women living in India waiting for their NRI grooms to return from Australia, the US, the UK, Canada, and Europe to take them overseas or explain why they were abandoned, and return the dowries paid.

Abandoned brides and their parents feel powerless to pursue answers from grooms and their families. Why is that? I have spoken to a hundred or more such women in India about this.

The courts in India can impound passports and issue look out circulars (LOCs). According to the Indian Ministry of External Affairs, it has revoked or impounded twenty-four passports and has suspended twenty-one passports of erring spouses based on the complaints received and issuance of look out circulars. This is a tiny drop in the ocean when one considers the estimated numbers of abandoned brides.

The helplessness of these women has reached the ears of the Ministry of External Affairs. On 13 March 2020, the Indian

Government passed a bill put forward in 2019 that authorises compulsory registration of all NRI marriages within thirty days and an amendment to the Passport Act, stipulating the impounding of the groom's passport if this is not done. It also recommends better coordination with the member countries of the Hague Convention to take up the issues of NRI marital disputes.[21]

This problem cannot be addressed properly unless a global effort is made through an international platform.

Currently, such impounding of passport notices is meant to be passed on to the local embassies in the foreign countries, who are required to follow up with the relevant local authorities. But, according to my contact with the group of NRI abandoned brides calling themselves Truth Still Alive, it is almost unheard of that the erring husbands return to India to face justice. There is no incentive for NRI husbands to do so, though in some cases they return to India by stealth and do not get caught. Extradition treaties are available to the Indian Government but are not being used. In a personal communication, the Australian Department of Home Affairs said that an extradition request is taken seriously when there is a serious crime.[22] But marriage break-up is not a crime.

We need specific, gender-sensitive laws in Australia that recognise abandonment of imported brides as a crime.

Returning to the money, for a moment.

The problem of return of dowry in Australia is complicated by differing legal systems. The Australian Family Law system, and Western countries more generally, operate on the general principle that property division after separation is based on, among other things, direct financial contributions made by each party, such as wage and salary earnings. The courts also take into account indirect financial contributions, such as inheritances from families and gifts.[23] Dowry constitutes such gifts.

Traditional cultural practice dictates that the gifts are to be passed into the practical control of the groom or his mother, and a woman's control over her dowry diminishes. This usually happens in private, behind closed doors, with no witnesses, and no evidence to prove it.

In case of separation, dowry is rarely returned to the bride, and there are few prosecutions. I once met a man in Melbourne who said his bride in India was mounting a dowry case against him and it was fake. When I asked him what had been given, he minimised it by saying, 'It was nothing. She brought it to my brother's house [in India], it was for her own use.' I asked again what was given. He replied, 'Just the bedroom furniture—bed, cupboard, bed linen.' 'Why was that furniture taken?' I asked. 'Was she not going to come to Australia to be with you?' 'Yes,' he said. (Though she didn't; she was abandoned in India.) 'Was there no bed for her in your brother's house in India?' He mumbled, 'It was her choice.'

No, it is not free choice. It was enforced. She could have been advised to not waste her money. This groom 'could not remember' what else was given, though it is likely the bedroom furniture was just the start of it. Most men and their families conveniently 'forget'. This produces two different realities—one for the woman and another for the man. This is used by the groom's lawyers to produce doubt, and that is sufficient in the adversarial system of law to avoid conviction.

One woman's family paid for the three-day wedding functions (approximately $30 000), dowry worth $40 000 and a car that was left behind in India for the mother-in-law's use. After the break-up in Australia, his parents in India returned the car to her parents, but in bad repair, along with some damaged furniture. In addition, the groom also paid her $20 000 in Melbourne. She was a rare case. But in her favour was evidence that $20 000 had been transferred from her Australian account into his account.

At the present moment, dowry demands are not recognised in the Australian Federal Family Law Act as an example of family violence.[24] Such an addition would help educate the police and the judiciary, entitle the bride to claim her dowry in Australia, and give her better access to justice.

One can ask, though: is it not natural for the husband's family to claim the gifts and cash after a marriage break-up? Given they were *gifts*.

There is confusion over what constitutes dowry, which many wrongly believe is only the cash and gifts given in the pre-wedding ceremony, previously defined as groom-price. But the extravagant cost of the five-step wedding ceremony, the cash and gold gifts for the groom and his family, and the bridal-wealth are all dowry; all gifts brought into the marriage by the bride. Both the Indian and Australian laws agree on this point—when a marriage breaks up, all of this needs to be returned to the bride. But, regardless, this is a disingenuous way of looking at it. An arranged marriage is an unspoken social and financial contract between two families: it is an investment, and the grooms and their families know it. The bride's parents spend all their wealth and borrow to supply the groom and his family with financial resources—and the social contract is that they will take care of the bride from now until her death. The groom can't simply walk away from this contract; if he does, he must return everything. But this rarely happens.

We also need a transnational system that will make it easier for women to reclaim dowries in Australia whether they are given here, in India, or elsewhere overseas.

Hopefully, the increasing threat of a marital break-up and the final division of resources will play a role in curbing the costs of weddings. Education and awareness campaigns are required so that the future happiness of the young couple is not dependent on the level of extravagance of the wedding ceremony and the size of the dowry, but their capacity to adapt to each other as a husband and wife. In India, women are more educated than ever before.[25] Increasingly, they are earning income and adding to the marital finances. (Though many daughters-in-law still are told, 'There is no need for you to earn money; we have enough.') They are not financial burdens. There is no need for dowry, no justification for it.

Society needs to give equal value to women, and the messages of equality need to be conveyed to the children by the families. Parents need to bring up their daughters with the mindset that they are as valuable as sons, as capable of looking after themselves as boys if given a chance, and as capable of supporting their parents as sons. Men have power over women because they interact with the wider world more than women do. This pattern starts early on in life. Girls are told to stay home and be safe; boys are given free hand. In Australia, one migrant mother recognised this in a community education session on enhancing gender equality run by our NGO.[26] A well-meaning parent, she said she would allow their teenage daughter to stay out with friends until 10 pm, and insist upon picking her up. Her brother, on the other hand, was allowed the independence to go anywhere he wanted with his friends and make his own way home. The immigrant parents were being careful, but had not recognised the impact of this different approach on their daughter's confidence in acquiring life experiences, in learning to protect herself along with those unexpected lessons that independence brings. They thought they had given their daughter freedom and experiences equal to anyone else. The discussion in the session was a 'light bulb' moment, she said. It opened up discussion regarding 'well meaning' disadvantages, or handicaps imposed on girls. Sex is one of the most difficult areas for migrant parents. Boys are not watched and protected; girls are. Boys can have girlfriends but for a girl to have boyfriend is shameful for her and family.

In all of this, boys end up learning more about life.

I once met an Indian lawyer in Melbourne who told me that 'all dowry cases are fake'. This is a pervasive mindset. (This is not to deny that occasional false cases of dowry abuse occur). In India, nearly 200 000 people were arrested over dowry offences in 2012, but only about 15 per cent of the accused were convicted.[27] (Dowry cases meaning financial demands, associated with verbal abuse, physical and sexual violence. Usually, it is all combined.) This is the consequence of the weak and slow implementation of the law and a backlog of hundreds of thousands of cases in the system, leading to a lack of justice for women.[28] But the low conviction rate is used by some as evidence that most dowry claim cases are fake.

In 2018, the Supreme Court of India stated there was no credible data to suggest that the laws against dowry were misused, adding that 'Law, especially criminal law, intends to control, if not altogether remove, the malady that gets into the spine of the society and gradually corrodes the marrows of the vertebrae of a large section of the society.'[29]

# 5
# THE MALADY (DOWRY DEATHS)

I was about eleven when a neighbour's daughter got married in 1958. Sheela was a 'very old' single maid, in the terminology of those days. She was about twenty-eight, and our neighbour had been worried sick that she would never be able to get her married off. That was a stigma so big that being married to any man, with or without good qualities, was better than being a single woman.

Sheela was pretty and educated. Her new husband was a schoolteacher, a short fat man of reasonable intelligence who had been married once before. His first wife died in an 'accidental' kitchen fire, as do many women in India. Such fires are not accidental at all. Research by Dr Ranjana Kumari found that the majority of these deaths are homicides perpetrated by husbands and mothers-in-law, usually for insufficient dowry.[1] It would have been easy for Sheela's husband to set his first bride alight as she sat on the floor cooking on a kerosene stove, wearing a sari of cotton or synthetic material—six yards of fabric to catch fire. It would be easy for him to do the same to Sheela, but her mother did not want to think about that. Sheela was given a huge dowry in cash and gold jewellery, a big wedding and lots of gifts for the groom and his family. After the wedding, her husband and mother-in-law criticised her, humiliated her, and excluded her. She was too old. Sheela went on to have two children with her husband, proving them wrong.

My father, who was seen as a substantial authority figure by most in our network, influenced their family matters just by being there. I am confident he was instrumental in intimidating her husband into behaving himself.

This kind of power of the patriarch of the family is a widely accepted cultural norm. The notions of complete equality are seldom evident in daily life. Societal hierarchy is evident in caste groups, amongst individuals, and in family and kinship groups. It upholds the ideals of conduct and maintains family honour, and strengthens the collective societal system.[2]

Migration tends to disrupt the collectivist system, with positive and negative consequences.[3] My father was a generous and benevolent patriarch. But what if he had not been? Power imbalance facilitates abuse. Societies world over are suffering inequalities, with benefits for those in power and losses for the subordinates. The powerful have better mental and physical health, more wealth, better sleep, and faster decision making, and the less powerful and subordinates, in contrast, have poor mental and physical health, higher morbidity and mortality, less access to resources, education, wealth, and the list goes on.[4]

Luckily, Sheela survived into old age, outliving her husband. Had she not had that support, she could have been another victim, one more statistic.

# THE MALADY (DOWRY DEATHS)

A dowry death, according to section 304B(1) of the Indian Penal Code, is a death otherwise than under normal circumstances (including suicide), within seven years of marriage and where it is shown that soon before her death the wife was harassed or subjected to cruelty by the husband or his relatives for, or in connection with, dowry. The National Crime Records Bureau (NCRB) defines it is a homicide or suicide in connection with mental cruelty, harassment and bullying in relation to insufficient dowry.

More than 7600 dowry deaths were reported over the twelve-month period of 2016, according to the NCRB. Dowry deaths rose from about 19 per day in 2001 to 21 per day in 2016.[5] Twenty-one dowry deaths every twenty-four hours, as the media put it. Female dowry deaths account for 40–50 per cent of all female homicides recorded annually in India, representing a stable trend over the period 1999 to 2016.[6] Although dowry practice is found in many parts of the world—the Horn of Africa, the Middle East—dowry deaths are found predominantly in India, Pakistan, Bangladesh, and Iran. Pakistan's dowry deaths are higher than India's—2.4 out of every 100000 women, compared to 1.4 out of every 100000.[7] Globally, 137 women are killed by a member of their own family every day. Such homicides, also known as femicides, seem to be on the increase. The largest number of femicides was in Asia (20000) followed by Africa (19000).[8]

In Melbourne, I have observed the same pattern among Pakistani victim-survivors of family violence as with Indian women. Despite it being a Muslim country, the practice of dowry in Pakistan follows the traditional practice of Hindu India, where it is conceptualised as pre-mortem inheritance. Emulation of the dowry system by the Muslim culture of Pakistan points to dowry being a manifestation of patriarchy—and a convenient way to increase power of grooms and men over brides and women, in turn facilitating domestic violence.

A famous case in Melbourne was the murder of Deepshikha Godara in December 2014 by her estranged NRI husband. Her death came after 'years of prolonged physical and emotional abuse at the hands of her husband', the coroner found, and when she had been separated from him for a year and had a protection order in place. Her husband's uncle told her that she was getting access to a grand Australian life for free, courtesy of her husband.

An Al Jezeera documentary, *Australia's Dowry Deaths* noted:

> Deepshikha's family gave her dowry, which included gold, diamond necklaces and money. But soon after Deepshikha moved to Australia … her husband and his family began demanding more. One year into her marriage, the demands for more dowry got so bad Deepshikha went to the police. Two years later she was dead at the hands of her husband.[9]

During the coroner's inquest, a police statement taken six years before her murder was produced. 'One night in January 2008 Sunil's uncle got drunk and verbally abused me and my family for not paying enough dowry which is *Indian currency* after my marriage to Sunil.'[10] The local police didn't understand how dangerous issues around dowry could be. There was limited awareness in Australia in general, but a secret kept within the community. There was resistance from some quarters to our campaign designed to break the silence. The resistance came from patriarchs of some Indian community organisations. They took their complaint to their local MPs and Ministers. They argued that dowry was not an Australian problem, it was an Indian problem; dowries were being given in India, and did not merit legislative change in Australia; that Indian community would be named and shamed. My argument to the policy makers and MPs was that the dowry was given in India, but extortive demand continues in Australia. Further, many brides after breaking up (usually due to domestic violence) are not able to claw back the dowry gifts, usually substantial wealth and gold. It is usually under the possession of the groom and his family, held in Australia and sometimes in India. The transnational nature of dowry crime deserves transnational responses. This is an indication that we must stay the course with our campaign to increase awareness around dowry and dowry-related abuse in Australia, despite resistance from some quarters.

Two years before Deepshikha Godara was murdered, our NGO, the AustralAsian Centre for Human Rights and Health, began a petition to include dowry abuse in Victorian law. It came into law seven years later, in 2019, with dowry abuse specified as an example of family violence. The campaign to attain the law led to hundreds of media articles and helped to raise awareness, but progress is inconsistent. For example, in 2019, a young newly married woman in Melbourne rejected her husband's demand for $50 000 (he wanted to obtain a loan for an investment property), but was nevertheless manipulated into giving him $20 000. Afterwards, when she demanded to know the exact expenditure and income arising from tenancy arrangements, he was abusive and threatening. She was afraid he would harm her. She approached her local police station and told them about the dowry demands, saying she wanted a protection order. The police officer refused, saying it was a civil matter. He told her, 'I am white Anglo-Saxon male, I do not understand the cultural practice of dowry.' He refused to take her complaint. She was distraught and contacted me. I was able to guide her, and she got her protection order in the court.

This brought home to me the need for consistent education for service providers in the police and justice system.

Al Jezeera documentary *Australia's Dowry Deaths* formed a part of our successful campaign that resulted in legislating against dowry demands in Victoria in March 2019.[11]

In a personal interview in 2015, Deepshikha's father, Ashok Kumar Godara, who arrived in Melbourne after her murder, told me that he supplied Deepshikha's new family with more cash out of fear for her safety, and at one stage he considered cashing his superannuation funds to meet her husband's demands. Elders of the groom's families tout themselves as the powerbrokers in the wedding ceremony, he noted. But when one complains to them about domestic violence and dowry demands, they say they are powerless to influence their son in Australia.[12]

His letter of support of our campaign was powerful and astute:

Why Anti-Dowry law is needed

Large number of Indian origins have migrated and settled in Australia obtaining Permanent Resident. Some of them get married in India and migrate to this country with their brides. Other who have already inhabiting go to India and get married with that country's girls and return with them. Indian origins have roots in their country. They have their roots in Indian culture, traditions and rituals. All the rituals are performed in their wedding ceremony in Indian tradition. It is known fact that despite of stringent law against dowry, people receive the dowry, so do the Indian Australians. When they go to India for wedding, their parents choose the brides for them. Since the father being the head of the family has command, authority and influence on all the activities, all the rituals are performed in his patronage. Marriage rates are fixed and decided by the fathers for their sons. Traditionally, these are fixed according to their status and position/post of their sons. Money incurred Rs. 20 lacs to 50 lacs [$40 000 to $100 000] to bestow upon groom and his parents according to their status. It's varying from the position like doctor, lawyer, engineer, professors, managers or teachers and executives. In wedding ceremonies, all luxury cars, A.C., T.V., fridge, utensils, costly watches, branded clothes, gold jewellery and diamond rings are given. Grooms and their parents enjoy with these dowry items and return to Australia. When they, in-laws commit domestic violence against brides/wives for dowry, there is no law to punish them for bullying. They escape from stringent anti-dowry law since they have not committed crime in India and vice-versa grooms/boys commit offense in Australia and their dowry seekers parents live in India and get Scot free.

In Indian law, two kinds of remedies are provided to the victims:-

1. All dowry assets are retracted or retrieved from the groom/boy and his parents

2. Criminal case is registered against the whole family including the parents of dowry seekers and prosecuted.

Due to non-existence of such a law, these two kinds of problems prevail consistently in Australia. Further, matter gets complicated when family is divided, son and his wife reside in Australia and his parents reside back in India.

They hide behind absence of laws. It's mockery of justice. In India, if the domestic violence is committed to satiate their greed and lust by dowry demands whole family is prosecuted, convicted and sent behind the bars. Therefore, in Australia, law should be enacted in a similar way to make liable every member of the family for dowry crimes so that lives of the innocent girls may be protected.

With Regards

Ashok Kumar Godara [13]

Part of the problem of understanding the harm caused by dowry is that parents give dowry for a number of different reasons. An audit of fifty-six of my South Asian patients, all survivors of family violence, revealed that half of them had suffered dowry-related demands and abuse.[14] I analysed why those women and their parents gave dowry, supplementing this information with my ongoing clinical observations and interviews with dozens of parents and siblings seen with young women victims of dowry-related violence in my clinic. The findings:

(a) Some parents give dowry as ante-mortem inheritance for their daughters, despite equal inheritance laws in Australia and India. One woman, an MBA graduate, said that her brother got everything that her wealthy medico parents owned in the North Indian state of Utter Pradesh, while she got some cash and gold as dowry—which was all taken away by her husband. She got no family inheritance after her divorce and fell into poverty.

(b) Others regard dowry as a payment to take on a liability. For example, one set of parents gave an Australian-Indian man a million dollars in an extravagant wedding and dowry for marrying their daughter, a marketing manager by profession. She had a shorter left leg as the result of a car accident. The groom had been married three times before, but he was not considered handicapped by her family or his.

(c) Some give dowry out of fear that insufficient gifts will lead to violence against their daughter.

(d) Yet others give dowry to demonstrate their social status. One young male international student told me that he gave a huge dowry at his sister's wedding recently in India. He also said that if he did not receive dowry when he married it would be a shameful thing for his family. 'It is a matter of family honour,' he said.

(e) Some give dowry because of peer pressure. One father told me that it is very hard to not give dowry. 'All the neighbourhood comes asking, "What did you give to your daughter?" We have to display the dowry given.'

(f) Some give dowry to catch the best possible groom in a competitive marriage market. It is like a marketplace. One father told me that good grooms were not available in India, and he chose an Australia-Indian groom for his successful daughter. The dowry expected was big—around $40 000—and given. Yet more was demanded after the marriage.

(g) For some, giving dowry is a genuine desire to increase the wealth level of the new couple. These are possibly happy marriages where there is no demand made and nothing is expected. There is no violence, and they live happily.

The practice of dowry places an unfair burden on the bride and her family, and is an unearned privilege for the groom and his family.

In spite of education and holding high-powered positions—becoming astronauts, doctors and IT engineers—it is disturbing that young women are not exercising the agency and choices they have acquired as a result of their education and walk away from grooms who expect dowry.

It is sad to see that patriarchy raises its head, and women's liberation from dowry is suppressed.

Occasionally one hears of a young woman walking away from the wedding because her mother-in-law has asked for dowry. But not often. A young, educated second-generation migrant woman, born and brought up in Australia—let us call her Rima—did not object to her parents giving exorbitant gifts to her in-laws and husband who had lived in Australia for decades. Not only were gold jewellery and gifts demanded for his immediate family in Australia, but also for his extended family back in India. All up it cost Rima's parents $125 000. But still the dowry was deemed insufficient by her in-laws.

I asked Rima why she did not object to giving dowry. She said the decisions were being made by the elders in the family. The bride's opinion regarding the financial and gift-giving transactions prior to the wedding is considered inconsequential. One young victim of dowry abuse said, 'It is like things are happening around the bride.' The groom, however, has a voice—he gets to say what he would like as dowry gifts. Rima's groom, a young, educated Australian-Indian, did not stand up against the dowry demands put forward by his parents. He accepted his parents' statement to Rima's mother: 'We are the groom side, and we get to make decisions on how the wedding will be conducted.'

Looking back at it in trauma therapy, Rima could recall being uncomfortable with the demands of her future husband and in-laws and their dominance over decision making. These were inconvenient, uncomfortable thoughts, and she pushed them into her subconscious. She just glided along, as the dream of her life came true, enjoying the festivities and the drama of being a bride, buying the most expensive clothes and gold jewellery for herself. She regrets not noticing the red flags that there were present from the beginning.

Many women have told me the red flags were there during the pre-wedding transactions, but that they ignored them. Demands for more gold jewellery for their relatives, boxes of sweets and fruit baskets were not sufficient gifts, the demands began just before the wedding. It was too late to cancel the wedding. What will people say, their parents said, and the preparations for the wedding continued. If young women were to value themselves as men do, they would not put up with bad behaviour. If young men were to receive education at home and school, and if there was broader messaging in the community about the unfairness of the unearned superior status of one gender that entitles them to privileges and dowry and causes similar harm to racism and caste-based discrimination, it may change behaviour. Sadly, though, at our community education programs male participation rates tend to be low—around one-third or less, sometimes even zero. In recent gender-segregated workshops for women and men, no one registered for the male-only workshop and it had to be cancelled. The female-only workshop was well attended. The meaning is clear—women instinctively know what domestic violence is and are eager to learn how to stop it. But we need to engage men. Why didn't they want to attend? Work, financial pressures, not enough time, were the reasons given to the leader of the workshop. But, in reality, it was the topic.

Perhaps my clinical work with perpetrators of family violence can shed light. I have seen that men expect to be respected, and feel hurt if they are not given the respect and voice that they believe is their due. This easily turns to anger. Young women are told that they must accept their submissive position and put up with a lack of respect, and many do. Those who do not submit suffer abuse and violence. Men have the power to stop violence against women.

Every parent needs training in parenting techniques that feel culturally appropriate to learn how to bring out equal best in their sons and daughters. They have enormous influence over their children. Every school should make it an essential subject of education on life. Australia has started respectful relationships education in schools, and the evidence is that it is a very promising intervention, enhances gender equality and respectful relations, and reduces bullying behaviours. All are essential ingredients if we are to stop family domestic and sexual violence.[15] Similar education programs ought to be part of tertiary education.

Rima's marriage broke up within a year of the big fat Indian wedding. Her modern education, and her wish to express her individuality, were at odds with the centuries-old traditions that she had nevertheless absorbed—avoiding boyfriends before marriage, and getting married as soon as practicable. She was also under the influence of the expectations that her groom and his family were imposing on her. Their controlling and coercive behaviour became manifest, and she could not bear the oppression. Not satisfied with dozens of boxes of fruits and sweets sent by her parents, her groom and his family continued their demands, wanting more gold jewellery gifts at key festivals. She left the house after a series of life-threatening arguments.

She is now amazed at herself—why did she and her parents put up with her future in-laws' greedy, oppressive demands for more than eighteen months? Why did she not raise her voice earlier? Or raise her objections and walk out even before the marriage had taken place?

Dowry abuse usually co-exists with other types of family violence, and subordination and coercive control are the common link. Death is the final price to pay when there is failure to comply.

Imagine the level of fear in the community. It is like the coronavirus. No one knows when it will hit you. This holds parents in nervous anticipation of the first evidence of dowry demands from the groom's family. Caught between opposing forces—the shame of marital break-up and loss of dowry, versus the safety of their daughter—many are paralysed.

Many families are neither happy nor peaceful. One social welfare minister, Ramsewak Singh, from the Indian State of Bihar, said 'to tackle this social demon, it requires 100 per cent participation of the common people.'[16]

# 6
# SOCIETAL FEAR PARALYSES SOCIAL CHANGE

*'Serving her husband is like living with a teacher, tending the house equals tending of the of sacred fires.'*

Manavdhramashtra[1]

*'Though destitute of virtue, or seeking pleasure (elsewhere), or devoid of good qualities, (yet) a husband must be constantly worshipped as a god by a faithful wife.'*

Manusmriti, chapter 5 verse 5.152 [2]

Even with India's embedded gender roles, it takes some parents no time at all to recognise what their daughter is going through and empathise with her. In Melbourne, working with hundreds of victims of family violence, I hear of and from parents visiting from India who are heartbroken about their daughter's marriage break-up. They are severely stressed, traumatised even. I have treated their depression, anxiety, panic attacks, insomnia and provided them with trauma-based therapy, alongside their daughter's. They put their faith in the system of arranged marriage believing it delivers stability, and yet the divorce rate of Indian marriages is rising.[3] Meanwhile, their much-loved child has gone through hell.

Some parents learn when they observe firsthand. At a family violence prevention project run by ACHRH in Victoria called 'United We Stand', a father of a young woman said that he became aware of the patriarchal dominance of decision making only after he witnessed that type of behaviour from his daughter's boyfriend. He laughed and said this changed his attitude in favour of greater gender fairness. Awareness of his patriarchal attitude occurred only after empathy for his daughter was aroused. Some come to understand later.

One young woman's parents in South India were not willing to discuss her wish to separate from her violent husband, due to their fear of the stigma of divorce and their concern that her children were too young to cope with the family break-up. This was after her husband had shoved her under a cold shower at 1 a.m., annoyed with her behaviour at a dinner party in a restaurant.

It was her brother who convinced them of her plight, and she was able to leave her husband with their support after some twenty years of domestic abuse.

Some parents never give in. That their daughter's marital home remains intact is their highest priority. As well as losing a considerable financial investment, it seems the stigma of separation and divorce affects not just the victim-survivor but also the whole family, and especially any unmarried sisters. Many women are told by their parents to patch up their marriage, otherwise their unmarried sisters will not find grooms.

The system asks these daughters to sacrifice her individual needs in service of the family and society. What pressures exist on parents that they lose empathy for their daughter's emotional and physical pain and insist she stay in a violent or abusive marriage? The lived experiences of bride-victims far away from their home in India, isolated and devoid of social support structures in Australia, makes one question the societal wheels within wheels that stop change.

'What will people say?' That is the sentence most frequently heard in the homes of Indian families in Australia, India and elsewhere. I am sure that many parents display more consideration and compassion to everyone else in their life than their own daughter.

Reena wed an Australian-Indian man in an arranged marriage, left her parents' home, and lived with her in-laws. At her husband's parents' home, Reena discovered information that caused her serious concerns, but she said nothing.

Reena told me that she was trained from childhood to not exercise any agency of her own, to not exercise her choices, and, importantly, to not think of choosing a husband:

> Being raised in an Indian traditional family where strict principles of being obedient, respectful and never questioning the husband have been repeatedly taught … that I was always to make things work out. I was back in India waiting for a spousal visa and he was back in Australia. When going through the immigration papers, I noticed that he had written somewhere that he had been in a de facto relationship. He hadn't mentioned it to me earlier. I was very surprised.
>
> As the custom dictates, after marriage I was living with my mother-in-law and father-in-law. I spoke to his parents, they reassured me that it was nothing like I was thinking but rather a girl's name that he had entered to qualify for a tax benefit. And that the girl was married and living overseas. I was anxious, but my mother-in-law would not let me speak to him by phone. 'It is too expensive,' she said.
>
> I am worried, I tell my parents that he is always aggressive, rude and curses a lot on phone.
>
> They said it will be okay, stay there. They say: 'It is always like this in an Indian marriage.'

> I arrived in Australia. I found he was rude, dismissive. He would not tell me where he is going, he would use his phone after dinner and I waited in silence for him to speak with me. When I speak he would use his hand gestures to show disrespect. He would use abusive language. He asked me to put it in writing that I will do everything as he says and that I will ask him before I do anything.

Reena was distressed when she spoke to her father in India. He was a loving man who doted on his daughter. But he was keen for her to do everything possible to save her marriage, and her family's name. The exchanges between them were tense and highly traumatic for Reena. Reena's education (she is a dentist by training) had made her aware of her human right to a safe and peaceful existence. Her father had given her the education that made her aware of this, but he would not give her the power to make herself safe and have a peaceful life.

Reena's father's letter to her on how to manage a new marriage shows why a woman is victimised for the break-up of a marriage, despite being subject to humiliation, disrespect and inhuman treatment. She found his response to her desperate situation painful to read.

> Dear Reena,
>
> I am your father and have your best interests at heart. I want to share with you our society's expectation of a young Indian woman who becomes a wife. There are some things that can make your marriage succeed. For example, you should always have sweetness in your voice while you talk to your husband. This will avoid arguments. You should not question him, and should consult him for every small thing you want to do. It is important that you appreciate his strengths and not look for weakness in him. It is important that you should try to avoid criticising him and should not allow anyone to criticize him. You should try to absorb his worries and his tensions. This will help make room in your husband's heart. Above all, believe in God and his acts,
>
> Your father

The story of a young woman named Nutan haunted me for years. Married in India—an arranged marriage—she followed her husband to Australia to find he already had another family. Her father, in India, advised his daughter to put up with her husband's abuse, control, and rejection.

How low must a woman stoop to avoid the dreaded stigma of being a divorced woman? What must she put up with to enjoy the respect given only to married women—not to single women, divorced women, a widow, or a female foetus? How much self-dignity should she lose as she begs her husband to be allowed to return to his beatings and name calling?

In spite of his behaviour, Nutan, a dentist, tried to meet her husband's demands. Against all her instincts she accepted his judgement as superior to hers and followed his instructions. She kept in mind the wife's role: to always please her husband, to always agree with him, to never argue, to be demure when he shouts, to listen politely, to try to fulfil his demands.

I asked if she believed that complete submission to this unequal situation was the right thing for her. She was a modern, educated girl with modern ideas, she told me, and she'd always had doubts about this marriage. But that she should get married early and stay married had been drummed into her from a young age. It had imposed itself so strongly on her young mind that she had never envisaged another reality as being possible.

'Living in Indian society for a girl it is difficult to buck the system,' she said. 'You just know this is your fate and to fight against it brings the spectre of rejection by your family, something that no girl can imagine doing. There is no place in society for single, young, educated women like me to live alone, live away from their family and work even in their own town.'

After hearing dozens of similar stories, I have come to believe that she is correct: that being single and living alone is a hard life, and one that many Indian women would not opt for.[4] Single women are considered fair game by men, labelled as loose characters and objects for sexual use. One way they are devalued as human beings is to have stories spread about them in their social groups, even in their families: a story that they've been raped or sexually abused, for example, further 'damages the goods', and gives justification to any rape that might then occur.

This was brought home by a young Muslim woman named Ayesha from Hyderabad, who came to Australia as an international student following a period of hell in India.

Ayesha had been an excellent student and wanted to get a tertiary degree and become an accountant. But her age was against her—at eighteen she was getting old and soon no one would want to marry her, or so her parents feared. Against her wishes, a marriage was arranged with a 42-year-old man, who came from Dubai for the wedding. Within days, he told her that he had a wife in Dubai. Ayesha demanded to know why he'd married her. Her new husband gave her a beating for being 'insolent' and complained to her parents about her behaviour.

Ayesha discovered her husband had been given a lot of dowry to marry her—in cash. He had wanted quick cash, and the easiest pathway to this in a system that protects the rights of patriarchy—where men are highly valued and women are devalued—is dowry. It provides an easy route to wealth for men while women are turned into objects, simply the means through which such an exchange happens. This man had, in fact, deliberately sought out her father's wealth. Soon there was daily violence and sexual abuse. Ayesha became pregnant. He already had a family; he did not want to feed another mouth, let alone have the burden of a child. Ayesha left him after being beaten, and returned to her parents' home. He went on to divorce her.

At her parents' house, Ayesha was subjected to victim blaming. The perpetrator of the violence against her went about his life while she was blamed for giving her family a bad name, blamed for not being a good wife, and blamed for not being able to make her marriage work. Ayesha felt she could never measure up to the standards her parents had set for her.

When I met her in Australia, Ayesha told me that she'd felt utterly powerless and helpless then, that life was futile. She thought of killing herself, but she was pregnant and wanted to live for her child. She gave birth to a boy. But before she could feel the deep pleasure of the mother-baby bond, her ex-husband came back to stake his claim on the child. He gave permission to her parents to bring him up until the age of eighteen, and then he was to be returned to his father's house. Ayesha said that tradition dictates that it is the father who owns the children, the mother has no claim. Desolate, feeling helpless and depressed, she stayed in her parents' home for a year to bring up her son. But she felt the pain of humiliations and rejections, perpetrated in equal measures by her family and society. She left her parents' home to study at a university far away, and started work at the university as a maths teacher. But she missed her son.

As Ayesha lived alone near the university campus rumours started to fly around that she was sleeping with many men, a 'loose woman'. She said that was untrue: she had male students who came to her apartment for academic discussions, just as female students did. But when her landlord heard the rumours, he evicted her.

It became impossible to find a place to live until Ayesha decided to lie and say she was married but her husband travelled a lot. This worked for a while until the rumourmongers discovered there was no husband, and she was thrown out of the house again.

> Women do not care for beauty, nor is there attention fixed on age; (thinking,) (it is enough that) he is a man, they give themselves to the handsome and to the ugly.[5]

The notion of sex and single women in South Asian communities is highly charged. There is nothing worse that a woman can be called than a 'loose character'. She is despised and humiliated, people whisper about her, and no respectable man or woman talks to her in case her shadow spreads.

Where is such a woman to turn? Ayesha was forced to beg her sister and her sister's husband to let her live with them. They were reluctant, having heard stories about her, but allowed her to move in. Then her sister's husband began to sexually harass her. Ayesha said she was devastated. Who could she turn to? She told him what he was doing was wrong. He told Ayesha that she had been with so many men it would make no difference if he had sex with her. She felt cornered, once again life felt futile, and she felt worthless. Ayesha told her parents, who once again blamed her for being a woman of loose character, and her father gave her a beating. She felt there was nothing left for her in this world.

Note how the man in question, her own brother-in-law, did not consider his ethics—or his wife. If sex outside marriage is not allowed, this rule does not apply to all men. It is there to stop women from exercising their free will and choosing a partner. Society does not punish men like Ayesha's brother-in-law. Instead, punishment is meted out to the victim. Blaming the woman takes the pressure away from the perpetrator. He is not held accountable.

The system continues.

The tools of the system are the parents of the girls who are afraid of society, and the parents of sons who have exploited and corrupted the family system.

The wheels within wheels paralyse change to the system and women remain trapped in the first-century thinking of *Manusmriti*—despite many scholars denying that *Manusmriti* has any legitimacy as a genuine document.[6]

> Though destitute of virtue, or seeking pleasure (elsewhere), or devoid of good qualities, (yet) a husband must be constantly worshipped as a god by a faithful wife.[7]

Every victim of domestic violence I have seen has confirmed in my mind that *Manusmriti* was written by a person who cherished the rules that enforced the oppression of women.

> By a girl, by a young woman, or even by an aged one, nothing must be done independently, even in her own house.
>
> In childhood a female must be subject to her father, in youth to her husband, when her lord is dead to her sons; a woman must never be independent.
>
> She must not seek to separate herself from her father, husband, or sons; by leaving them she would make both (her own and her husband's) families contemptible.
>
> She must always be cheerful, clever in (the management of her) household affairs, careful in cleaning her utensils, and economical in expenditure.
>
> Him to whom her father may give her, or her brother with the father's permission, she shall obey as long as he lives, and when he is dead, she must not insult his memory.[8]

*Manusmriti* also contributed to the unfair and unjust phenomenon of a man blaming his new bride for everything that goes wrong in his life: if he cannot find a job, if they cannot have children. She is blamed if they cannot have a son, even when the sex of babies is determined by the male gamete—the sperm.[9] One of my patients was told by her mother-in-law that she was unlucky for her son because he'd had a number of car accidents since their marriage. Her husband agreed. But when he got his much-wanted Australian residency visa, she was not credited as being lucky.

The burden placed by society on women is unfair and unjust.

To stop victim blaming, we need to keep a focus on the perpetrator and his actions.

Since the days of *Manusmriti*, over the past nineteen hundred years or so, a change in attitudes towards women has occurred in some areas. Women are becoming educated and they are allowed to work, but only as long as they remain subservient to the societal rules that state that women have much lower value than men and exist to serve the dominant masculinity. Whether it is a mother-in-law abusing their daughter-in-law or a husband or father doing the abusing, it all serves to strengthen this paralysis, this refusal of Indian society to change its attitude towards women.

All this pain has made women of India resilient and resourceful, and they have developed strength in their character. Ayesha's intelligence, her education and her resourcefulness gave her problem-solving skills. She decided to move away from India. She gathered all her courage and asked her father to give her money to pay for her education in Australia. After much begging, he relented. He thought it best for their family's honour and respect that she leave India. He was not trying to give Ayesha a better life; a woman's life, of itself, is of little value. That was how Ayesha came to Australia as an international student.

Ayesha's life experience is consistent with the theory of Over-Eye, in which society tells women that subordination to male dominance is necessary if they wish to be known as feminine and good women.[10]

Women silence their inner voice in order to preserve their relationships. Outwardly, even in the midst of fraying relationships, violence, and lives that are falling apart, they present a pleasing, compliant, submissive image to live up to these cultural standards. Meanwhile, their inner anger grows. Ayesha suffered from a powerful, powerless anger. Rage. When she expressed her feelings, she received a string of verbal and physical messages to shut her down.

Society trains young women to mistrust their own judgement, to not have agency, to not have a voice. When they do, they are told they are wrong or, as in the case of Ayesha, they are excluded from society by their family. Research shows that when your inside thoughts are at odds with the demands of the outside world, and when one must keep the inside thoughts and feelings locked away, then the likelihood of a depressive illness and suicidal behaviours are high.[11]

The women are trapped, and will keep dying by suicide until the society's 'Over-Eye' softens its stance, giving women options, respect, agency, voice, and control over their own life.

Ayesha eventually moved to Australia to pursue her studies. She got a good job and started earning money. But she also started to relive her past multiple traumas and developed post-traumatic stress disorder and a depressive illness. She would get flashbacks of beatings from her father, of the rumours, of being evicted, of being blamed for her sister's husband sexual advances. She craved to see her son. But she is not allowed to see him. She often speaks to him by phone and would like to bring him to Australia. There is very little to no chance of her getting custody of her son.

When Ayesha started to see me for treatment, she had suicidal ideation. In addition to antidepressant medication, I provided her with culturally responsive trauma therapy, and she eventually found a sense of agency and control over life.[12] She has found meaning and purpose. She financially supports her son back in India. She hopes that one day, when he is eighteen, he will decide to come to Australia.

South Asian women who come to Australia are well educated and are rapidly moving into the twenty-first century. Australian society provides them with freedom of a kind they have not known before. They can earn an income and have a greater awareness that they are entitled to control their own income. They observe the agency of their Australian counterparts and want to have their voices heard. They have a greater awareness of their human rights.

Women are ready to move up the ladder of power within their home. Women are ready to challenge the patriarchal system and gain equal status and the same freedom enjoyed by men. Women are willing to dream of a place where marriage is not their only destiny, dream of a society where being a single woman is of no less value than being a married woman. Women are already dreaming of a place where their whole being is not defined by their ability to 'tend to the marital home fires' as noted by *Manusmriti*. Women are moving into the twenty-first century, where respect and regard for mutual wellbeing means young women no longer need to 'defer to the needs of others, censor self-expression, repress anger, inhibit self-directed action, and judge the self against a culturally defined "good woman".'[13]

Society should be educating men and boys at schools to modernise their thinking and behaviour towards sisters, girls, and women. Boys and men should be trained to speak confidently to their mothers and fathers, to be able to tell them to back off if they are being harmful to their wife. They should be left to bond with their wife. 'Men need to be their wife's back,' said one participant in our community theatre project *Natak Vihar*. Let them bond with their wife, who deserves respect, who is their equal—*ardhangini*—not a lesser being. It can be done tactfully so as not to rupture family ties.

There is a deep contradiction though.

Goddesses are revered and worshipped in Hindu religion. And some women reach goddess-like status—PM Indira Gandhi, for example. Men will pray to goddesses, for example Durga, for power and good luck, but have no reverence for wives. A wife is subject to the disparaging notions espoused in *Manusmriti* and does not receive such privileges.

> If a wife obeys her husband, she will, for that reason alone be exalted in heaven. Or that through their passion for men, mutable temper, natural heartlessness, they become disloyal towards their husbands.

There is contradiction in *Manusmriti* too. It has done untold damage, but it has also provided a few verses to restrict the harm done to women's position, to give positive guidance to society and to men.[14]

In Chapter III, verse 55 advises that:

> Where women are honoured, there the gods are pleased; but where they are not honoured, no sacred rite yields rewards.

Chapter III, verse 57, warns us that:

> Where the female relations live in grief, the family soon wholly perishes; but that family where they are not unhappy ever prospers.

Chapter III, verse 60, assures us that:

> In that family, where the husband is pleased with his wife and the wife with her husband, happiness will assuredly be lasting.

These contradictions need to be re-examined. Women are not worthless. They need only to be equal. According to UN Secretary-General António Guterres, 'Just as slavery and colonialism were a stain on previous centuries, women's inequality should shame us all in the twenty-first. Because it is not only unacceptable; it is stupid.' Guterres says 'The women's rights movement came of age in the twentieth century. Women Heads of State dispelled any doubts about women's ability to lead. The Universal Declaration of Human Rights asserted the equal rights of men and women, and the Convention on the Elimination of All Forms of Discrimination against Women outlined a vision of gender equality' He goes on 'But despite these advances, the state of women's rights remains dire. Inequality and discrimination are the norm, everywhere ... Progress has slowed to a standstill—and in some cases, been reversed. There is a strong and relentless pushback against women's rights'.

Are men willing to enter the twenty-first century with women? If not, what will be the consequences? More father-daughter conflict?

More marital break-ups? And how can anyone enter the twenty-first century when the weight of dowry is dragging a whole country back into the past?

Complying with demands for dowry is like feeding the monster. Reena's father paid more than $40 000 in dowry gifts and cash to the groom and his family in India. And they were demanding more, which he refused to give. He had already given all his retirement savings. As a loving father, he wanted to make a good investment for Reena's happiness, and give his daughter and her husband a good start in life. That is why parents give money and gifts. None of them believe that by doing this they are supporting the evil tradition of dowry.

Perhaps Reena's father also feared the violence and torture Reena may suffer from the groom and his family should they feel dissatisfied with the amount offered by him. (Remember Durga, abused because her family had followed the law and refused to pay dowry?) Their conceptualisation that dowry is a gift to the young couple to give them a good start is at odds with this fear—the fear that their daughter will be abused and subjected to violence should she not bring sufficient dowry.

Economic abuse is a known form of domestic violence.[15] The abuse of power and control is central to economical abuse. Dowry abuse or coercive demands are a cultural expression of economical abuse. The 'big fat Indian wedding' is enjoyed by all, generally paid for by the bride's family, who also give generous gifts to the groom and his family. Some grooms abuse the tradition and start to make unreasonable demands. The increasing emphasis on economic development and the accumulation of material assets is fuelling abuse[16]. It also demonstrates the groom's power; when the coercive demands continue for years after the wedding is over, it is to maintain dominance, power, and control over the bride.[17]

And the tools are threats, intimidation, violence criticisms and control.[18]

In effect, parents are giving dowry to avoid violence against their daughter. Yet there is no set amount that will ensure her safety. And in giving dowry, parents are feeding the frightening, violent monster that is the prototypical abusive husband. I have also heard stories from young men in Australia who told me that their wives brought their dowry here and no further demands were made of them and their family. Dowry is society's reward to men for good behaviour and for bad behaviour.

Whether fear or hope was driving his thinking, Reena's father would be conflicted—liable to feel trapped by his financial investment when his daughter rang him in tears to tell him her husband was abusing her. After spending his precious retirement money on dowry, he couldn't bear to think that his investment was wasted, that there would be minimal return if they were lucky in the Indian courts—or, more likely, a complete loss.

Dowry-related violence is a harmful 'traditional practice', meaning it has occurred for so long that dowry demands and abuse are regarded as accepted cultural practice; it has become acceptable due to communal pressure, and sometimes by threats of violence. The parents only wake up to their unconscious thought processes and motivations in the combined family counselling session I do with them and their abused daughters. Usually, they are visiting from India to support their daughters, who have been abandoned by their violent husbands who have taken the dowry and deny ever receiving it. It is only after their daughter's gruelling experience at the hands of her new Australian-Indian husband—and seeing her homeless, stateless, destitute, suicidal, depressed and with severe states of anxiety, acute stress disorder and post-traumatic stress disorder—that parents acknowledge their unconscious bias. They are finally able to see that they have helped preserve the toxic mix of patriarchy and greed by rewarding men to marry their daughter and take the 'burden off their hands', so to speak, all the while being aware at some level, perhaps, that they were breaking laws designed to protect the women of India.

After treating the parents alongside their daughter—they too are experiencing depression, anxiety, and severe sleeplessness—the realisation fully hits them that they were kidding themselves to believe that what they gave was not dowry.

Sense of entitlement in the groom perpetuates coercive demands for dowry; most parents fail to keep this in mind. One parent (who I treated for severe anxiety) said they just wanted to see their daughter, Nina, happy and settled. She did not for one second imagine that her in-laws would turn out to be such greedy people.

'We met his family and the groom-to-be before the marriage,' this parent said. 'They presented themselves as sophisticated, highly educated, well-placed-in-society type of people. Their son was a modern person who was highly successful in Australia as an IT engineer. We were very happy that our daughter Nina will be very happy—being a highly educated IT engineer herself she had found an equal match, a good boy and a good family.

'After the dowry gifts were delivered to his parents' home in Delhi, they started demanding more gifts for this uncle and that relative.'

Nina's mother said she was so surprised, and at the same time sad and angry.

'This was in addition to household furniture, white goods, an air conditioner, television, cash, gold gifts for the groom and his extended family.' In addition, they had spent about $60 000 on the wedding celebrations in posh hotels over three days. The groom and his family did not contribute anything significant. 'They gave her a small gift of one gold chain and a couple of pairs of clothing,' Nina's mother said.

Parents often say they are distressed, sad and angry when the groom's family make more demands. It appears they have heard stories related to dowry demands, abuse, violence, abandonments and even murders. But they never imagine it would happen to their daughter. Unconcerned about other parents' experiences, the parents of daughters fall into the same trap again and again.

Nina's story also adds another layer to the discussion about what a husband feels entitled to.

A few days after her marriage, Nina's new Australian-Indian husband urged her to give him the password to her bank account. He said: 'Now that we are married, we should not have any secrets between us.'

Nina was reluctant to do so, but he pressured her and she gave in. She knew she had to make the marriage work. Nina was unhappy that his family were demanding more gifts; her father had spent his hard-earned fortune on the wedding celebrations with the clear expectation that this marriage would last forever. And the person who had to make it work was Nina.

Nina's husband cleared out her bank account, all the income she had earned in the three years before they got married. She was devastated. And she did give voice to her anger, though in muted tones.

Nina said to her husband: 'But I earned that money before I got married.'

'Now that we are married everything you own belongs to us and I, as your husband, will control our finances,' her husband told her.

Nina said she was seething inside, but knew she couldn't make her husband angry. But she kept thinking: 'Why? Where does his sense of entitlement to my hard-earned money come from? I did not know him, he had nothing to do with my education, he did not pay for it, my parents did. If anyone has any claim on it that has to be my parents.' He had known her for just ten months.

But a groom's culturally enforced feeling of entitlement extends to all his wife's income, and her property if she has any. This financial control is interlinked with dowry abuse and extortion. The cultural expectations around dowry give him the permission to steal, and the woman is expected to have the mindset of acceptance and submission.

Nina silenced her thoughts; they were making her so angry she feared she might destroy her new marriage. She knew she had to be compliant. She convinced herself that was her only option, and that maybe he was right.

'If I am going to live in his home that he has made before I married him, perhaps he does have claim over my income before my marriage to him,' Nina told herself.

But she felt she was his equal and thought, I should know how much he has in his bank account, and we should both have access to the joint bank account.

Inequality in right to control finances adds to vulnerability of the imported bride.

Nina asked her husband about his income, his bank account and where he had transferred her money. He refused to share this information with her. He became angry and abusive and irritable, telling her that she did not need to know about the finances, that he was in charge of the household, and that he would do his best for both of them.

Nina was not satisfied. She had agency, and she had controlled her own income up to now. She thought she was better off being single. But she also held in her mind the belief that marriage was an inevitable part of an Indian woman's life.

Her husband's demands kept increasing. One day, when she said no to his demands for money for air tickets for their holiday to Fiji, he pushed her out of the front door and locked her out of the house in a cold, wintry month. Nina's mother rushed over from India.

Financial abuse is a common form of domestic violence. In Australia, 16 per cent of women and 8 per cent of men suffer economical abuse, despite it being against the law.[19]

Analysing financial abuse in my clinical practice between 2019 and 2020: of 150 South Asian women experiencing family violence, I found dowry abuse to be present in 49 per cent and financial abuse in 100 per cent of cases. The financial abuse perpetrated by their husbands took many forms:

1   forcing her to work in unacceptable jobs for quick money;
2   stopping her from going to work;
3   taking control of her hard-earned income;
4   making her work in a family business and not paying her and claiming tax benefits;
5   not allowing her to spend wages on her personal needs, with actual or threatened violence;
6   sending her hard-earned money to his parents without her consent (oftentimes to build palatial homes in India);
7   not allowing her to send money or gifts to her parents or family;
8   not sharing his financial position but demanding to know hers;
9   running up debts in her name—for example on credit cards, or taking housing loans in her name without her name being on the house title; and/or
10  marrying her under false pretences—for dowry or for her educational qualifications so she can earn money for his gain.

Financial abuse of intimate partners occurs in every community, every culture, every country and is a recognised form of family violence in law. In the Indian community, dowry abuse and the related sense of entitlement over the bride and her parent's wealth has made financial abuse more possible and severe. It bears close resemblance to human trafficking and modern-day slavery.[20]

Parents are trapped and I wonder how they can extricate themselves from a tradition that so blatantly stacks up in favour of husbands-to-be.

This is Ashok Kumar Godara, the father of Deepshikha, the young woman murdered by her husband in Melbourne, on why he gave dowry and kept on giving gifts to her husband's family at every family function for six years:

> Society pressures make you do this. All your neighbours come to your house at the wedding and check out what you have given your daughter; they actually demand to see the gifts you have given. You have to give (dowry) for the sake of your family honour.

The parents of brides must stop lying to themselves that they are not breaking the laws of India and Australia by giving 'gifts'. They must be honest with themselves and call it what it is—dowry.

It was a difficult decision for Reena to leave her marriage. But she managed it. Nina found that despite societal and familial pressures to stay in her abusive marriage, it was better to get on with her education, and to further her career as IT engineer in Australia as a single woman. Ayesha is feeling happy for the first time in her life. All three young women remain single, have found new jobs, have permanent residency in Australia, and truly feel that they are empowered global citizens of the world, belonging to Australia and India while enjoying all that life has to offer.

Their parents are slowly coming to accept an uncomfortable truth—that society has hoodwinked them into believing daughters are a burden and sons are a gift to humanity. The parents I have met are recognising that there is nothing to be gained by marrying off their daughters to the wrong men; to those men who think they own a woman as their property. And they are acknowledging that as parents they must stand up against society's rule that states an unmarried daughter is a stigma and a shame. They feel in their bones that it is quite the reverse; an unmarried daughter can look after herself and her parents; she makes a contribution to the family, and an even stronger contribution to society.

Parents need to understand that when they break the laws—and when enough people break the laws that have been put there to protect the young women of India who marry non-resident Indians—they are leaving our daughters and sisters exposed to violence and murder.

They need to realise that giving extravagant gifts and financing extravagant celebrations at their daughter's wedding increases the expectations of men. This puts pressure on less well-off parents to copy them and destroy their own futures by throwing their savings at men who are trained to be greedy monsters.

When the parents of daughters, the young women themselves, and young men especially, have the honesty and courage to challenge the folly of dowry—a slippery pathway to coercive control and physical violence—then we will move from *Manusmriti*'s first century into the modern twenty-first century.

# 7
# WISH YOU WERE A SON

My father was a warm and caring parent. He supported his children, nieces and nephews, and gave help if it was needed—but was sparing in his praise. My father's generosity was unending. But underneath there existed an unconscious bias.

I was visiting India as a forty-year-old, and stayed with my parents. My parents enjoyed my company, we would often sit around chatting and laughing. This day we were having cups of tea, chatting about my life in Australia, and the pressure my father was experiencing. His difficulties related to their newly constructed four-storey home/office complex in Delhi and his conflict with the builder, who had lied and been dishonest in his financial dealings with my father. (It took many years for him to get a prison sentence.)

Suddenly, he turned to my mother and said lovingly, 'It would have been wonderful if Manju had been a boy.'

It was a bombshell! I was rocked by so many contradictory messages.

My father meant it to be a compliment: he saw me as a stable person who could handle the pressure he was experiencing. But how terrible that he did not see that I could handle it as a daughter and a competent woman!

I looked at my father and said: 'That is a terrible thing to say!'

My mother agreed with me.

My father was taken aback. At a conscious and rational level, he saw me as competent and capable, but he had just revealed his unconscious bias against daughters. Perhaps it was the first time he fully understood the bias he held. Did he see his wife as less competent and capable too? The answer must be yes. My mother knew of his financial dealings, but she was not allowed to make financial decisions or deal with business matters.

My father was not alone in having this unconscious bias. It operates in most homes, in both sexes and, therefore, in most levels of society—from individuals, to families, to communities and to society at large. Of course, women have this bias too, handily doing the work of the patriarchy.

Let us imagine that my father could overlook his bias that only sons should handle his financial affairs or business dealings, and that he had given me the authority to handle the builder. Could I have been more successful than him in dealing with the builder? My father said the builder was a rogue and very difficult to pin down. Would the builder have listened to me, and dealt with me more respectfully or honestly? Are women able to work in business and financial worlds and be treated with equal respect?

An Australian-Indian woman's story explains the reality. Sita wanted to sell her property in Hyderabad and invest her money in Australia. Her brother accompanied her to all her meetings and discussions with real estate agents. However, the agents would only address her brother when she asked questions, and pretended she was not there.

She tried to make eye contact and asked more questions to make them realise she was the customer, not her brother, but they only spoke to her brother again and again. She was annoyed at being ignored and could no longer contain her anger. At last, she said: 'Dear sir, if you do not speak to me directly I will go elsewhere. It is my property we are talking about.'

The agent was rudely awakened to his mistake, he apologised and from then on, she was back in control of the negotiations.

The societal schema has inbuilt sanctions against women taking on bigger matters of the world.

The unconscious message to women is that they are not as important or valuable as men. They are not as intelligent as men. In my father's loving statement was the message that I was not capable of handling difficult issues to do with money and business. He may have also been concerned about systemic or societal reasons that these negotiations could be more difficult for a woman to achieve than for a man. Not for a second would he have wanted to see me as inferior to my brothers or less intelligent; he unconsciously had absorbed societal value that places men above women—the nature of patriarchy. He respected my intelligence and capabilities. He did not mean to say that I was not wanted as a daughter—quite the reverse. He really appreciated me for what I had achieved in my life.

We learn gender norms not in isolation but within the context of broader society, our communities and families, each interacting and reinforcing the others.[1]

The societal status given to men and boys is not given to women. The privileges given to men and boys gives them advantages that lead to gender-based inequality. This inequality translates in every little and big aspect of life. Research shows that gender norms—or how boys learn to be boys—are formed by their father's role modelling.[2]

A kind, loving father shows how to choose non-violent ways of solving disputes. A father who is a dominant force and the primary decision-maker will unknowingly teach his son to dominate and expect to make important family decisions. Research shows that childhood exposure to violence is the single highest predictor for future family violence. Such boys are three times more likely to become perpetrators of partner violence in their adulthood. They learn through observation, learn through personal experience of undergoing brutality themselves. They learn that is the only way to handle conflict. By watching their friends and society, they learn that in their culture disrespect for women is a normal part of everyday behaviour.

The good news is that children and even adults can be taught empathy, compassion and respect for others.

Recently, a patient told me that her Indian female workmates in a factory in Dandenong, Victoria, congratulated her on giving birth to a son. 'Aren't you lucky you have got a boy? He will inherit all of his father's wealth and you can live in luxury forever with your son,' they said to her.

She replied: 'But we do have a daughter as well—she will get an equal share.'

Her co-workers quickly recognised their mistake and said, 'Oh, of course.'

The old ways of son-preference might be baked into society, but change can occur, is occurring.

If I *had* been a son, tradition dictates that part of my role would be to support my parents in their old age. Every Indian parent expects this of their son, and it makes them feel safe and secure. The assumptions we make are unconscious and, as such, we do not critically analyse them, we do not think about them logically or rationally. The parents do not question themselves, do not ask: Is my son in a position to help us out? They just assume that he will. What if he lives in Australia? That is all the more reason to imagine that he will—because he lives in a wealthy country, therefore he is wealthy. But not all sons can afford to keep their parents in Australia. Understanding this means asking uncomfortable questions and accepting the answers, no matter how unpleasant. What about, can my daughter help out? This question is unthinkable for most parents and even more unacceptable to the in-laws. This is taught to girls and boys as children. They watch it in their own families. It becomes an assumption.

Our assumptions govern our actions—they're like the jockey on a horse, where the horse is our body running fast into activity.

In Indian culture, there is a huge expectation that a son will deliver peace and happiness to the father and mother for as long as they are alive.

The extended family delivers the expectations.

A healthy extended family is caring and supportive. I grew up in one of these. Living together, against the background of the rising cost of housing, helps extended families to meet the need for childcare as more women work, and to provide support for elderly parents. That perhaps is the reason why many migrants prefer to live in extended family, even in Australia. The rise in migration has given rise to increasing numbers of extended families living communally. Generally, the extended family live together in four types of arrangements, with both related and unrelated adults: family households with three generations (parents, children of any age, grandparents); family households with other extended family members (e.g., uncle, aunt, cousin, siblings); family households with unrelated persons; and family households with adult children aged twenty-five years and older. These categories are not mutually exclusive.

In 2016, 18.1 per cent of South-East Asian families were living in extended family arrangement in Australia. Pacific communities from Papua New Guinea, Tonga, Samoa, as well as communities from China, Georgia, Armenia, India, and Sri Lanka, more often live as extended family, and add up to 20 per cent of all Australian families.[3]

The majority of my patients come from extended households. And all, except a handful, are headed by sons who bring their parents from India, and fulfil their obligations to provide support and care for their families.

I know of exceptions, too, signalling change. A number of daughters head their extended households, and have brought their own parents across from India.

The provision of familial support and love occurs more easily in a caring, joint family system with multi-generational members who see living together a source of support.[4]

But extended families are not always supportive. Acting on the assumption that her son would look after her, an elderly patient of mine suffered much sadness. She had depended on her son to give her a home in Sydney. She told me she used to be very close to her daughter-in-law in India, but since her arrival in Australia to live with them things turned for the worse. She was not allowed to mix freely with her grandchildren and, effectively isolated, lived alone in the garage-turned-granny-flat. She had no idea why this was happening to her.

With rising cases of elder abuse, the assumption that sons will look after their ageing parents needs to be discussed openly and widely. This mother believed all her prayers were answered when she gave birth to her son. This belief led her to migrate to Australia, instead of remaining in India where she had a circle of friends and relatives and lived in her own home in reasonable comfort. For her, migration was filled with dreams, while her son had to pay for her insurance and other bonds related to her visa. No doubt he felt financially pressured but was determined to live up to the societal expectations imposed on him as a son. But this brought a strain on his marriage and in turn his wife's rejection of her mother-in-law.

Many elderly parents come to Australia and gain a comfortable lifestyle, but they lose other things—connection within the family when the daughter-in-law is busy working, the children are at school or with friends, and their own son is probably working two jobs to support the extended family. During one of our community education sessions on the prevention of family violence with Indian senior citizens clubs, some seniors were angry with us. 'We are not the perpetrators here but the victims,' some said. How so? we asked. 'We live here in Australia,' said one man. 'It is a five-star prison. We have everything but we have nothing.'

They felt disconnected from their culture, and unable to find strong family and community ties. They felt powerless because the expression of patriarchy and power of the elders is, perhaps, less strong here; this is an unintended consequence of the need for sons to take care of their parents.

A couple of years later, my elderly patient told me that everything had improved at home with her daughter-in-law. They are a happy family again. She is allowed free-flowing contact with grandchildren and feels welcome. Why that happened, she did not say, but perhaps the Victorian Government community education campaigns against elder abuse may have had some influence.[5]

Families are resilient and can adapt to change. They just may need some help.

Indian society is changing rapidly. The expectation that only sons can take care of elderly parents is changing, fuelled by the rapid rise in girls' education and migration of children overseas.[6] I may not be the son that my father wanted, but I was able to host my parents in Australia a dozen times as they stayed in our house for three months at a time. On the rare occasion, I supported them financially, and they supported me when I was stuck during the last recession in Melbourne.

It is give and take; it is an equal relationship now.

The United Nations estimates it will take 99.7 years to reach gender equality in the world.[7] A lot of progress has already occurred, but the change is slow and uneven. Economic empowerment remains elusive. At home, women continue to do more domestic chores, and still do most of the caring for the elderly, sick and the children—even when they are working full time.

Of course, there are thousands of assumptions, big and small, important and not, underpinning all societies, but for our culture so many are long out of date. Sons are better; daughters are inferior; NRI grooms are very desirable; grooms have higher status than brides. But the one assumption that is the most unhelpful is that daughters are 'paraya dhan'—someone else's wealth/property.

The point about recognising our unconscious bias is that we can make it conscious and reflect on it. In all my dealings with men and women of the Australian-Indian community, I have found that people want to learn and change. But a lot of work is required to create awareness.

Recently I spoke at an Instagram meeting organised by a young woman, a celebrity of sorts in India, Ms Swati Suri. I spoke about the COVID-19 lockdown and its impact on families and mental health. It was an interactive one-hour session. The audience was about 150 young women, and some men. Most of the women were tertiary educated, and one asked me why the preference for sons persists, especially in wealthy parts of India like Delhi and Haryana. In both states the ratio of women to men is extremely low: 868 females to every 1000 males (the national average is 940/1000). Pregnancy, this woman said, should be a time to be happy, but sadly it is quite the reverse. For many young women it is a time of increasing anxiety and even depression. They fear they may give birth to a girl. Similar stories were discussed in our interactive workshops in Melbourne, 'Mutual Relational Respect'.[8] Women in Australia become tense before their ultrasound tests. What if the sex of the baby revealed is the 'wrong' one?

As the audience were a wealthy set—from business families of Delhi—I addressed my answer to that section of society. Most wealthy parents become extremely worried if they don't have a son, because they have a fixed idea that the future of their business empires can only be protected by sons. If there is a married daughter in the picture, these parents may believe her in-laws will make a claim over their business—because in their mind, after all, a daughter belongs only to her husband and in-laws. We need to shift this way of thinking. Parents need to stop seeing their daughters as 'praya dhan' and adopt the thinking that daughters are as competent as sons; that all that is necessary to manage the family business is education. The business will stay in the family's hands and the parents will feel safe. They will not fear losing control. The moderator, Ms Suri, agreed, and said that a similar situation had occurred in her own in-law's extended family. They did not have a son and their only married daughter was allowed to run the business with impressive results—the business empire extends globally. Her parents are very happy, and have no anxiety or fear.

If only parents and society would see that a daughter is equal to a son, in all ways that are important for family and society, there would be no need for parents to wish for a son instead of a daughter or see their daughter as *praya dhan*, someone else's wealth, not their own.

The fact is that world is changing—or, more accurately, the women and daughters of India are changing. They are getting educated and taking their rightful place in the twenty-first century. I have observed that women arriving from India to Australia are well educated, and they want to work, and control their income.[9] They are demanding equal status in their homes and society. But what about the society, including men? Are they able to keep up with this modernisation of women? Are they able to critically examine their unconscious bias against women and have equal respect for women, and to afford the women in their lives agency and choices?

# 8
# CASTE AND HONOUR KILLINGS

Does the caste system have relevance for Australia? Some years back, a journalist asked me this question. The short answer is yes, I said. The long answer was that after seeing young women with caste-related abuse in Australia, I had begun researching the origins of caste, its impact, and why it stubbornly sticks around.

There are four rungs of caste in India as understood today (and transported globally with migration), perfected in *Manusmriti* or *The Laws of Manu* written some 2000 years ago.[1] George Buhler's translation of the first chapter starts:

1. The great sages approached Manu, who was seated with a collected mind, and, having duly worshipped him, spoke as follows:
2. 'Deign, divine one, to declare to us precisely and in due order the sacred laws of each of the (four chief) castes (varna) and of the intermediate ones.
3. 'For thou, O Lord, alone knowest the purport, (i.e.) the rites, and the knowledge of the soul, (taught) in this whole ordinance of the Self-existent (Svayambhu), which is unknowable and unfathomable.'
4. He, whose power is measureless, being thus asked by the high-minded great sages, duly honoured them, and answered, 'Listen!'
5. This (universe) existed in the shape of Darkness, unperceived, destitute of distinctive marks, unattainable by reasoning, unknowable, wholly immersed, as it were, in deep sleep.
8. He, desiring to produce beings of many kinds from his own body, first with a thought created the waters, and placed his seed in them.
9. That (seed) became a golden egg, in brilliancy equal to the sun; in that (egg) he himself was born as Brahman, the progenitor of the whole world.
31. But for the sake of the prosperity of the worlds he caused the Brahmana, the Kshatriya, the Vaisya, and the Sudra to proceed from his mouth, his arms, his thighs, and his feet.[2]

The highest caste is Brahmin, the priestly or the knowledgeable ones; the second is Kshatriya, the warrior caste or the caste of kings, the brave and fearless; the third is Vaisya, the merchant class, artisans, farmers; and the lowest is Dalit (once called Sudra), who were ordained to do the menial tasks of society.[3]

Once, this caste system was flexible and of little relevance to ordinary people; it was perhaps only relevant to the small group who called themselves the Brahmins.

Inter-caste marriage was allowed and practised. 'Know that the following rules apply to weddings with females of a different caste,' says *Manusmriti*. 'On marrying a man of a higher caste Kshatriya bride must take hold of an arrow, a Vaisya bride of a goad and Sudra female the hem of the bridegroom's garment.'[4]

The Muslim traveller Alberuni (973–1048), who came to India with King Mahmoud Ghazni, wrote about the Vaisyas and Sudras that as 'much as these classes differ from each other they live together in same villages, towns, mixed together in same houses, lodgings.'[5] He noted Brahmins as the highest caste, but also put forth the Hindu philosophers' views: 'liberation is common to all castes and to the whole human race, if their intention of obtaining it is perfect. Then you may follow whatever religion you like; you will no doubt be liberated.'

The British ruled India for two centuries. Among their first tasks was to conduct a census. The first census of 1860 was ignored by the government. Why? The census did not produce four tidy rungs of *Manusmriti*'s castes. The result, instead, was many confusing varieties of castes. It would be too hard to rule such a complex diversity of people.

The caste system was simplified into four rungs. It became rigid. The Brahmins misled the British into thinking that this was always the way it had been (which led to the rise of anti-Brahmin movement). For the British, it was self-fulfilling prophecy. A lot of harm followed.

One of the ways in which the rigidifying of castes—and the associated harm—occurred was via the British stereotyping and labelling certain castes as more loyal and brave, like the Jats (a North Indian sub-caste found in Punjab and Haryana), and cultivating the higher castes like Brahmins to help with the administration of India. Some people were given no caste at all—they were considered outsiders to society, and seen as bad, harmful.[6]

Another way in which the system became rigid was around marriage. You could only marry within your caste or Jati (defined by occupation, for example goldsmithing or leather work). Marrying outside your caste, without the approval of the family and the leaders of the community, became a dishonourable and shameful act, one that deserved the worst punishment perpetrated by one's own family—honour killing.

My family hardly knew the value or the antiquity of our caste. I think it was arbitrarily assigned as Kshatriya.[7] My paternal grandfather worked as a legal counsellor to the local prince in the North-West Frontier province of Pakistan, and this probably earned the family this caste. Prior to him, little is known about my family's inheritance. My grandfather was fluent in many languages. He could read and write in Farsi, Urdu, Hindi, Punjabi, Derawali, English. Many British people who lived in the area came to him to be tutored in Farsi and Urdu (the British needed to know the languages to make it easy to rule over the natives who did not speak English). It earned him good money. He stopped teaching them after he started work for the local Muslim prince, who had a strong dislike for the British. I suspect he was given the Kshatriya caste just because he worked for the prince and was much admired by him. He married a woman of unknown caste from the same village. The story goes he chose her because she was the prettiest girl in town—a century ago, and not an arranged marriage! One century later, not only did three of us four siblings not have arranged marriages, we also married outside our so-called caste. In our family, the caste of the new spouse is hardly ever a topic of discussion when a marriage is being arranged by parents or arranged by the young couple between themselves.

But my family is not unusual in this regard. One study from Bengal found that 30 per cent of marriages are not based on caste.[8] Nevertheless, in this modern era, there is still a widespread belief that marriage within the same caste maintains the stability of male-female roles and masculine and feminine norms, and that it maintains tradition and customs.[9] Society expects it, and society must be obeyed.

So what happens to those who don't obey?

If a couple marries outside their caste or religion, harm is always lurking nearby. This is also true for those who transgress other social norms: contact with the opposite sex or sexual activity when unmarried, expressions of homosexuality, rejecting an arranged marriage, fleeing a violent marriage, an extra-marital affair—all of these can invoke the spectre of an honour killing. Men are also victims of honour killings, but to a lesser degree.[10] Young couples are most at risk when they have tried to move towards modernity. It is all the more frightening and pernicious when an entire village cultural council turns against a couple. Found in some parts of north India, these cultural councils are called Khap Panchayats, and act as quasi-judicial bodies. The council generally comprises senior men and sometimes women of the village, and they can ferociously order murders if they believe the honour of the caste has been damaged by the young couple's decision to marry.

A young woman named Maya was from such a village near Delhi. She ran away and married a man of her choice—a white Australian man whom she met through friends. She was barely eighteen years of age. She had the threat of an honour killing on her head while living in Australia, and was highly anxious when she came to see me.

I asked her why she would take such a risk.

She said that it was about love and affection; it was about being valued as a human being, and being made to feel worthwhile. This she got from her thirty-year-old boyfriend, whom she later married.

Her family are wealthy farmers, respectable, and honoured as economically superior. In her family, the women stay at home and look after the children and the family, and the men go to work. It is very traditional. She gave a vivid description of an aunt in the family, the matriarch of the whole family, who belonged to the local cultural village council. She would feel free to abuse or slap Maya any time she walked past if she felt Maya was somehow not following the rules of the family. Maya's mother suffered beatings at the hands of her father. That violence made her completely submissive, and she was afraid to protect her daughter. In contrast, her brother was looked after by her parents.

However, modernisation had reached Maya's family to an extent. Her family had sent her to a secondary school in another village, where she also attended her first year in a college. She loved the freedom of leaving home and going to school. It had been a pleasure to walk to primary school with a group of girls, laughing and joking. The secondary school and college were in her maternal uncle's village, and so she moved in with his family. She loved being away from home, but also recognised it was a form of rejection by her family. She was craving love and attention, and that is when she fell in love with her boyfriend.

Maya's love affair with a boy from a different race and different country threatened to destabilise her family's image in a society that enforces uniformity and tradition and suppression of women.

Honour killing is a system that perpetuates control over women's sexuality, gender inequality, and abuse of power. Most victims are women, and the majority of perpetrators—though not all—are men. Women have the burden of upholding the family honour, by not expressing their sexuality in ways that are unacceptable to the norms laid down by patriarchy; laws that older women willingly uphold, murdering their own daughters and nieces.

Maya knew her life was at risk at the hands of the Khap Panchayat in collusion with her own family, especially her aunt. But the warmth of love, and a heady experience of gender equality and respect, were too powerful to resist.

In March 2018, India's Supreme Court, taking note of the plight of young people like Maya, declared it illegal to stop a marriage between two consenting adults.[11] But the edict did not stop Maya's family, or other families like hers. Her story shows that the tension between modern and traditional values has costs. The question is, who pays the cost? In this case, it was Maya who paid the cost. Rejection by her family, the threat of being killed, and being unable to return to India for her own safety made her anxious, depressed, and suicidal.

Generally, it is young women who pay the cost—when they are devalued, and controlled, and murdered for bringing dishonour to the family. This, in the end, damages the fabric of society.

The great power of caste in modern arranged marriages is apparent in advertisements placed by families in newspapers looking for a match for their son or daughter. In one study, most of these families belonged to the upper middle class and were highly educated. The caste of the bride was a stronger preference than dowry.[12] Assortative mating was common—in other words, men and women were of the same educational standard. But there are signs of change. I know women happily married to men of different castes. One well-known Melbourne obstetrician—gynaecologist Dr NK—married her classmate from Pune Medical College about a decade ago. He was a Brahmin from Pune and she was Kshatriya from Punjab—they had different languages, different castes, and came from different states with different customs. It was going to be an uphill battle. Her extended family and especially her grandmother objected—until they met her chosen partner. And then they gave in. Dr NK's grandmother decided the boy was 'suitable', good enough for their family. Why? Because 'he was tall and fair, and good looking, and a doctor'—the right match for their medical daughter. They are now a happily married couple with children, and both have successful medical careers in Victoria. The inter-caste rivalry just fizzled away.

Dr NK's grandmother loved her enormously. Her initial hesitation about her granddaughter's marriage probably stemmed from the fact that she could not bear to see her granddaughter hurt.

Why are some mothers, and some grandmothers, able to protect their daughters while others are not? Maya's mother was a victim of domestic violence herself, disempowered. She was poorly educated and financially dependent on her husband. The barriers to speaking up were huge. Had she dared to speak out in favour of her truant daughter, she would have placed herself at risk of more beatings, abandonment, or even murder. If more mothers and matriarchs felt empowered, they would feel compassion, and more daughters would be saved from harm.

In Dr NK's case, education won, and caste lost.

A young woman called Mira was, by the time I met her, acutely suicidal. Mira had fallen in love with Krishnan, whom she met near her village in Utter Pradesh; he was from a lower caste, though he had high status as an Australian resident. Mira did not dare ask her parents' permission for marriage, so she ran away with Krishnan. This created a bigger problem. Her family were abusive, insulted her, bullied her, and threatened to kill her, and Mira took out an intervention order against them in India.

Mira joined her husband in Melbourne on a partner visa. Krishnan, recognising his power over her and that she had no support other than him, began to be verbally and physically violent. Krishnan's mother knew that her son's love marriage had deprived her of dowry and felt that Mira was getting to live a life of luxury without paying any price for it. Because they had decided to run away together, their parents were not involved in any negotiations over dowry.

Mira's mother-in-law made every effort to highlight her faults and criticised her at every turn. She convinced Krishnan that Mira was not good enough for him and eventually persuaded him to cancel his sponsorship of her partner visa. Mira was homeless, stateless and without family support.

'What is there to live for?' she asked me. 'I should lie down on the road and let a truck run over me.'

Fortunately, she met people who became her friends and helped get her a job in a factory, which gave her money to put a roof over her head. Mira was prescribed antidepressants and, as she had not slept for weeks, I gave her a strong anti-anxiety sedative pill.

Mira's situation raised a lot of questions in my mind. Erik Erikson's seminal work *Identity: Youth and Crisis* states that psychologically speaking, the development of one's identity occurs during middle and late adolescence. There is a need to be accepted by others—family, friends, peers—and this need must be balanced with what the young person wants for themselves as they discover their own unique sense of identity. There can be an initial period of identity confusion followed by clarity around late adolescence or early adulthood. A clear understanding of identity brings with it feelings of satisfaction, industry, and competence, and includes an ability to assert control. A confident identity is one where a person can relate to others without feeling confused about themself. It is essential to the mental health of an individual; and developed through the process of exploration and commitment, it is associated with low depression, low anxiety, and low suicidal thoughts, and the absence of an exaggerated sense of oneself.

I wondered about Mira's self-identity and how it been shaped by her choices. She was eighteen when she fell in love—still an adolescent. Her exploration of the world around her led to meeting a man from a lower caste. Then, in a need to exercise control over her life, she made the choice to be with him and made a commitment to him. She felt the satisfaction she needed in her life by being with him. She was on track to form a strong identity for herself.

However, this process was thwarted—first by her own family, and then by his family, and then by Krishnan himself. It is no surprise that she was severely depressed and acutely suicidal. She could not see a way out. Fortunately, the majority of women in Australia are not so constrained in their lives—they are more or less free to choose a life partner without having to consider their partner's caste, socio-economic status, or race. I see my role as helping Mira forge a new identity for herself here.

Identity is also formed by feelings of belonging to a group. Individuals define their own identities in relation to their social groups, and such identifications work to protect and bolster self-identity. We come to define the group we belong to as the 'in-group' and any others as the 'out-group'. There is a general tendency to view one's own group more positively, while the out-group is viewed more negatively. Thus, we form a collective, depersonalised identity, one that is based on the group membership that we have imbued with positive aspects.

Caste is an 'in-group'. Mira's parents threatened to murder her—an honour killing—because she had dishonoured their social identity. She had chosen to marry a person of an 'out-group'—the lower of the out-groups, a Dalit. He was inferior, according to Mira's parents, and Mira's association with him threatened their membership of their 'in-group', and hence their social identity.

The social identity process is more influential in Indian society because it is a collectivist society, and belonging to a social grouping is an essential aspect of one's identity. But there is a negative side—it causes more social conflict. All people who belong to the 'out-group' are seen as inferior, and therefore as deserving fewer resources, less social contact, and so on.

Adventurous youngsters or individuals who cross the boundaries are shunned because they threaten the group identity. My father, from a young age, tried to cross boundaries. He dared to have a girlfriend in the early 1900s in a small province where women were not to be seen in public, nor heard at home or outside, and men could not marry outside the constraints of arranged marriage. His father put immense pressure on him to study law in Lahore, and be part of the family law business. But my father defied his wishes and went to Aligarh University in pre-Partition days (now in modern-day India, then part of united India) to study economics. He did compromise and do a double degree in law and economics, which pleased both him and his father. But his psychological identity was strong enough to stand against the group. And perhaps his compromise is a model for the art of living in a modern migratory and ever-changing world.

Why is it that Mira's husband Krishnan could not adopt more of a hybrid identity—as an Australian resident with a modern marriage of mixed castes? Why could he not envision a new self-identity and a new future? Was his social imagination stunted? What happened in Krishnan's adolescence? Normally, this is the time when young people explore new identities, experiment with new ideas, are creative, and imagine a different future, a better future than their parents'. What happened in his education? Did his school encourage exploration, imagination, self-reliance, and pride in taking decisions and control over his life? Perhaps it did, because he daringly fell in love with a young woman of a different caste.

So what was the problem? Krishnan's violence appears to have reared its ugly head after his parents arrived in Australia to live with the young couple. They were just forming a new relationship when Mira's mother-in-law started criticising her openly and continuously to her face and in front of her new husband.

Was it just his mother's greed for dowry that made her do this? Krishnan's mother and father were somewhat dependent on him for financial and emotional support. His mother brought him up knowing the mother who gives birth to a son is rewarded by society and that he is their old age insurance. She had been waiting for him to grow up and be their support. She had been waiting for the opportunity to exercise power by choosing his bride and negotiating dowry—reward in return for supporting patriarchy—the patriarchal bargain. How must she have felt when all of that was taken away from her by her son's one folly—his decision to marry a woman, not for dowry, not for custom, not to please his mother, but for love; to exercise his choice as an individual. She must have felt cut adrift. So she did what her society had taught her to do for her own survival.

Why does a young man independent enough to come to Australia in the first place not take control over his own life? What are the options open to young men like Krishnan who are being controlled by their mother's fears? Schools and parents have to take responsibility and educate young men. How can we support young men to recognise these fears, and offer their mothers comfort, but to also set boundaries? To communicate that they will be there for her, but not by diminishing the status of his wife—the woman he loves.

With this strong wish to stick to one's in-group or caste or gotra or Jati is the embedded fear of being thrown out of the group, and all that this implies.

One of our neighbours in India had a beautiful daughter named Sangeeta. One lovely spring day she ran into another neighbour's son. He smiled at her, and she smiled back. He seemed like a decent, handsome, educated young man. Over the next few months, they regularly met at the bus stop. His name was Raj, and he was an aerospace engineer; Sangeeta was a schoolteacher. After some months of smiling and talking to each other, usually at the bus stop or in the street, he casually said he would like to marry her. She said he would have to check with her parents. He sent his parents to talk to her parents, to make his proposal official and respectful.

A drama exploded. Everything was good except his caste. He was a Dalit, the lowest caste, and she was a Kshatriya—the warrior class, or the class of kings and soldiers. The biggest explosion came from her father, the head of the family.

'What will my brotherhood say?' he said.

It would be shameful and humiliating, and he feared he would be shunned, laughed at, no longer respected as an equal.

Sangeeta's mother was far more sanguine. She said Raj was a lovely boy—highly educated, highly intelligent, well paid, good-looking, with huge potential, and he really wanted to marry their daughter. He did not want any dowry; it couldn't get better than this.

The explosion continued for weeks until massive pressure from the extended family forced the father to relent and give in. Sangeeta and Raj got married.

The most striking and pleasing aspect of this mixed-caste marriage is that the groom's traditional sense of entitlement is completely absent. Raj has no need to feel superior to his wife. He is devoid of a male sense of entitlement over Sangeeta's income or gold. He has no expectation that she is his maid, there to simply serve his needs—to cook, clean, and look after his emotions while he acts like lord and master of his home. I once asked Raj about his family and learned that they are all mathematical whizzes. Raj and Sangeeta's children will move ahead in life with no recognition of their caste. This type of inter-caste marriage will help to bring about change in attitudes.

Change is inevitable—it always comes. So how do we prepare for it? How do we manage the process of it? Those who stand rigidly in the face of change are liable to damage themselves—as an old hard-wooded tree that does not bend in a storm will break, but a green tree that does bend is spared the storm's ravages. An engineer patient of mine said that this principle is used in the construction of high-rise buildings: the taller the building, the more it needs to be able to sway with the wind.

Sangeeta's father was not able to bend.

Ten years later, he was still estranged from his son-in-law. He never visited Raj and Sangeeta, and continued to talk about the loss of respect he had suffered within his brotherhood and networks as a result of their marriage. Raj climbed the career ladder, as expected by his extended family, and did very well for himself and Sangeeta. But Sangeeta having married a Dalit, out of caste, was still spoken about in hushed tones in her parents' house lest someone hear. Sangeeta's father blamed her mother. Sangeeta's mother, though very happy with her daughter's husband and their married life, began to wilt under her husband's constant criticism and the strain of the fractured family relations. She was highly stressed by her husband's behaviour and her divided loyalty. Her high blood pressure became worse, and she suffered from depression. The rigid social norms around caste took their toll. Her husband was angry, lonely, and isolated from his daughter and grandchildren. He told Sangeeta that he loved her a lot and would speak to her if she visited her parents' home, but when alone with his wife he was angry, abusive, and distressed. He sometimes wouldn't get out of bed for days and would not eat or speak to anyone—all symptoms of a depressive illness. His depression was triggered by a change in a social system. How was he going to recover from it?

It took another five years for him to allow his granddaughters to visit him and their visits make him happy. He is still estranged from his son-in-law and still suffers from depression, though it is milder now.

If he could have changed his beliefs earlier—understood that his daughter had not done him irreparable harm—that would have helped him. If his social standing was, indeed, damaged, he could have challenged his peers by presenting the virtues of his son-in-law, and by recognising Raj's value as a decent person, as a respectful husband to his daughter, and as a man who had found his *ardhangini*. Perhaps that would make them reassess their own positions. Perhaps it might lead to an understanding that judging someone for their caste is akin to judging someone for the colour of their skin, and an understanding that this is an abuse of their human rights. The toll paid was immense—mental illness, physical illness, and damaged relationships between husband and wife, father and daughter, father-in-law and son-in-law, and grandfather and grandchildren.

One very wealthy father in Andhra Pradesh (caste unknown) did pay the ultimate price. He had his nineteen-year-old daughter's new husband murdered for being a Dalit, and when he was charged by the police, he then killed himself. He wrote a suicide note to his estranged daughter: 'Go back to your mother, I am sorry.'[13] But of course his apology was too late. He had inflicted untold damage on his family.

I discussed this case with a Melbourne GP friend who comes from Andhra Pradesh—let us call him Dr Rakesh. My friend married outside his caste. His wife was from a goldsmithing Jati, or sub-caste, while he himself belonged to the weaver Jati. Dr Rakesh did not know the name of the bigger caste group he belonged to. It was not relevant.

When we spoke about the case from his home state, he became very angry. It brought up unsettling memories. His father had wanted his doctor son to marry a woman from the weaver class, but promised to come to the wedding when Dr Rakesh married outside his Jati. At the last minute, he did not turn up. Dr Rakesh said it was an empty, hollow feeling. Instead of his wedding being a joyous occasion, it turned into a sad affair. His father went on to disconnect from him. Interestingly, Dr Rakesh had four younger sisters back in Andhra Pradesh, and when the elder three married, they all did so out of caste. Their father disconnected from all of them. It took until the youngest daughter married inter-caste for him to change. All of a sudden, he accepted that inter-caste marriage.

Perhaps he managed to challenge his own biases. More likely, he realised his actions were hurting himself the most. All his children were happily married and getting on with their life; only he was left behind.

I asked Dr Rakesh about his father's reasoning for rejecting the inter-caste marriages previously. His father 'was afraid that his peers would laugh at him'. Peer pressure, fear of mockery or humiliation, had paralysed him. It took a long time, but his children freed him from his narrow thinking.

Another doctor friend of mine, a Hindu—let us call him Dr Vijay—fell head over heels in love with a Pakistani woman and married her in Australia. His family rejected him completely; her brother made threats of honour killing them both. Fortunately, these threats were never carried out. He and his wife have suffered numerous family rejections, which have been emotionally traumatising and have adversely affected their marriage—'It is just hanging there by a thread,' he said. After many years, his family now speak to him but not to her, and her family speak to her but not to him. It is a source of ongoing stress for everyone.

Why has the Indian caste system gone so wrong?

It is because it is supervised and controlled by patriarchs in the name of preserving culture. Yet when it suits, the patriarchs change their caste. Under British rule, they became higher caste because that is how they would get jobs in the British Raj. After Partition, they wanted to be known as lower caste because that would give them jobs in the newly formed Indian Government, and seats in educational institutions.[14] Maintaining caste is about maintaining power. It is not about preserving culture.[15] Would it not be better if every group is just called a community—the weaver community, the goldsmithing community. Dr Rakesh, from the weaver Jati, and his wife from the goldsmithing Jati, like many couples, want only for their children to become better educated and for them to be happy. Let the movement from one community group to another be unremarkable. Let it no longer be labelled as dishonourable. The reasons Dr Rakesh's father wished that their ancient past should dictate their modern life in a faraway land like Australia serve no purpose now. It took many years, but luckily he woke up.

Another way to overcome this obstructive, outdated system may be to teach empathy to all schoolchildren, teachers, and parents. Empathy means valuing the other person and valuing what they represent. In this, Sangeeta's husband would be seen for his achievements, and for his worth as a kind, generous, loving respectful and intelligent man, rather than devalued as a Dalit. The first step towards empathy is to understand one's own thoughts and feelings, and to then take the perspective of the other person and appreciate their thoughts and feelings. It is something that a child learns from their mother and father, and it can be taught in schools.[16]

Many stories I hear confirm to me that mothers and mothers-in-law have to open their minds. A good vehicle for the education needed already exists in TV series and Bollywood films, given the impact of film and TV on societal attitudes.[17] *Devdas* is one such famous Bollywood film. It examines the disastrous results on young people's minds when families stick to their rigid caste inequality and deprive young people of choice over their life partner. More films, TV series and other forms of popular culture are needed that sensitively examine the deep cultural issues regarding the inter-mixing of the caste system and show alternative pathways.

Empowerment of women is another solution. Empowerment through employment, business skills, or home-based business activities such as childcare, beautician training, or cooking for other families, all enhance women's economic status. Many newly migrated women have higher educational status than their mainstream peers, and start simple home-based businesses. The Australian Government is supporting immigrant women with a number of support services to enhance their expertise in business.[18] This, in turn, helps women to better integrate socially and culturally, bringing about societal transformation[19] and diminishing caste-based segregation.[20]

However, inter-caste or inter-Jati marriages between young men and women will be the biggest change-maker. As in the case with Dr Rakesh, women must use their education to exercise their rights. They must use their intellects to question caste. Dr NK took on her family's beliefs against another caste and demonstrated to them, her children, and society that caste is an irrelevant concept in matters of life and marriage. Dr Rakesh's father took a long time to learn the same lesson, but he did get there. Sangeeta and Maya are shining examples of modernity. Sangeeta asked herself why a man of Dalit caste is less than any other man. Maya knew her life was at risk at the hands of a Khap Panchayat, but the promise of unconditional love, dignity, and the excitement of change was too powerful to resist. Through their marriages, these women are helping to rethread the fabric of society.

# 9
# HUGE COST OF MENTAL ILLNESS

How do society's ideal female roles affect the mental health of women who don't live up to them? Or those who discover that the man they've married is not a benevolent patriarch? The effects of violence and abuse have been touched on in previous chapters, but let us now look at them in detail.

Myma is aged forty-two, from Delhi, and one of five children. Her two sisters and two brothers are married. They all complied with the societal norms of a happy family, as did Myma's parents. Each family is headed by a patriarch, with the feminine role filled by a working wife, who is subservient to the needs of her family.

After high school, Myma was married to a man chosen by her father. Her husband was lower middle class; he had a clerical job, and he went to work on his scooter.

One day while riding home, he was hit by a truck and killed. Myma was widowed before she had a chance to have children. She was a single woman in a society where the only important role a women can perform is to be married. Whether or not she is educated and/or working, society sees her primary roles as being a wife and a mother. These roles are more important than her own self-worth as an individual. If she tries to break out of those roles, she will face barriers.

Myma knew she was in a bad place. And, to confirm her fears, her neighbours started calling her 'unlucky'. She was unlucky her husband died; and, worse luck, she was childless: a 'childless, unlucky woman'. She had no job, nowhere to live, and both her parents had died. As a single woman in India, society decrees she may not live alone. If she defies that convention, she will be an object of suspicion and gossip, and vulnerable to predators.

Myma begged one of her brothers and his 'ideal family' to let her live with them. He reluctantly agreed. The family was saving money for dowries for their two daughters, aged ten and eleven. Another mouth to feed was too much trouble. After a short while, Myma found a job in a factory and started to study to keep busy—maybe she would earn a promotion.

Then, suddenly, one day all her dreams come true. She was to be married off to a divorced man who wanted a wife. He lived in Australia with his teenage daughter. His brother arranged the marriage. Myma saw her future husband only once. He had a crooked nose, strong body odour, and funny teeth. But she did not dare think he was ugly, and suppressed her negative emotions. Society would value her more if she was married. Would she have married him if she had completed her education and was earning a handsome income in Delhi? Perhaps, yes, to be rid of her lowly status as a widow. Would she have married him if she could exercise choice, despite her lack of attraction to him? Perhaps, yes, for the same reason.

Myma was not able to merge her newly obtained modern and educated outlook, her self-determination and independence, with the traditional values practised in her new husband's world. Myma's mother-in-law decided she was not submissive enough and did not do enough housework, while her husband thought she was ugly.

Myma took an overdose and was admitted to hospital after her husband rejected her for a woman he found on the internet. She had severe chest pain that would not settle. It looked like a heart attack, but it was severe anxiety disorder. It took nearly four years of regular treatment from her GP and her psychologist, four emergency admissions to hospital, and numerous tests and treatment from me, but I am pleased to say she is now well, working in a regional town and enjoying a good life.

I've seen hundreds of victims of domestic violence in Melbourne over the years. The enormous emotional trauma the young women suffer is associated with suicidal thoughts in at least 75 per cent of them, and serious attempts in about 17 per cent.[1] Often women have not slept for weeks, and are under-nourished, anaemic, and severely anxious by the time I see them. This is perfectly understandable. Domestic violence is associated with high rates of anxiety disorders, panic attacks, including post-traumatic stress disorder, and major depressive illness.[2]

I once treated a young woman called Sheena living in Melbourne for severe post-traumatic stress disorder that would not respond to treatment. Her illness was triggered by her husband. He tortured her for months, depriving her of food and locking her outside on wintry nights. Her mother-in-law threatened to kill her. They were insulted at the wedding, her mother-in-law said. They did not receive sufficient cash and the gifts were not of high quality. Her new husband demanded she buy him a new Range Rover.

Sheena was the only daughter of parents who lived in a small town in Punjab, India. Within weeks of the news that Sheena had been seriously abused and her life had been threatened, her father suffered a stroke. It took about six months for him to recover and once again be fully independent. About a year later, her mother was diagnosed with cancer of the uterus and died within eight months. Sheena was traumatised again and again. Fortunately, there were some kind people in the community who gave her a chance at work, and she restarted her life.

Interesting research with animals sheds light on how the human brain responds to threats. An animal such as a rat is placed in a cage next to a caged predator such as a cat. This leads to a sequence of reactions. First, the threatened animal tends to freeze, their heartbeat races, and they shake. Next, the animal tries to escape, continuing to experience high levels of arousal. If unable to escape, the animal becomes angry, struggling or fighting. If neither of the 'fight or flight' reactions is successful in terminating the danger, a fourth stage of immobility and behavioural paralysis begins.

This is what happens to those trapped in violent relationships, and to rape victims. After attempts to fight or flight fail, there is a sense of helplessness and loss of motivation which can lead to feelings of guilt, failure, and self-blame.

All the while, the brain is producing harmful stress chemicals through the hypothalamic pituitary adrenal axis.[3] The victim's physical health suffers as well. Changes in stress chemicals have been associated with conditions such as hypertension, diabetes, central obesity, and reduced immunity, as well as memory problems and depression.

Another woman, Saraswati, came in for treatment, and her father also attended the first consultation. She had spent nights homeless after being thrown out of her house by her husband. She had not slept for weeks, and her father had also stopped sleeping. He was receiving treatment for diabetes, and his daughter's situation was impacting badly on his blood sugar levels. In addition, he had developed a clinical depressive illness.

He said that at the time of the wedding in Delhi, the seniors of the groom's family put themselves forward as the key leaders and influencers. They negotiated the dowry payments; they demanded substantial cash and gold. But after the violence, they washed their hands of the match.

Demands for dowry—and enforced isolation from family and support networks in order to have these demands met—is coercive control.

'Sorry, we have no say here,' they said. 'The groom is an Australian resident, we cannot influence him.'

Both acutely felt the betrayal. Her father was incredulous and tearful. 'How deceitful,' he said.

I treated them both for depression and anxiety.

There is no discounting the trauma that these women (and their families) have lived through.

Dowry abuse and family violence are wicked problems that rob the victim of their personality, resilience, and self-worth. Along with the many forms of abuse already mentioned, social controls may also be inflicted on a bride. For example, she may not be allowed to go outside the house alone; she may not be allowed to speak to her family or told to keep the contact to a minimum; she may be told to wear certain type of clothes.

She is like the trapped animal in a cage, with the predator ever watching her.

Abuse via technology has the same texture. The woman might be stalked through social media, the internet, or her mobile phone—the abusing partner might put a GPS tracker on her phone to watch her every movement; he might use spyware.[4] One woman told me her husband had planted cameras all over the house, in each bedroom and bathroom, to observe her and her visitors.

Another woman told me that her separated husband had sent nude pictures to her previous employers in India and her extended family, defaming her as a 'loose woman'. She was shamed and humiliated, and suffered anxiety, fear, loss of face, and panic attacks as a result. This was a breach of an intervention order (IVO) issued against him in Victoria. The police gave him a warning. Police warnings help, but when the crime is being conducted in India by a third party (the man's brother was involved), the police are powerless to act in Australia. In such cases, I advise the women to speak to the Indian police. Inevitably, the barriers to them doing so are a sense of embarrassment and a lack of confidence that they will be taken seriously. They feel their honour is being smeared.

This woman tried to fight back, but eventually felt paralysed and gave up. The stress chemicals in her body, however, did not stop; the brain still registers the threat, causing harm to the body and mental health. The perpetrator is not present in person, but the fear and distress are as powerful as if he were physically there. Cyberstalking has serious consequences for victims: increased suicidal ideation, fear, anger, depression, and post-traumatic stress disorder.

It is a new form of family violence and has become more common in recent times with increasingly accessibility to the internet.[5] Support can be difficult to find as it can be hard to pin down the perpetrators, but I have heard from women that the police do help and that courts are taking a strict line against cybercrime in Australia. It is a new area of study and research.

As mentioned previously, the relatively unknown form of family violence is dowry abuse.[6] It might also take the form of modern-day slavery.[7]

Alka was a doctor in India. In order to work in Australia, she had to pass the Australian Medical Council exams. But her new husband would not spend money on her exams. He forced her to work in an old-age nursing home and took her entire income. She would put her income in a joint account, and he would remove all of it. If she bought a cup of coffee, he would intimidate and rebuke her, telling her not to spend money without his permission. She had been excited to get her first pay packet in Australia, but she was struck down in mid-flight, so to speak. This is defined as modern-day slavery by the International Labour Organisation: 'all work or service which is exacted from any person under the threat of a penalty and for which the person has not offered himself or herself voluntarily.'[8]

There are laws against slavery in Australia and every other country in the world, but perpetrators like this man are not being held to account. Alka challenged her husband and spoke up for her rights. He withdrew his sponsorship of her partner visa and she was deported back to India. There was no physical violence and family violence could not be proven. The stress, hardship and sense of failure felt by this bride was profound. Alka's dreams were shattered by threats, fear, and oppression. Her disappointment was extreme. She thought she was coming to Australia to live the life of a modern women like her Western counterparts.

Here is the story of a young woman—let us call her Aruna—who lived in Brisbane with her new husband of one year.

> I was studying to be a computer software engineer in India. They started pressurising me and my family to marry him. I sacrificed my dream of studying because of him. My parents did a simple wedding in a restaurant. After I came to Australia I was working five to six days a week. He would send all my salary to India to his family. He needed money so he took a loan of $7000 from a Bank, to help him get permanent residency visa. He lied to me. He said he had permanent residency of Australia but he had 457 visa [a temporary work visa] when we got married. I found out to my shock that he could be deported back to India any time. He was fighting a lot with me. He started to threaten me. He will send me back to India, he can't stay with me anymore. He needs money. He asked me to ask my father to send him money. So my father sent $5000 to him. I had no money in my bank account, he had taken every cent of my wage. I would come home from work tired and have to do the household chores, cooking cleaning, wash the dishes, cook hot dinner, and hot breakfast in the morning for him before work. He did nothing to help me. One day, he brought a piece of paper typed that we are going to separate.

I refused to sign it. He forcefully made me sign it. I had hidden everything from my family. He deported me back to India. He divorced me and got married to a woman in Australia who had permanent residency. I live in India with my parents now. He is living happily in Australia. I am depressed all the time, I cannot work and I cannot study, I am not able to sleep at night, I have no pleasure in life, I have lost all my savings. I am a burden on my parents, I feel like a failure, the society here does not respect women who are divorced, men think I am a tainted woman who can be used for sex for their pleasure. I have lost will to live. As a girl I had a dream like other girls do, I dreamt of having a great husband, happy home life, children. That was the main thing at the back of my mind. If I am not a wife who am I? I was getting education but being married is the big thing, all girls dream of it.

Aruna's descriptions match classical symptoms of major depressive illness. Although the cause is social—family violence, slavery, economical abuse, stigma and shame of failed marriage, being divorced—it has affected her mental health, and she feels like a failure and has lost self-worth. If she has a genetic vulnerability, her depressive illness may become more severe and she will need pharmacological agents. Society's view of her has impacted her self-image. Her identity as a happy married woman has been battered.

All of the above can be shifted. It is her mindset, her conscious and unconscious thinking learnt as a child and reinforced by years of conditioning within family and society, that is paralysing her. Yet she must have a support system within her social network to get better. Her parents do support her, but they have not asked her to see a doctor for her mental health. She has a friend in Australia who has been asking her to get help in India.

Good, effective medications for moderate to severe depressive illness and anxiety make a difference. Psychological treatments like trauma therapy are designed to help people like Aruna deal with what they have been through; to help them process it and restructure their thoughts. Trauma therapy would allow Aruna to recognise that her emotional problems, fear, panic attacks, loss of confidence in her judgements, low self-respect, and self-doubt are a result of external social trauma and not her fault—she is not a failure, she is the victim of a crime that is societally perpetuated, and often goes unpunished.

As mentioned earlier, Australia's Immigration system is propping up the perpetrators and failing the victims. It does not support victims of domestic violence who have temporary work visas or student visas (such women do not have access to special provisions of Immigration Law), though it gives some protection to women on partner visas. Service providers and activists, including my own NGO, the AustralAsian Centre for Human Rights and Health, are working with a national alliance and urging the Australian Government to change the rules so that all victims of domestic violence are given this same protection regardless of their visa status.[9] Currently, numerous women like Aruna are falling through the cracks of the system and not receiving the right kinds of support.[10]

Aruna also needs supportive therapy, to help her feel believed, respected, validated, and not negated; to help her gain empowerment and self-confidence; to help her to move from feeling powerless to having choices, power, and control over her own life. In addition, her illness also needs to be treated with antidepressant medications. The likelihood of a good outcome for her mental health is high with effective treatment.[11] It will allow her to reclaim her life; society will gain from her becoming a valuable, productive member again; and her family will gain from her ability to contribute socially and economically.

But Aruna lives in a small provincial town in India. There is no psychiatrist or psychologist. She has not complained of her depression to her family doctor. She does not recognise this as a treatable illness. Instead, she believes that this is her fate and destiny.

Global research has found that levels of anxiety and depression globally are rising. Even in advanced nations like Australia, the rates of mental and behavioural conditions are very high. One in five people (20.1 per cent of the population) have a mental health condition.[12] The problem is worldwide. Women suffer anxiety and depression twice as often as men (who succumb to substance abuse far more often). Social factors—such as greater risk of psychological abuse, physical violence, or sexual abuse—add to the stress caused by fluctuations in sex hormones such as oestrogen and progesterone in women.[13] Globally, less than 10 per cent of people with anxiety or depression get appropriate treatment, and this number is lower in low-income countries.[14]

The global cost of intimate partner violence is estimated at $4.4 trillion, or 5.2 per cent of global GDP.[15] Homicides and assaults cost about 7.5 times more than war and terrorism. An excellent VicHealth study in Australia found that about 75 per cent of the costs of family violence are due to resulting anxiety, depression, and suicide attempts: treatment costs, days off sick, and unemployment as a result of mental illness, homelessness, and attempted or completed suicides.[16]

What a figure: $4.4 trillion. What an enormous price paid by women, their families, and society generally.

Aruna lost her job because she was unable to concentrate; she could not sleep at night, felt tired all the time, and lost interest in eating and self-care. She felt hopeless and financially and emotionally insecure. She was no longer a loving daughter, sister, or a friend. Aruna felt like killing herself. She thought of hanging herself.

Aruna was taken to her mother's guru in the next village for treatment. But she remained demotivated and sad. Faith healers may provide some comfort, but common mental disorders need proper psychosocial therapy and/or medications. Her mother thought it was okay to take her to see her guru but not to talk it out with her doctor. Her village needs doctors and trained therapists. Governments must spend much more on mental health: on staff, treatment, raising awareness, and helping communities to fight the stigma surrounding mental illness and its treatment. They do not spend nearly enough.

It is a wicked system that takes young, intelligent, confident and educated women and turns them into wrecks with serious mental health issues.

Family domestic violence is strongly associated with mental illness and suicidal behaviour. In one large Australian community survey, half the victims had developed some form of mental illness.[17] It is a coping response to an abnormal situation.

In my clinical case load, in 2016, I analysed suicidal behaviour and associated mental illness in a small subset of fifty-five women.[18] They were victims-survivors of extreme family violence living in Victoria and were mainly of South Asian origin. They had all escaped their situations, were no longer living with the perpetrators of their abuse but were fearful for their lives, with half needing police protection orders. We compared them to another subset: a group of twenty-eight Middle Eastern women who had presented to another clinic with major depressive illness, strong suicidal thoughts, and serious suicidal attempts. These women were also victims of domestic violence, but were still living at home with their perpetrators. They were not fearful for their lives, but were severely demoralised.

The average age of the South Asian women was twenty-nine. Their mental health diagnoses revealed that 75 per cent suffered post-traumatic stress disorder; 70 per cent suffered major depressive illnesses; 70 per cent felt acute fear all the time; 50 per cent had suffered dowry abuse; 75 per cent were suicidal; and 17 per cent had attempted suicide.

The Middle Eastern (ME) women, on the other hand, were an older group, and suffering mild-to-moderate depressive illness. Of this group, 100 per cent showed suicidal thoughts, while 64 per cent had attempted suicide—mainly overdoses of medications and self-mutilation. Two women had nearly died after overdosing.

Across both groups, 80 per cent of the women had suffered physical violence—slaps and hitting were common for the Middle Eastern women. The South Asian women, in addition, suffered more serious violence like pushing, shoving, choking, threats to kill, and having objects thrown at them. Ninety per cent of women in both groups suffered emotional abuse. For the ME women, verbal abuse consisted of critical words like 'stupid' and 'good for nothing'. South Asian women endured greater verbal abuse—vulgar words, humiliation, criticisms, and demands for dowry—and were isolated from the in-law's extended family.

Both groups of women were given psychological treatment and medications.

The young South Asian women, in spite of their immense fear, severe anxiety, panic attacks, problems with sleeping, inability to enjoy food, loss of weight, and recurrent flashbacks, were now able to exercise choices in their lives, having left their husbands. They were educated, and they were able to make decisions, enjoy a sense of freedom, wear what they wanted, work in a job they liked, keep all their wages or send money to their parents if they wanted—all things they were not allowed to do before separation. These women responded well to treatments, with their depression and fear levels reducing. Therapy's first role was to help them understand they had been a victim of abuse. The women started to recognise their rights to protection from abuse and violence. As the medications took effect and they started to sleep better, their appetite improved, and 68 per cent went back to study and work within six to twelve months.

The main difference in the two groups emerged. Improvement in depression and anxiety was seen in half the women of both groups, but suicidal ideas showed a different trajectory.

Of the ME women, 82 per cent remained suicidal, compared to 39 per cent of South Asian women.

It was our opinion that the most likely reason they did not want to live was entrapment. They remained in a demeaning environment where they were humiliated and insulted on a daily basis. These women had low education levels, less than secondary school; they were not employed outside the home, and they had few social connections outside their family. For each woman, their home was not a warm, loving, or respectful place; it was where they were slapped, or lived with the threat of it, for 'making stupid comments' or not cooking the food the way their husbands liked, or for the way they spoke to their children. It could be any minor thing that their husbands found unacceptable. They would be pushed out of the way like a child might be, endlessly disparaged or criticised.[19] It is no wonder they did not want to live. There was no way out; they were trapped.

The fifty-five South Asian women stopped being suicidal within six months after separating from their husbands. Their therapy included discussions on strategies to increase understanding of cultural expressions of coercive control, entrapment in abusive marriage by societal pressures, family and the perpetrator and the nature of family violence; attending to their physical safety and housing safety; and establishing a trustworthiness in service relationships. The therapy focused on how the trauma of family violence impacts mental health, and incorporated principles of societal gender norms as a reinforcer of gender based inequality, and principles of social justice. In addition, a detailed report stating the nature of violence, mental state, and cultural construction of the case with treatments given helps them to fight their court cases.

All needed medications broadly termed as serotonin enhancers, and some needed benzodiazepine clonazepam for a period of 15–30 days, depending on the severity of ongoing fear.

This treatment strategy had a powerful healing effect on victims, and started their journey towards not only being survivors but thrivers.

Their treatment lasted between six months and three years. After three years, most had recovered and had good mental health; they felt in control of their life. They had generally found a job or returned to study. They were empowered; they were free of anxiety, fear, and depression; flashbacks to trauma stopped in 90 per cent of the women.[20] The majority of the women on temporary visas (forty-seven women) went on to receive permanent residency of Australia.

The resilience of the immigrant South Asian women is remarkable.

The main difference that allowed the younger, educated South Asian women's improvement in suicidal ideas was escape from their marriage, coupled with an ability to envisage a new life for themselves in Australia and then actualise that vision. They were not trapped. They were free and empowered, with agency over their life and choices. Whereas the older group of women with less education, who were stay-at-home mums and housewives, could never actualise life away from the home. Separation was not an option. Their agency over their life was minimal. There was nothing to live for. Suicidal thoughts and suicidal attempts were not related to their depressive illness; they were related to their life circumstances. The issues that worked in tandem were defeat, humiliation, entrapment, a sense of isolation—leading to suicidal ideation that became, in some, suicidal behaviour.[21]

Arti, an IT engineer, had an arranged marriage in India to an Australian-Indian resident. A day after the marriage, her husband stopped talking to her and his mother repeatedly complained that the dowry gifts were insufficient and of poor quality. Arti moved in with her in-laws pending the visa papers that would allow her to travel to Australia. As soon as she arrived in her husband's family house, her mother-in-law took all her gold jewellery and ornaments—'for safeguarding'.

Arti became anxious and fearful, realising she was in a hostile environment from which escape was difficult.

The following week, her father visited. Arti's mother-in-law exploded at him: 'We were dishonoured by insufficient, low-quality dowry gifts.' (Arti's parents had spent their life savings on her marriage. Over three ceremonies, her parents had given extravagant gifts of gold and cash; her wedding cost more than $130 000.) She threatened to send Arti back home. Her father cried and pleaded because that would dishonour his family. He explained he had spent his life savings. Arti was deeply sad; she felt helpless and powerless, and humiliated.

Her mother-in-law relished the impact of her power. She finally relented and said: 'Okay, Arti can stay here and will be allowed to go to Australia.'

Some months later, Arti arrived in Melbourne. Soon, her husband made escalating demands for money. Her 'backchat' angered him; he hit her, saying she was costing him too much.

Over the next weeks, she was given little food to eat and no access to money. Her husband kicked her out of the house on cold nights. Arti would sit in the park nearby—alone, fearful, tearful, and becoming suicidal. She was shocked and traumatised by the sudden change in his behaviour—he had been a loving fiancé.

His sister and mother arrived, and both threatened Arti's life on a number of occasions. She recognised the threats were dowry related and knew that dowry demands can lead to murder. She went to a police station and obtained an intervention order against her multiple perpetrators—her husband and his family.

Arti was referred to me for treatment by her GP. A mental health examination revealed an acutely fearful, sad, anxious young woman, who was shaking like a leaf. Arti had panic attacks every few hours and would become breathless, have dizzy spells, and feel her head was going to burst. She thought she was going crazy. She was acutely suicidal, and at one point overdosed on sleeping tablets. She felt her life was not worth living and that she had brought so much trauma to her parents. Her sleep was disturbed with nightmares of monsters chasing her or someone trying to kill her. She could not focus on anything. Arti had no energy and no appetite; she had lost ten kilos in seven months.

Flashbacks are a key feature of post-traumatic stress disorder. Arti said her brain would not stop thinking of the events of the past seven months. She would relive episodes like a film in front of her eyes, moments of physical violence, threats to her life, criticisms of her and the dowry given. She would then disconnect from her body and have feelings of dissociation and suffer panic attacks. I diagnosed her as suffering from post-traumatic stress disorder and panic disorder and started her treatment.

Arti represents any one of the fifty-five young South Asian women in my study.

After fifteen months of treatment, Arti slowly improved: her anxiety lowered; she started sleeping well; her flashbacks became easier to handle, and she had no nightmares or panic attacks. She learnt to handle emotional distress, observe her painful feelings as an outsider, and to handle her suicidal and hopeless thoughts. She was taught a technique called Eye Movement Desensitization and Reprocessing (EMDR), a therapy that helps to cancel flashbacks of violence, abuse and negative thoughts, and her thoughts were restructured to help her recognise her power and control over her life as a single woman.[22] She recovered well enough, found a great job, and had excellent support from within the Indian community. She got on with her life.

Another thing that aided the improvement of these women was the detailed technical letters I wrote in their support, which they needed for their visa applications for permanent residency of Australia, or court cases against perpetrators, migration reports, family law cases. (Their worst fears were of their visa being cancelled and being deported. Often the women do not know that the Australian Government and most Western countries allow victims of family violence to apply for permanent residency and that they often get it.)

These letters would describe their problems and the mental health impacts of the dowry abuse and family violence they'd suffered in great detail. As well as helping women fight their cases, the reports have a highly positive impact on their mental health. The women make sense of the chaos in their lives by reading a coherent, culturally nuanced description of different types of abuse and the ensuing emotional trauma and mental suffering they experienced. Sometimes the women have not fully recognised the abuse they were going through until they read their story. A slightly different version of this process is one written by victim-survivors, called narrative therapy. The women feel validated, feel their story has been heard, believed, and respected, and know their suffering was not imaginary. The women start to recognise they have human rights in Australia, that family violence is an abuse of these rights, and that they will be protected. It gives an enormous sense of validation—a concept many are not used to. For some women, treatment will be the first time they allow themselves to recognise they have suffered mental trauma, and is part of a process in which they receive mental health treatment for the first time.

And what about their broader community? Will they find support there? This is the most interesting thing about Indian society. When things go wrong, some will turn against the victim. Yet the help that came for Arti was from within sections of her community, and it was life-saving. The benefits of a collective society such as the Indian community are numerous for women like Arti. She found connectedness and a sense of belonging after a long, distressing period.

# 10

# MIGRATION, FAMILY AND SUICIDE

Suicide is the second-leading cause of death among 15- to 29-year-olds globally, according to WHO, and 75 per cent of suicides occur in low- and middle-income countries.[1] The South-East Asian region accounts for 39 per cent of all suicides, and has the highest suicide rate at 13.4/100 000. For Indian women overall (14.7/100 000), the rate is more than double that of Australian women (at 6.4/100 000).[2] Though the Australian male suicide rate is rising (18/100 000), it is still lower than the Indian male rate (21.2/100 000).[3] Suicide is responsible for 70 per cent of deaths of women under forty in India; they are 2.1 times more likely to die by suicide than the global average.[4] Analysis of Indian data shows that social and economic causes lead men to suicide, whereas emotional and personal causes are the main reasons why women end their lives.[5] This data from India is relevant for understanding the recent cluster of suicides in Victoria. Recently, in the Melbourne suburb of Epping, seven Indian women—half of whom were young mothers—died through suicide within a year. About five of the seven women had history of family violence; half of them had previous contact with police for protection from domestic violence; and two others had disclosed to their work colleagues or family the presence of family violence in their present or past relationship. All of them were new immigrants into the country and lived in a new settlement on the outskirts of metropolitan Melbourne. Sergeant Damian Lehmann from the local police station, who discovered the cluster, found that six of seven did not have a driving licence, and the majority were not employed, and isolated.[6]

Migration adds another layer of complexity and stress.[7] There is the loss of social networks and support of biological family. New migrants often have little knowledge of local support systems. In running educational workshops for migrants, I have come across women who did not know the telephone number of police, or the role of police in supporting domestic violence victims. Our NGO, the AustralAsian Centre for Human Rights and Health, received a grant in 2010 to provide interactive education workshops for migrants around the above issues, called the Mutual Relational Respect workshops.[8] I recognised that many migrants from developing countries had limited knowledge of the crime of domestic violence; of ordinary mental illnesses like depressive illness and anxiety disorder; of the fact that suicidal thoughts/behaviour can be treated, or that mental illness/distress improves with modern effective treatments; or that a good source of help was their local family doctor. The barriers to help are many and varied for newly migrated women. The Federal and State Governments of Australia fund support services, but there is a lack of adequate funding for effective educational workshops that are nuanced and tailored to specific needs of migrant groups.[9]

Since 1990, the rates of suicide across the world have come down by 10 per cent, and by one-third in China.[10] The greatest reduction occurred in the Chinese female rates—64 per cent. In India, the reduction was 15 per cent.

Suicide is a complex phenomenon. Multiple factors play a role—biological, psychological, social, and cultural factors. One can speculate on the reasons. In China, greater improvements in social and economic conditions for women are credited for the reduction. Professor Su Zhonghua notes that even women in economically dependent homemaking roles are becoming less confined as a result of changing social structures, becoming migrant workers or making money on their own. Professor Su regards the role of migration a positive factor in many women's lives. 'The traditional tension within a rural family is alleviated as people of different generations no longer live together as long as they used to.' Values, too, are changing: 'divorce has become a more acceptable way of dealing with family problems, including domestic violence.'[11]

Though small, it is hopeful sign. Things can change.

In Australia, the suicide rates of young people aged 18–24 have been rising. It increased from 10.8 deaths per 100 000 people in 2010 to 16.4 in 2020. The age-standardised suicide rate was higher among both men and women. Three-quarters of the young people who died by suicide were boys or young men, and 57 per cent had diagnosed or possible mental health disorders, suggesting that the mental health and wellbeing of young Australians should be a key target for youth suicide prevention. The social stressors included history of abuse, loss of a loved one, and financial pressures.[12]

There are different pressures in different contexts.

Indian farmers die of suicides in large numbers. The known causes include crop failures, high cost of fertilisers and seeds, and economic bankruptcies.[13] Different pressures apply to young people. Professor Vikram Patel, a noted Indian psychiatrist, explores why suicide is the leading cause of death for India's young people.[14] In the Indian context, Professor Patel speaks about lack of autonomy, and lack of freedom to make choices about important psychosocial factors affecting young people's lives.

Let us examine pressures faced by students from Indian families.

They have particularly high expectations of their sons. An ideal Indian son is an excellent student who receives perfect scores. He will become highly educated, and will enhance the social status of his parents. The ideal Indian daughter will be obedient, docile, a good student and well-educated, but marriage is her primary goal.

In my family in India, we children were to study hard and be successful at school. But my now deceased younger brother was not good at school. He failed Year 9 and 10, got into bad company, would stay out late at night, smoke and drink alcohol. This was in 1960s India, when such behaviours were totally shunned. He was the source of much anguish to my parents. They spent their hard-earned money on an expensive private school for him. My sister and I were sent to a government school after Year 8, because it was near home, we were told. My mother denies this difference in our education was biased towards my brother. Regardless, he failed to keep his end of the bargain at the private school and was pulled out. What to do with him next was a huge worry for my parents. He was not the studying type. My father used his adaptive thinking and sent him to study hotel management abroad. That, too, was an expensive exercise, and my parents had to borrow money to pay for it. No expense was spared on his education. Our neighbour's son, around this time, was twenty years of age. He attempted suicide because he could not live up to his parents' expectations that he would become a doctor. Luckily, he survived and found an alternative profession as an accountant. His parents were finally happy with his choice, but at what cost? Their relationship always remained a little strained.

I was very sick with flu the week before my pre-medical examinations, which were critical to getting into medical college in Delhi in the 1960s. All my dreams were pinned on these exams. But the flu was severe, and I had a high fever. 'I don't care, whatever happens,' I remember thinking.

Unbeknown to me, my parents were anxious because they thought I would miss my chance to become a doctor. My father put in extra effort and care and made sure I got the right food. He gave me a pep talk before the first exam and said, 'You will be all right, sit the exam. You must not give up this opportunity.' He took me to the examination hall at Deshbandhu College, not far from my home. He gave me a thermos flask full of some nutritional liquid that I was supposed to drink through the examination.

The first paper was the English exam. The first question was an essay about walking on the moon. The United States had just landed the Apollo 11 spacecraft. We were all very excited about it. I don't remember much about what I wrote, but when I came out my father asked: 'How did you go?'

'I don't know,' I said.

'How did you describe the walk on the moon?'

'They had to make no effort to walk on the moon,' I replied.

'You will be fine,' he said.

I improved significantly by the next paper on organic chemistry, then came a physics exam and a biology exam. When the results came out, sure enough, I had fulfilled my parents' dream. I got my first class, although not a brilliant one; I just scraped in. But I managed to get an interview at the Maulana Azad Medical College.

My mother and father later told me they sat outside the examination hall during the exams, for the full three hours, often peeping in to check on me and see if I was still sitting upright, worrying about how I was doing. My father said I was half lying down in the chair and writing away. I recall feeling quite out of it, much of the time I was writing without much thinking.

I reflect on that process now and realise that my mother and father devoted a lot of emotional energy and financial resources into our upbringing. It was largely a strong and positive influence. But it also put the responsibility on us children to return the favour and deliver their dreams.

If I had not become a doctor, I am sure we would have all survived; I would have taken up some other career. My brother went to become a successful hotelier; sadly, his life was cut short at age fifty-five. But some do not survive this expectation. Many young people feel the pain of letting down their parents so intensely that they attempt suicide, and often, tragically, are successful.

An international student once came to see me, let us call him Mohan. He was extremely suicidal and depressed, with some signs of clinical depression and existential despair. He'd failed his accounting subject and had to pay a second set of fees; he'd lost his job as a security agent and had no means of support. All he had was a car in which he slept and spent most of his time. His parents in India were not poor and could afford to send money, but he was too embarrassed to ask them. He usually avoided ringing them, and when he did ring them, he pretended everything was going well. It would be too great a disappointment for them, and shame for them and him. He was their bright son, and they could never imagine failure in an exam or in his life. He had also left his friends.

Mohan had been contemplating suicide for the past month. He felt he was unable to share this information with anyone but me. Somehow, he found my name on the internet and came to see me. He said: 'I need to save this year. A psychiatric report will help me so I can receive special consideration from university.' Saving face and avoiding shame were the most important issues for him.

It took about three months of treatment and reports for his university to accept his mental illness as a legitimate cause for his exam failure. His depression gradually improved, his mood picked up, and, no longer suicidal, he could see a path forward that would be acceptable to his parents, though he didn't tell them about his ordeal at any point. He regained his place at the university, found a job, paid off his fees, and went home to visit his parents with pride.

He had been perilously close to suicide; not because of serious depression, but for social-cultural reasons. Recently I heard the sad news that a teenage boy killed himself in Melbourne, leaving his Indian parents devastated. They had no idea why their son killed himself.

I thought about Mohan for a long time afterwards, wondering what alternative actions he could have taken to prevent his suicidal thoughts.

Support from family and friends is an important protective factor. Yet something had stopped him from reaching out to his parents when he was down and out and needed their support the most. In our sessions, he kept talking about his parents' love for him. The flipside of this was disappointment in him if they heard about his failure and unsuccessful life. He feared their expectations of him would be trashed. Their aspirations for him, intertwined with his own ambitions, distorted his judgement.

Some parenting skills are not commonly learnt—for example, how to value a child, be they a girl or a boy, for their strengths and qualities without comparing them with others. This occurs at a subconscious level—automatic thinking—and needs to be made conscious to deal with it effectively. The socially learnt bias towards boys is deeply unconscious; it puts a strain on boys and young men.

Strong parental engagement significantly influences students' academic achievements. But is it optimal engagement? What about emotional and social development?[15]

Expectations around education and employment are not the only ways in which young people are feeling pressured. Societal pressure to always look strong, in control and successful, and to maintain dominance over women, take a toll on men. That can be avoided with effective parenting skills. During my teaching stint with psychology students at Dev Sanskrit Vishva Vidhyalya in Haridwar, India, I saw patients in the mental health clinic run by the university. A dozen young men and women, with anxiety, depression and suicidal ideas, usually described having to hide their relationships with their girlfriend or boyfriend from their parents and from society, and talked about their thwarted sexual desires. Pre-marital relations and choice of mate are social crimes that young persons are conditioned to not commit.

What are the young Indian women's and men's experiences? It was a chance discussion with a smart young woman named Samya in a workshop I was leading that sent me down a new path of thinking. Samya told me that during her training in psychology at an Australian university, she was asked to observe fifteen children at a childcare centre. She particularly noted the children's eating habits—they were being taught to feed themselves independently as young as six months. At home, it would be the same: Western parents train their children to eat independently. It struck her that children of Asian parents are completely different, especially those from the Subcontinent. Children are fed by their mothers—mothers literally put food into the mouths of children, sometimes even up to the age of seven or eight. Children enjoy being fed by their mothers, and even ask for it. Perhaps a piece of bread or roti with vegetables or rice with lentils tastes much better from the hands of a mother? Samya, herself a mother, said she also enjoys feeding her children in this way.

Samya observed the children at the childcare centres trying to feed themselves and hold their own milk bottle. They may make a mess, they may drop spaghetti everywhere, but they're sitting in the highchair and learning independence.

It was a small insight, but one that brought forward many questions.

Learning to eat by yourself is just one of many things that can inculcate an attitude of independence or self-reliance from a young age. It's interesting to consider what might stem from this independence. Could it foster rebelliousness of a positive sort later on?

If hand feeding children—along with many other societal habits—encourages them to rely on and remain extremely close to their parents, especially their mother, does this mean they do not find the same need or skill to rebel against their parents' wishes or traditions later in their lives? What impact might this have on their future relationships? Is it a good thing that children remain so interconnected with their mother and family?

Interestingly, brain imaging with functional MRI scans show that this type of upbringing influences our very brain structure. In an innovative project, neuroscientists from Hong Kong put forward scenarios of themselves, their mothers, and other non-family persons. The brain images they took revealed that the words 'mother' and 'I' were located in the same place of the brain—the ventral medial prefrontal cortex—in Asian participants; but not in Western participants, where the two words were located in different parts of the brain. In another experiment, Asian participants were asked to recall events they had been through or objects of interest. What they recalled occurred in a social group or interaction, whereas Western participants recalled events oriented to the individual. In other words, people in Asia see themselves primarily as a part of their family and social network. People in the West see themselves as separate individuals. These differences are pervasive, and account for and, in turn, influence our different social relationships, motivations, and upbringing.[16]

Different upbringings also determine how we experience traumas and how we deal with them. In Asian cultures, with our dependent view of self, we interpret everything in relation to someone else—in other words, how it (whatever 'it' is) affects our parents or our family, or how society will perceive us. This has been shown in another MRI study that examined cultural differences in brain activity. The study identified two groups of sociocultural values: one set was independent, individualistic, and self-focused, and emphasised personal agency and uniqueness; the other was interdependent, collectivistic, and group-based, with a sensitivity to relations among people and social harmony.

# MIGRATION, FAMILY AND SUICIDE

There will be little surprise in which set of values belonged to which group.[17] Interestingly, it has also been shown that ethnic minorities migrating to Western countries show Western-style brain patterns.[18]

That is not to suggest that either style of socialising/family/parenting is superior to the other; merely that our brains are programmed socially.

The reasons for completed suicides shed some light.

Families play a significant role in suicides in Indian women: 'family problems' were a risk factor in 32 per cent of cases; dowry-related issues in 8 per cent; other marriage-related issues in 7 per cent; love affairs in 6 per cent.[19] In contrast, in Australia, individually determined factors played a bigger role. The most common risk factor was mental illness like depression, anxiety, or schizophrenia, or illicit drugs and alcohol. Family issues (identified as the disruption of a family unit due to separation or divorce, or problems with a spouse) were seen in only 14 per cent of cases. Problems in relationships with parents and in-laws were identified in just 47 cases out of 2474—1.8 per cent of Australian suicide cases.[20]

Both parenting styles, of East and the West, have advantages to offer; they also give rise to unique problems.

Our brain responses are shaped by the family and social situations we are immersed in.

Families are strongly influential in both. The motivation 'comes from within an individual in Western families', while Asian children 'find strength in parental expectations'.[21]

In a highly complex session with a distressed Pakistani mother, I saw an echo of Samya's observations. My patient, who was accompanied by her three-year-old girl, was describing the abusive conditions of her married life. She was crying and her daughter also became distressed. She stopped playing and demanded her mother's attention. She started crying and hitting her head on the table and then cried even more because she was hurt. Her mother picked her up, comforted her, sat her in her lap and said, 'Naughty table, it hurt you.'

Suddenly, hundreds of similar scenarios ran in front of my eyes. 'Naughty ground, it hurt you!' I had often heard mothers say to their young children in India.

Mothers and fathers need to teach children how to own their mistakes, identify problems, and identify their negative emotions; not to blame someone or something for their hurt and pain or failure, but to manage their pain or disappointment, solve problems or seek help, and move on knowing that pain will pass and new doors will open.

To be prepared for the inevitable hurts and failure in life, to move away from an attitude of blaming to owning the issue or the problem, what alternative statement could the little girl's mother have made? She could have picked her up, comforted her and said, 'I'm sorry you are hurt, it will get better soon,' and given her a drink or food. The problem was that the child was hungry, and when the right solution was applied and she got a biscuit, she was happy.

Growing up, girls and boys should be made aware that problems occur within families, and be empowered to recognise them, and seek help, and solutions.

The situation can change.

A father, Shyam, was referred to me for individual therapy from a Men's Behaviour Change Program group. He hit his 20-year-old daughter. She was driving the family car on L plates, and refused to listen to his directions regarding the route to take. Shyam insisted. She backchatted, calling him useless. She was a Western teenager, after all. Shyam's parental authority was threatened. He hit her.

He had wanted the best for his daughter all her life. He had spent a lot of money on her education and her driving lessons, but she had kept failing, and was insolent. Sure, he had been angry often and yelled loudly, he admitted grudgingly. 'It was in her best interest.'

His daughter took out a protection order (Intervention Order) against him.

Shyam slowly responded to therapy.

How could she go to police? Shyam asked. He was distraught, sad, and confused.

We did role play to help him find answers. I asked him to pretend to speak to his boss who calls him 'useless'. How will he approach that? It was successful. He recognised he had abused his power as a father, in the interest of making her achieve better scores, better jobs, a better life, etc.

We discussed parenting styles in the East versus West. Shyam shared that most families he knew of in Melbourne used corporal punishment to discipline their children. He knew no different.

Parenting techniques have been developed and researched for Western-style parenting. What would Eastern parenting styles look like that would produce children who are resilient, emotionally stable; not impulsive and not overly pampered, but still remaining part of a strong, supportive family system?[22] Western-style positive parenting techniques teach parents to allow independence and age-appropriate exploration by children. When a child has a setback, whatever the form, the parents can help support the child develop an attitude of resilience, to get up, dust themselves off and keep going. Resilience-enhancing skills that help children cope with tough situations can be taught—for example, how to regulate negative, painful emotions in situations of relationship difficulties, exam failure or bad results.[23] How to communicate, and how to be empathic and compassionate with others, are skills that parents need to learn and impart to their children in an appropriate manner according to the age and emotional maturity of each child.

By and large, parents love their children and want the best for them. Their devotion comes from a soft spot in their hearts. Their child-rearing habits represent their intentions to give their child the best chance of success. But it is possible that parents go too far in that direction and confuse where their needs finish and their child's needs start. Are they making parenting choices in the best interests of their daughter or son, or are they serving needs of their own—perhaps a need for societal approval and social status?

International students like Mohan who come to Australia from India have never cooked or cleaned for themselves, having lived a protected life within the cocoon of their family. But soon, they learn to look after themselves and do all kinds of jobs available to students that they may have considered beneath them in India. They have relationships their family would have forbidden. They enjoy having agency in their life, the sense of empowerment that comes with decision making.

Mohan came to see me after he was awarded his degree and had been to visit his family and attend a wedding in India. He was smiling, happy, confident. He had impressed his parents with his achievements. Just a small amount of timely help prevented his suicide. Suicide is sometimes the result of an impulsive action in a difficult situation. It is an attempt to problem-solve. Suicide is a permanent, heartbreaking solution, chosen in haste, to what is a temporary problem.

Schools play an important role in shaping attitudes and behaviours of their students. Increasingly, schools in Australia and world over are taking on the mantle of promoting mental health and resilience.[24]

In India's state of Bihar, the home of ancient Buddhist University Nalanda dating back some 1500 years, Professor Vikram Patel is leading and evaluating a school-based program to support adolescent students. The program involves the whole of the school—parents, teachers, and students—all working together as a team to create an environment that enables change. Its content relates to learning about mental health, empathy, bullying and gender-related violence, rights, responsibilities, and effective study skills. Parents are engaged in learning effective parenting, engagement, and good communication skills, and individual referrals are made where necessary. The result is that rates of bullying, depression, substance abuse, and violence are being lowered.[25]

There is always a solution. The solution may not be the one that had been imagined—but there is a solution.

And what of the devastating rates of young Indian women killing themselves no matter where they live? How can parents and families adjust so young women do not choose this permanent, heart-breaking solution? For women of Western countries, never having married, being single, separated, divorced, or widowed is a known risk factor for suicide.[26] In other words, marriage is a protective factor. But in Indian society it is the reverse. Marriage is known to be less protective against suicide because of arranged and early marriage, young motherhood, low social status, domestic violence, and economic dependence.[27] Social norms that discriminate against divorced women, coupled with lack of parental support, encourage young women to remain in unhappy marriages in dependent living arrangements with extended family. Women are effectively trapped, with little or no agency in their husband's home, and little control or power over their lives. Entrapment and powerlessness are known pathways to suicide.[28] Suicidal behaviour arises from one's attempt to escape from unbearable situations, or from unbearable thoughts and feelings. Society has to allow women freedom to think for themselves and make decisions for themselves. Sure, they will make mistakes, but that is part of the learning process.

What can autonomy for young women look like? Rational boundaries between a grown-up daughter and her parents, for example, would lead to a dialogue about her needs, education, employment, and how they fit in with marriage to a particular man chosen by her parents. She would bring her own critical thinking to this. Does she have someone else in her mind? Does she object to the tradition of dowry? Do her parents ask her how she feels about them spending so much on her education that she feels a mutual obligation towards them? About whether she wants to see them comfortable in their old age rather than spending their retirement savings on her wedding and dowry, even if they call it gifts and not dowry?

Family and social relationships do influence the actual structure of an individual's brain development, which can be changed for the better. The outcome for hundreds of women I have seen in my practice is usually highly favourable. The majority go on to become fully independent, take on new study and new jobs, and make difficult decisions about their own lives. Often, they support their families, and the families learn that being a daughter rather than a son does not stop her from being a source of strength for them. They enjoy their newfound sense of freedom. The families recognise that it is not only a son who can provide financial and emotional support for parents and siblings.

I am sure their brains are changing for the better. The human brain has remarkable capacity to regenerate, reorganise pathways, create new connections —a concept called neuroplasticity. It is about developing more connections and brain cells in the right places.[29]

# 11
# EDUCATION IS THE KEY TO EQUALITY

It was a jolt to read the World Economic Forum report on gender equality published in February 2020. The Gender Gap Report showed that the world has, overall, gone backwards—in the pay gap between men and women, poverty, and sanitation, to name a few areas. In this deteriorating situation, it will be a huge 257 years before gender parity can be achieved. There is no country where men spend the same amount of time on unpaid work as women. In countries where the ratio is lowest, it is still 2:1. The UN Secretary-General also reported some sobering figures. Currently, only 50 per cent of women of working age are in the labour force, compared to 77 per cent of men. Women are employed more in unpaid and precarious employment, or congregate in industries with lower average pay—social services like childcare, elderly care or disability care—rather than high-income areas such as finance or technology, which are traditionally dominated by men.[1] For example, in Silicon Valley most companies are male dominated and the gender pay gap is big.

Two hundred and fifty-seven years—that is too long to wait. Too many women's lives will be blighted with domestic violence and residual mental health trauma. Currently, one in four women in Australia suffer intimate partner violence.[2] Globally, the statistic is one in three; in the Eastern Mediterranean region 37 per cent, in Africa 36.6 per cent, and Europe 26 per cent of women report domestic violence.[3] In India, the figure is 4 in 10.[4] That is far too many. We must do all we can to speed up the process of gender equality.

And it all starts with schooling, and the education of every child.

My mother's gorgeously chatty and playful maid Kamla is thirty-two, has five children, and lives with her husband in a tiny hut in a shanty town of Delhi. Her husband is illiterate. Kamla studied to Year 5 at a village school near Agra and married at sixteen. Once I asked her why she did not study for longer.

She told me her mother was widowed early. Her father was killed by hooligans in Delhi where he had gone to find work. She was left with her mother and two younger brothers. Both she and her mother decided to go to work driven by an unstated imperative—to give her brothers a good education. The assumption was that they would support their mother in her old age, whereas Kamla was a girl, and she was just going to be married. Kamla was happy that she was educated to Year 5. She said she is happy that she can read numbers and street names. Her husband has to rely on her for counting money. She likes that small bit of power in her marriage.

Kamla was unemployed until her youngest child went to school, when she started work as a maid. She is enjoying the power and respect her income has brought her, and the dignity it has given her family. Previously, her husband worked intermittently as a street-based hot tandoori roti cook. The money was not enough to feed his four children and wife, and he pressured his mother, who lived with them and who also worked as a maid, to support his family. He drank regularly, and would give up work for months at a time. Kamla's participation in economic employment and her smart money management has given the family extra income, and, in turn, it has helped her husband lift himself out of his alcoholic stupor. Of late, he has been working as a chapatti maker at a tandoor and earning an income. As he feels better about himself, he is less bossy and drinks less. Her husband would have felt the way many men do: that he should be a powerful, dominating husband, and the main provider.[5] Poverty makes this role even more fraught.

These changes have brought peace and happiness into their home, and he has started helping his family.

Kamla, by taking power, has created an alternative to the male-dominant truths of her married life. Her children are all at school now and she can look forward to a more dignified life. The economic power of women is a force that will propel us to gender equality, says UN Women:[6]

> That means participating equally in existing markets; their access to and control over productive resources, access to decent work, control over their own time, lives and bodies; and increased voice, agency and meaningful participation in economic decision-making at all levels from the household to international institutions.

Kamla's older brother finished Year 12, but sadly was killed in an accident. Her younger brother got married after Year 12 and lives with his wife. Her elderly widowed mother lives alone in the village. I asked if her brother looks after their elderly mother. Kamla was sad. 'No one in this day and age looks after anyone. She lives alone and I worry for her.' Being widowed makes her more vulnerable to rejection by her married son, and to isolation.

Although significant strides in narrowing the educational gender gap have been made, the World Economic Forum Report shows that the education rates for Indian women remain lower than men. Sixty-six per cent of women are literate compared with 82 per cent of men. (In neighbouring Pakistan, literacy rates are 46 per cent for women and 71 per cent for men. In Australia, 99 per cent of all children are at school, and more women than men pass Year 12, with 90 per cent of young women and 84 per cent of young men aged 20–24 years having qualifications.)[7] Low economic participation makes gender inequality worse. Only a third of women are working or actively looking for a job in India. Married women, less educated women, and women from higher castes are less likely to participate in the labour market.[8] The rate of change needs to be accelerated.

Society needs to give women the permission to become educated, to enter employment, and stay in jobs after giving birth to children.

Kamla has greater bargaining power in her home now. She might have had a limited education, but she has a natural capacity for managing money. She is also supported by a government-funded preschool care project. Her two younger children are picked up by a bus at 9.30 a.m. daily and looked after until they are dropped back at 3 p.m. Childcare support is essential for women to be able to work. Kamla is lucky her husband and mother-in-law are supportive of her work. Many so-called upper caste families do not allow women to work. But work is not just about money; it is empowering and induces self-confidence and self-respect.

The World Bank has numerous projects that are supporting women on the ground with loans for education and loans in new types of businesses and agriculture. Although that is a helpful enabler, on its own it will only be a drop in the ocean. The question is: how to motivate more men and women to participate for a fairer, more gender-equal world? All the sacrifices made by Kamla and her mother to support the two sons in the family were due to a deeply patriarchal mindset. The support of the patriarchal system is repeated millions of times over on a daily basis. This is Deniz Kandiyoti's patriarchal bargain.[9] By giving him special attention and more privileges, the son remains attached to his mother. He, in turn, will reward her by allowing power over his future bride. This would complete the cycle that is the patriarchal bargain. The majority of mothers-in-law will not exploit that power. Some will.

Radha was nineteen and a bright law student who became a victim-survivor of domestic violence in Melbourne. She was intelligent and vivacious, and an outspoken, confident young woman whose parents were extremely worried that she would soon be twenty and there were no marriageable young men in their village in Haryana.

At university, she instinctively knew to keep herself 'nice' and not fraternise with young men. She was to attend classes and come straight back home; she was not to speak to strangers, go to restaurants, or to events hosted by students. In other words, she was deprived of education in the broader sense. She was there to get her degree in law. She knew she may never use it; it was simply there to make her look educated, to help her parents catch a good match. She completely accepted these rules. Women in her extended family get married very early, she said. She came from a wealthy farming family and was the only daughter with three brothers. She was going to get a good dowry.

Her marriage to an Australian-Indian did not turn out to be happy. Her mother-in-law was domineering and complained about Radha to her son, her married sister-in-law was a jealous bully who had been abandoned by her husband. The family was controlled by his mother-in-law's greed and power. She demanded a big dowry, and used her son's Australian residency as a bargaining tool. Radha too had multiple perpetrators. Along with her husband, her sister-in-law and mother-in-law were involved.

Radha turned out to be more educated than her husband, who was seven years her senior, and his entire family. Her husband drove a bus in Melbourne and, although he earned a reasonable income, he was not the IT engineer promised to her and her family. In addition, he had been in love with another woman for some years. His arranged marriage was a farce—perhaps to grab dowry, cash, and goods, and possibly to please his possessive mother.

Radha's education gave her an edge over her uneducated in-laws and husband. Despite her parents' efforts to restrict her education to what she learned on the page, her university education had exposed her to many new ideas and young men and women and ways of seeing the world. She did not keep quiet when her mother-in-law lied about Radha to alienate her son against his new bride, or when her sister-in-law bullied her and hit her for eating food out of the refrigerator. In India, she talked back and told them off for demanding dowry, telling falsehoods, and not allowing her to live with dignity. In Melbourne, she learnt of her husband's lies and his love affair within months of arriving. He refused to treat her with respect, talked down to her, abused her with ugly words and used her like a maid and sex slave. She had enough self-confidence to challenge his abuse; she didn't take it quietly or accept her fate. Radha fought for her dignity. His sense of entitlement as the supreme commander of the family was injured, which gave rise to immense anger and violence and fractured bones. Police were called by the neighbours and Radha left him for good. Radha's modern Indian education was at odds with the societally accepted patriarchal oppression imposed on her.

In Melbourne, she lives her life with dignity, and vows to complete her education.

Radha's education helped her to break the cycle of the patriarchal bargain. Imagine if she was not educated—she may have stayed in her violent marriage, playing a subservient role while her husband had affairs and pressured her for more dowry. She has paid an immense emotional and economic cost in her marriage and in leaving it—post-traumatic stress disorder and the loss of substantial dowry. She is determined to support her daughters to achieve whatever they would wish, with equal treatment, and without the pressure of marriage.

Indian women like Radha and Kamla are finding their voice, expressing their thoughts, and growing in confidence. But a system that does not share the same level of confidence in itself and in them inhibits young women, and stultifies them and their ability to make decisions of significance.

'No one gives up power willingly,' says eminent Indian psychiatrist, now president of Royal Australian New Zealand College of Psychiatrists, professor Vinay Lakra. 'Women will have to snatch power'.[10]

Education endows women with the tools to snatch power and support other women. Kamla lives far away from her mother in Delhi—her brother and his wife live closer in Agra city. But it is Kamla who makes the most effort to visit her mother and give her money and emotional support. Even though her husband is still the dominant adult in their household, Kamla's meagre education is helping her to survive better in this modern world than him. She is planning to buy a small business with her husband, setting up a mobile cart selling vegetables. He will need her help to count money. She has some power in the home—education gave her this power. She is determined to equalise the power balance with her own children. She wants her daughters to be as well educated as her sons. Her oldest son is seventeen and left school in Year 10 and helps his father. A second son is in Year 7. Her twin daughters are five and attending school and enjoying it, while her youngest daughter, aged two, receives free early childhood education and childcare, and attends a mobile kindergarten—a bus that comes to their shanty town, equipped with teachers, books, toys, and food to help the intellectual and social development of young children from impoverished families.

A young man named Sash once spoke to me at length about why the head of the 'ideal family' was right to make important financial decisions. He said women sometimes do not understand financial issues. 'Take my wife for instance,' he said. 'She decided she wanted to buy a car and it had to be a BMW. I told her it was expensive to buy, to think of something else. She stuck to her idea stubbornly.' Now, he says, 'We have to pay very high costs of servicing the car.'

His wife had found a great paying job at a bank recently; she was just coming out of the shadows of her husband and perhaps she wanted to take control and feel her power in some aspect of their home life. Sash was not able to understand that; he lives in a society that give him messages that women need protection, women need to be looked after; women are mothers, women are wives, women are not the equals of men.

If women are not given the chance to make decisions, they will not learn. We learn from our mistakes and successes. But women will be told they are incapable of making good decisions forever. Patriarchy functions at conscious and unconscious levels.

For Sash, 'patriarchy' is a word; but its manifestations are varied and complex, conscious and unconscious, manipulative and straight-out dominating. Sash has to accept that his wife will make mistakes when making financial decisions, but only for a short while, as he probably also did when he was starting out. She will learn from her mistakes and perhaps become a better money manager than him. She needs to be given a chance, or she may snatch the chance from him.

From a very young age I knew I was going to be a doctor. Dr Barlow delivered me in Peshawar in times when women generally were not seen or heard. My parents held up Dr Barlow as an ideal for me to follow. They were impressed by her no-nonsense, intelligent approach.

My mother, a qualified teacher, was well educated. My father had a double degree in law and economics. Their families approached girls' education slightly differently. My paternal aunt, a very intelligent woman who taught herself Sanskrit and leant all the Vedas at the age of fifty, told me that she was resentful that she and her two older sisters were deprived of a chance at education. They were taken out of school after year 6, in Dera Ismail Khan in Pakistan. Both their brothers were sent off to university and became lawyers. My mother's father, a schoolteacher, wanted to educate his three daughters and his sons. Sadly, this was interrupted for my mother's two sisters and her brothers by the Partition between India and Pakistan and the family relocating to India from Karachi and Abbottabad with none of their vast wealth. And although my mother had her degree, she was not allowed to use it. My father wanted his daughter to become a doctor, but he did not want his wife to work outside the house. Whereas all four of us children, two girls and two boys, were given every opportunity to become educated and find a career. Why he would not allow his wife to work is a mystery to me. One thing I knew was that he wanted to protect us children from predatory outsiders. He may have wanted her to be a stay-home mother to avoid hiring babysitters, or 'Aayah' as they are called in India. There may have been unconscious bias too; the need to be the sole earning member, and the dominant patriarch.

In Australia, I observe that Indian men also give the best opportunities and attention to their children—both sons and daughters. But what about their wives? A GP friend noted that in medical consultations for their wife's problem, some Indian husbands take over and dismiss their wife's opinion as unimportant.

The subconscious bias, or even the conscious bias, that leads even the most loving husband to overlook his wife's wishes and needs puzzles me. It appears as an unwillingness to reflect on his own thought processes, on how his decisions affect his wife. Societal structures that support men's biases against women's independence, whether in small or big ways, need to be discussed in media, in films, on talkback shows, in newspapers and books, and at every dinner table. It will make obvious what is being swept under the carpet. Some programs are taking initiatives—such as Champions of Change Coalition in Australia, whose mission is to engage leaders to help achieve gender equality and a significant and sustainable increase in the representation of women in leadership; and primary prevention programs in

India are mobilising communities to make the biases conscious, so that change can occur.[11]

Unconscious biases start to emerge during childhood. One volunteer at our NGO told me that while working as a preschool teacher, a white child told her, 'I like you. Can you change your brown colour to white?' She was stunned. It was evidence to her that racism and attitudes develop at a very young age. Another white child brought up in an expat white community in Singapore, upon returning to Australia, asked her mother 'Is she our maid?' when she met a Chinese family friend. 'Othering' is done by all children, not just white children. This leads to invisible exclusion and bullying of anyone who looks or seems different. Beyond skin colour, the excluded child might be obese, disabled, suspected as being gay, or Indigenous—all are seen as outsiders, or members of an outgroup; 'not one of us' and liable to be rejected.[12] Parents have a crucial role in educating their children towards equality and respect for everyone. Biases around gender and gender roles are forming alongside those around race and colour. Gender development in early adolescence (10–14 years) has been studied in rich, middle income, and poor countries.[13] The issues appear to be universal. Gender norms, relationships, sexuality, and empowerment in early adolescence follow universal themes and beliefs: boys are strong and independent, and girls are vulnerable. How does this come about? As explained previously, societal factors—media, schools, peers, and a range of other influences—reinforce gender stereotypes. The messages are personalised for the child in the family setting, through parents using controls and violence in different guises.[14] In Delhi and Shanghai, opposite-sex interactions are restricted by parents and violations are punished with physical violence. I have treated many young patients—second-generation South Asian migrant girls and women—who have suffered similar restrictions in Australia. Sushi Das writes about difficulties as a second-generation migrant woman living in the UK, including the wish for autonomy and circumnavigating parents' plans of arranged marriage.[15] Gender roles and mobility, especially in relation to sexuality, are more strictly enforced for girls than boys. Girls are repeatedly told to stay away from boys, and there are sanctions if they do not—punishment, social isolation, sexual rumour, and innuendo. Schools, parents, media, and peers are influential in supporting myths around gender norms, but also provide opportunities to create better gender equality through education and challenging unconscious biases.[16]

Some of my young patients effectively divorced their parents and claimed their freedoms. A patient of mine, a young woman, moved out of her parents' home at age sixteen. She was severely depressed, and suicidal. Her parents' extreme overprotective behaviours included micromanaging her friendships, what she wore, and who she spoke with.[17]

There is raised awareness among young women that gender equality is an attainable goal. Can parents accept this reality?

Our NGO, the Australasian Centre for Human Rights and Health, received federal funding to run our flagship project Mutual Relational Respect for migrants as a strategy to prevent family violence. In this program, migrants discuss case stories depicting many different aspects of gender-based relations and try to understand the underlying forces that propel us towards unequal gender relations and domestic violence in many cases.

One story we looked at shows a grandmother minding her six-year-old grand-daughter and four-year-old grandson. The boy wants a toy, a fire engine, that the girl is playing with. He snatches the toy, but his sister snatches it back. He hits her with a cricket bat, and she is hurt and starts crying. Grandmother smiles and says to the neighbour she will have to get used to being hit in her future life—this will be a common occurrence for her in her married life. He, however, needs to become strong, and it will do him good to pick up a heavy cricket bat and swing it around. This was based on an event witnessed by one of our volunteers in a Melbourne suburb.

The facilitator then encourages the participants to dissect the layers of cultural conditioning that we expose our children to. It has been fascinating to listen to the responses of migrant participants who came from about twenty different countries. One African woman said this was a common story in her hometown in Africa. A South Asian grandmother said that she had not realised the impact of her behaviour. She recounted a story when her grandson went to help his mother wash dirty dishes in the kitchen. Quick as a flash, this grandmother said: 'You are a boy, you don't go into the kitchen, it is your sister's job. Your mother should not ask you to help her.' For the first time, she realised that boys are overvalued and being taught to be waited upon, while girls are being taught to remain subservient and confine themselves to serving men. Another woman lamented that 'girls must not speak too loudly.' They must be submissive to male dominance. If they are not, they will be beaten into submission by bystanders—parents, grandparents—in order to maintain the centuries-old status quo. A Japanese student said that she was brought up with strict gender roles and now that she was a mother of a young baby, this workshop had made her aware of her powerful role in shaping her daughter's attitudes. We as parents have enormous power over the way our children's brains are wired in relation to gender roles. Mothers are considered very influential in forming attitudes; fathers too are powerful.[18]

In the global scenario of women doing two times more unpaid work in the home than men, UN Women recommends 'reducing the burden of unpaid care work for women by providing free and universal childcare, and access to employment opportunities, create decent jobs in the social services sector, and improve children's health and nutritional outcomes'.[19] What needs to change in each home alongside these macro-level policies can happen through education of parents and grandparents.

Dare we imagine the following scenario: A son goes to help his mother wash dirty dishes in the kitchen. Quick as a flash, his grandmother says: 'You are a boy, you don't go into the kitchen, it is your sister's job. Your mother should not ask you to help her.'

The boy feels repressed; he likes to help his mother. He is sensitive and does not like to see his mother in the kitchen alone, cooking, serving dishes, washing dishes after a day's work while he sits down to eat at the dining table with his father.

He says to his grandmother: 'I am a boy and I like to help my mother. My sister is a girl and she enjoys playing football; she does not enjoy going into the kitchen. Granny, I will not become a girl and my sister will not become a boy; we are just changing the roles society has given us and we are having fun doing it.'

In the scene where the young boy's grandmother condones or encourages him to beat his sister, the young boy will likely grow up into a man who expects to dominate his wife. At work he will expect that women are there to take lesser roles. That is why it is so important that communities are educated to understand that gender equality is the basis of a fair and just society. It can only lead to more prosperity and harmony and peace, whether within the home or within broader social groups. It all starts with schooling, and not just the schooling of girls.

Culture is not fixed; it changes in response to changing social circumstances.

Here is another story—this time of a family violence prevention project called United We Stand, in which a mixed audience of South Asian heritage was shown a video of an 'ideal family'. It was a family that mirrored my own. On screen, the head of the household is, yes, the loving, caring, benevolent patriarch. He takes a keen interest in his teenage daughter and son; he cooks breakfast for them. But when addressing his family over issues of concern, he privileges sharing information with his children over their mother—he only belatedly includes her in the discussion. In the video, he tells the family that he has planned a holiday for them—they are going to Rome.

The aim of the exercise was to facilitate opening up of minds, dissect hidden 'truths', remove unconscious bias against women, promote change, and enhance gender equality through community education. How did the community participants respond?

One woman felt that that the man in the video neglects his wife by not asking her what she would like for breakfast, instead focusing on his children; he is more animated towards them, and he does not give his wife equal significance. She also noted that in the video the wife asks for attention, stating she would also like pancakes for breakfast and she is then given the attention and the pancakes she wants.

A well-spoken, assertive young male student said this was a happy family, like his own, and the audience were looking for things to criticise. Most participants expressed the same sentiment.

But then the audience began to analyse the scene in more depth, and were taking note of the harm caused to other family members by having one person, the father—albeit a very loving father—as the only decision-maker in the family. A middle-aged gentleman looked unhappy at the turn of conversation. He probably saw the analysis as unnecessarily critical of a family system that most of us in India are brought up in. He refused to comment.

The father had been planning this holiday for five years, a woman noted. Why had he not told his wife? What does that say? What else does he hold back? He was saving money, but she did not know about it. Where is the financial accountability?

What would happen to this family if they migrated to Australia? Would the roles change? What if he could not find a job and had to depend on his wife's income? What would happen to his self-image? How would he manage the transition from being the main provider? How would he cope with the change in the balance of power? How would he cope with his quiet, submissive wife gaining more importance both within the family and outside it, and having more freedom and financial power? He could be flexible, and accept that a change in roles does not diminish his power or his self-esteem and decide that he would help the family as best he can, maybe as a homemaker. If he was rigid and had to be seen as the head of the household, he would not be able to cope with the resulting loss of face; that would lead to family issues like conflict, violence, or depression.

We take our everyday home life for granted. It is so familiar we feel safe. It is human to not question it. Not everyone is open to a critical examination of their culture, but many in this audience were. That, in turn, produced a ripple of useful questions.

One elderly woman at the Mutual Relational Respect workshop for prevention of family violence and gender role training sessions was not for change: 'That is the problem, they come here and forget their culture,' she said. The young man who had earlier asserted in the United We Stand that it was a happy family changed his thinking: 'Happy family not,' he said. He saw the harm that was possible when one person dominates decision making, forcing others to adopt accepting, submissive roles and suppress their independent thinking. I am hopeful he will change the rigid gender norms within his own relationships and networks.

'Change can be easy or it can be hard,' said former Premier Ted Baillieu at the Second National Dowry Abuse Summit in 2019.[20] Another truth is that migration changes everything. Women go to work, earn money, learn the ways of the world, gain confidence, feel empowered, spread their wings. But some suffer backlash from controlling, patriarchal husbands. In United We Stand, we showed another video clip about a young woman who gets a great job that earns her $90 000 a year. Her husband is very excited at first, but then becomes more controlling over her social life. He asks: Where are you going? Who are you going with? Are there men at the weekend conference? The audience analysed the clip and recognised that he is feeling insecure in relation to her expanding universe. It makes him feel uneasy and he wants to stop her. One man laughingly said, 'You know, it does hurt! He likes the money deep down, but it hurts his ego.' The community laughed with him. It was a joke that spoke the truth to the group. The conversation started up again with many questions. Onscreen, the young husband needed desperately to appear dominant and in charge by controlling his wife's choices in an overbearing manner but proclaiming it as love. When she rejected his control, he became threatening.

Minni is a victim of family emotional abuse in Australia. She told me that she could not go for a coffee with her colleagues because her husband and his mother would become sarcastic and call her 'too Westernised'. She was taunted for wearing Western clothes and speaking in English, for having white friends. Her husband 'jokingly' accused her of having affairs. She would have to come home at 5.30 p.m. sharp, cook for her husband and his parents and clean the kitchen. She would be exhausted by 9 p.m. and would get to bed as she had to start early in the morning to cook a hot breakfast for her husband and his parents. She felt defeated and treated like a slave, unappreciated and excluded from family conversations. Work was an escape for Minni, and those coffee mornings were an important part of team building, especially for her as a 'visible' migrant. Without them, she felt left out of the camaraderie at work.

Minni was punished for breaking out of the traditional gender role. For many migrants, the freedom women find in their new countries can be threatening for the men in their communities and gives rise to pushback and excessive control. Many do not want change to occur at all, and this results in greater acculturation stress for them. A young male was admitted to a hospital in an acute suicidal state, because he could not bear to watch his wife, an international student, interacting with male students and male co-workers.

Culture is not static; it will change.

Migration to a foreign country like Australia is a time of cultural change for many people, and causes upheaval in identity formation. Identities are less fixed and stable than they once were, containing traces of the past and what it is to come, leading to what is called hybrid identity. Migration stresses the dynamic and positional nature of identity. Well-supported migrants will have healthier hybrid identities, less confusion, and better integration between their new home and foreign cultural traditions. New migrants need to be supported with education programs around gender relations, based on adult learning principles. In such programs, the participants are considered not blank slates, or empty vessels, but people with knowledge, ideas, and experience. Mutual Cultural Respect, the precursor to Mutual Relational Respect (MRR), is another program that provides a format for new learning around gender relations and related laws that are likely to be different to those in migrants' home countries.[21]

Of the hundreds of women victim-survivors I have seen over the years, most would want to return to their marriage, but only if there is respect, compassion, and no abuse.

Gender equality education for tertiary students is a way to reach millions of young adults.

In 2005, I began a commute to India to re-embrace my heritage and became immersed in the cultural ecology of family violence. I chose to teach at DSVV University at the foothills of the Himalayas which integrated Vedic, Ayurveda and other Indian medical and healing traditions with Western mental health and sciences.

I met and mixed with students from all walks of life. I saw a segregation in males and females that was both spontaneous and enforced by authorities. Romantic liaisons were prohibited, and would lead to students being expelled. The families of the students who boarded lived far away and entrusted the care of their children to the university's authorities. This was one of their responses to the immense responsibility of being given authority over young women and men by their families.

But the university was highly progressive in other ways. They were at the forefront of training female Pundits—the learned scholars of Hinduism, once the preserve of only the highest caste, the Brahmins. It is a practice that is frowned upon, albeit not forbidden, by Hinduism. One such young woman told me that she'd returned to her village for the holidays and put her hand up to conduct a religious ceremony. Some of the village leaders were strongly against the idea, while some others were concerned that she would not be able to remember the verses in Sanskrit and would spoil the ceremony. This gave her an opening, and she demonstrated her ability to recite verses on demand. This impressed the villagers and she was given an opportunity to perform a village ceremony. She rightly felt proud and enjoyed the bliss of recognition as an authority figure. I wondered whether this would open the door for her. Would she be invited to preside over more events? Or would her parents or new husband clamp down and stifle her sense of achievement and power?

Indian society's sociocultural practices—those that guide daily rituals, aesthetic concerns, festivals, and taboos, and also gender roles—are to a great extent informed by Hinduism.[22] But recognising that socio-cultural practices need to work for the good of everyone is key. The DSVV University is using education of women to successfully bring a change in the patriarchal customs of their religion.[23]

The construction of Indian masculinity needs to be studied. The patriarchy in the Indian cultural context needs to be understood deeply if prevention programs are to be effective. Simply taking ideas from Western literature is not necessarily helpful.[24]

We must make sure that girls have the same access to choices and education as boys. And then we must allow them to use it. We must always, all of us, continue our own education, calling out the colleagues who congratulate us for having sons rather than daughters. I am constantly pained by 'jokes' depicting strong women as monsters who stand over fragile husbands. In them, the husbands are hen-pecked and nagged. In one, the husband is selling his entire set of *Encyclopaedia Britannica*. Why? He recently got married and his wife knows everything. Humour and jokes can be a mature way to educate and get a difficult message across, but this sort only reinforces the myths that block gender equality: they confirm the bias against strong women, even showing them as dangerous. They demean knowledgeable women. (There are also jokes that demean men: depicting them as domineering and unaware of their wife's emotional reactions.) I once refused to attend such a Hindi play as a special guest in Melbourne. The producer-director was confused. He did not understand my objection. I had to explain to him that his jokes reinforced the unconscious bias against women and promulgated the dangerous myth that women who look powerful are monsters, or dangerous for men and husbands.

We must all be educated around the idea of subconscious bias (or 'unconscious bias')—those attitudes and stereotypes we hold in our minds that affect our understanding of situations, of other people. It is a very fast way of thinking, but not rational. In times of stress and threat to life, rational thought processes are easily overridden by unconscious thinking and stereotypes that have been reinforced through lifelong learning, role models, and fear of punishment.[25]

Education helps to make us conscious and more amenable to change.

Education is a liberating force. Let us allow it to flourish.

# 12

# THE BURDEN ON MEN OF INDIAN SOCIETY

This book predominantly looks at the issues of social pressures faced by women compelled to play the expected role at home at work and in broader society. There are cultural pressures on men too—ideal roles they must play in Indian society—which are also a burden, but less often spoken about.

I was around ten, playing a game on the floor of the veranda with a neighbourhood friend, when a car stopped on the street and out came a beautiful woman; a white woman, which was a rare sight in Delhi's eastern suburb of Patel Nagar in the 1960s. My friend and I were fascinated. She walked towards us. 'Does a Mr K live here?' she asked in an American accent. I said, 'He is my uncle.' In the meantime, my parents came outside to see what was going on and she introduced herself as Betty and said she would like to see Mr K. She had come from New York.

My uncle, who worked in the Indian Foreign Service, at times closely with PM Jawaharlal Nehru, had recently returned from a three-year posting there. He was my mother's younger brother and lived with his parents a couple of kilometres away.

My father asked me to go in the car with our driver and fetch my uncle. We were all sure he would love to come and see Betty. After all, she had come a long way from America. At my grandparents', I told my uncle about Betty arriving at our house and to come quickly; the driver was waiting outside. I was so excited. Imagine, then, my huge disappointment for Betty when he said he didn't want to see her.

There was no telephone so my parents could not converse with him. I had to rush back home to my parents who conveyed the disappointing news to Betty. She went back to the US.

I could not ask my uncle why he hadn't come, though I wanted to know for years and years. I suspected he'd had an affair with her in America. This was not the type of thing one would talk about in the 1960s, let alone accuse an older person of. It was brushed aside as a non-event in our family, but I never forgot it for the sake of Betty. She seemed like a beautiful person; she opened a new world in my mind where you might have a relationship with a foreign person. I never forgot her. Her disappointment haunted me.

Decades later, I met my uncle in Delhi at my mother's house. He had turned seventy-five and had come from America, where he'd lived for the past thirty years with his Punjabi wife and two adult children. I'd come from Australia where I had lived for more than two decades. I plucked up enough courage to ask him about Betty. Why had he refused to see her?

My uncle reminded me that the family—his parents and siblings, including my mother—had just arrived from Pakistan and had lost their extensive wealth. They had been housed in Delhi's Kingsway Camps for more than a year before being allotted a small house for a family with five adult children at home. They had become poor—something they were not accustomed to. His father, my grandfather, had found a job as a secondary school teacher nearby but it was not enough to support the family. What is more, my uncle had two of his sisters to think of. They had to be married off, and that would mean finding money for a wedding and dowry. The burden, my uncle felt, was his: to find money and provide emotional support to his entire family who were dispossessed and lost. My grandmother had suffered a severe bout of depression, as did my grandfather. My uncle's older brother, an engineer, had been transferred interstate and was already married with a family. His younger brother was studying to be an electrician. It was his duty as a son to bear the responsibility of his unmarried sisters, his mother, and the remainder of the family.

My mother was already married and comfortably off, but she could not be asked for help. It is considered shameful for parents to take financial support from a married daughter, as she belongs to her husband's family. It was this rule that dictated my uncle's decision. He could not imagine that my mother could give emotional or financial support to her parents, or that he could ask my father for money. He could not imagine Betty fitting into a poor Indian family. She would have to accept his family, and accept that he must support them as sons must do in his culture, and he could not imagine how this would work. My uncle was a man of few words. He did not elaborate on how much he'd loved her. He did not want to dwell on it. But it is clear to me that if he had felt like it was an option, he would have at least met her when she followed him all the way to India, and perhaps this would have given him, and Betty, proper closure on their relationship.

The burden of being the main provider, financially and emotionally, for the family is unfair to sons. Although it brings with it the power of being the dominant force, the decision maker, and the patriarch, it also means many men have to make sacrifices that cost them their own mental and physical health. They, too, must from a young age behave according to the script written by society and enforced by parents.

Society generally sees 'masculine' traits as desirable and positive: physical strength, leadership, authority, power, courageousness, and problem-solving. Benign as they are, are all these traits so desirable? Are there others that will make happier and more balanced men? Adolescent boys learn through socialisation to adopt these stereotypes as characteristics of manhood and live the rest of their lives conforming to them. But at what cost?

For some men, the expected standards are unattainable, restrictive or too oppressive. Technically, they can opt out of the societal pressures, yet the majority do not, as they believe they have no choice to opt out. They are trapped and become confused by the privileges granted to them for acting like the 'ideal man'. This has been called the 'man box'.[1] I call it the man prison. The men who choose to follow these dominant ideals have greater physical and mental health risks such as higher risk of depression, suicide, substance use. They are more likely to suffer stress-related disorders like high blood pressure, heart attacks and diabetes, and they have a higher suicide rate. They may drink excessively, indulge in the misuse of substances, and suffer alcohol-related diseases.[2] As a result, they die earlier than women. Men also seek medical help less often. Imagine the stress on those millions of boys and men who are not perfectly masculine and are constantly striving to appear this way. They are liable to use violence to get their way and induce fear in their victim.

When a wife out-earns her husband, the community response is: 'He likes the money deep down, but it hurts his ego.' The stereotype at the heart of this is part of the man prison. He likes being a man, but his behaviours must demonstrate why he is the boss. He must be the sole provider, or at least the major provider; he cannot look weak, effeminate, or gay; he must demonstrate his superiority at every turn. If he belongs to a superior caste, he must assert his authority over the lower castes by being violent towards them. The intersection of caste hierarchy with patriarchy reinforces male dominance and sense of entitlement in those who consider themselves to be superior to other people. And this results in hyper masculinity—that is, an exaggerated image of the dominant form of masculinity, mainly depicted in the media. It overemphasises the ideals, such as physical strength, aggression and sexuality set out for men, thereby reinforcing them. This in turn resulting in greater aggression, and worsening gender equality.[3] We must educate each man to understand that if his wife earns more than him it does not diminish him; she is his *ardhangini*, his other half; her strength strengthens him and the family unit.

'Like girls, boys too are victims of sexual abuse,' says Mr Khan, a volunteer at Sneha, an NGO supporting young men in Mumbai, India. 'But boys rarely speak about it as they feel ashamed.'[4] Why do victims feel shame? It may be that they blame themselves and hold themselves responsible for the humiliation. Seeking help requires acknowledging this humiliation to oneself, the loss of control and power. There is no place in the man prison for these boys, for the kind of thinking that will help them to get the support they need. The urgent need for specific interventions among young boys and men who are also victims of rigid gender norms.

It is encouraging to note some exciting educational programs being addressed with adolescent girls and boys in India. For example, a school-based program entitled 'Gender Equity Movement in Schools' (GEMS), aimed at students in Grades VI and VII, promotes gender equality by encouraging equal relationships between girls and boys, examining the social norms that define men's and women's roles, and questioning the use of violence.[5] However, there is paucity of such programs. It leaves a vacuum in education. Young men are struggling with not knowing how to behave like a 'real man'. It is unsurprising they learn lessons in the wrong places, such as from Bollywood films.

An example of how this can go wrong for young men occurred in Tasmania, Australia, not long ago. Over an eighteen-month period, an Indian man, Sandeep Balia, aggressively pursued two white women. He repeatedly texted, called, and approached the women, who he thought would acquiesce to his wishes for a relationship. The women complained to the police, and he was charged with stalking. In court, his barrister argued that his client was obsessed with Bollywood films that portray the hero aggressively pursuing the heroine and being rewarded by her acquiescence; he did not know his behaviour was criminal. Balia escaped conviction after the magistrate considered 'cultural factors.'[6] But this is not Indian culture—the same men would be respectful of their mothers, pray to goddesses. Rather, it is bad behaviour arising from a lack of sex education for young men, and them not knowing what normal heterosexual dating and gentle wooing of the opposite sex is. Pornography has become a widely used and abused medium of sex education. Neither pornography nor Bollywood films are a substitute for proper sex education, but they are influential. Bollywood needs to make films that help men to recognise alternatives to aggressive, macho, dominating, sexually-entitled, predatory behaviours—such as kind, considerate, empathic, respectful behaviour, and being able to accept rejection and manage the emotional pain that goes with it.

My uncle could not marry Betty. He could not leave his parents or abandon his younger sister, whom he adored. It was his duty to take care of his family. This unspoken rule, this wish, this demand, is drilled into the minds of all Indian men. It is this patriarchal burden that leads some young men to become violent towards their wives.

Parents are fearful of losing the support of their sons when they get married, and often do not let them go. They maintain emotional control by direct and indirect means. Parents in India concerned about the displacement of their power or value to their son living in Australia often stay in intensive contact by telephone or Facetime.

Dozens of young women have told me that their husbands would speak to their mothers in India for hours on end daily. It is hard to imagine what anyone can talk about for so long. But one possibility became clear one day when I took a ride in a taxi. I was talking to someone on my mobile about how expensive it was to get from the airport to Parramatta in Sydney. The taxi driver was Sikh and did not recognise me as Indian. He was also on his mobile, and I came to realise he was talking to his mother and translating every single sentence I said into Punjabi. How annoying! Then it dawned on me that that is what mothers do to their sons. They do not want to let go of them whether at work or at home with their new wife. The sons fill in their time by describing their activities minute by minute. It can be an inane conversation, such as translating my phone call, or it may be more serious, in which case it becomes intrusive and dangerous. In such a conversation, any small or big frustration with his wife would get reported to his mother. Instead of solving the problem as an emotionally mature married man, he tells the person who has a vested interest in not letting go of him. His mother is inwardly delighted at this turn of events in his marriage. She exploits it. If she is an insecure and controlling kind of parent, she will not recognise that the patriarchal system is using her to maintain the system, and that eventually the system will act against all women and men. If she is a secure and thinking person, and not greedy for dowry, she will tell her son to solve the problem with his wife respectfully, to make sure that his home is happy. I have heard these stories too. The problems in such marriages have been far easier to solve in therapy than in situations where the in-laws were actively creating friction.

There is every chance my own mother would have had terrible problems with her mother-in-law had my father not been the sort of man he was.

When I was growing up, my father's mother lived with us half the time in Delhi. (She spent the other half in Agra with her older son's family.) My grandmother loved us children, but she had disdain for her daughter-in-law. She felt threatened by her presence. She was jealous. Her favourite son was sharing his affections not with her primarily but with another woman. Sudhir Kakkar, the eminent psychoanalyst of India, explains:

> The sexual life of Indian women appears very disciplined – (trying to stay a virgin before marriage, becoming a perfect Mother ...) and this fact contributes to a very strong affective and sexual investment of the son by the mother. [7]

Grandmother's disdain was well controlled. She would not or could not say anything negative about my mother in my father's presence. He was a strong patriarch with a strong sense of fair play. If she did venture to say something like 'My daughter-in-law ignores me', or 'My daughter-in-law gives me bad food' my father would have been the first to tell her that she was wrong, that it was my mother who took care of her. But it must have been difficult for my mother. As my grandmother approached her late seventies, she developed dementia and became paranoid. She would have bouts of agitation and express delusional ideas about my mother, accusing my mother of poisoning her. My father ignored her rants most of the time, except when my grandmother became more loud than usual. He would then tell her off. We children got used to Granny's loud tirades, and thought she was out of her mind, mentally unwell. We also knew that she was an integral part of the family and would stay with us until her death.

A woman named Neru, herself a young mother of two, bore the brunt of her mother-in-law's insecurity. Neru's husband had been incited by his mother soon after their marriage. His mother recognised that Neru was a strong, professional woman and that her son was a somewhat submissive man. She feared that their migration to Australia would mean she'd lose control over him. He was made to feel guilty for 'abandoning' his parents and, in return, he promised he would make sure he supported them financially and emotionally. That meant ringing his mother on a daily basis and talking to her about things, small and big, to do with his wife and his family. Meanwhile, his parents' hostility to Neru increased.

Unbeknown to Neru, her husband regularly transferred money to his parents from their joint bank account. This included her hard-earned income. She was kept in the dark because the bank account was fully controlled by him. His own income was lower than hers. Neru was working two jobs to reduce the financial pressure on them as new migrants in Australia and he knew that if he told her about the money she would object. His mother was fully aware of Neru's views about giving them money, but that did not reduce her demands on her prized son. In fact, it probably increased them. Neru suspected something was wrong, and one day found a message from her mother-in-law on her husband's phone thanking him for the money and demanding more. She became extremely angry, and when she questioned her husband, he could not give her a straight answer and refused to share any information with her. This led to violence from her and then from him. The police became involved, but she was the only one charged as the perpetrator. It was overlooked that Neru was the victim of extended family's social exclusion and control mediated via financial appropriation, executed by her husband.

The high rate of misidentification of victims is disturbing. Research finds that 1 in 8 female victims are misidentified as the perpetrator.[8] There is a need for laws and education that can better explain coercive control to the front-line workers. The perpetrator of abuse of power, control, and fear should face justice.

In therapy, Neru recognised that she had felt powerless for a long time in her marriage. Her mother-in-law had made sure that Neru had no voice or influence with her husband or in their family. She was made to feel like an outsider, never spoken to warmly, never shown love. If a girl is brought up to recognise that her rightful home is that of her husband, it is therefore important for any daughter-in-law to feel included in her husband's extended family. Neru was denied that sense of belonging. All they wanted was her money—because the patriarchal system that values sons also puts a demand on the sons that makes extortion possible. Societal influences are upheld by parental reinforcement.

The development and maintenance of unhealthily close bonds between sons and mothers and fathers, where the sons are not allowed to grow up to become independent thinkers and where they believe they cannot function without their parents' opinions, weakens the bond of marriage. Research in British South Asian migrants is revealing. Strong parental ties are shown to be associated with weaker bonding with a new spouse.[9]

Neru's husband was a sensitive man and recognised that he had done Neru an injustice. He agreed to join her in therapy and empathy training. Putting himself in her shoes and reversing their roles made him recognise the trauma that he and his family had inflicted on Neru. Their marriage stabilised, and he chose to cut off all connection with his parents.

Neru's husband was a victim of Indian masculine burden, the gender norms taught to him in his early life by his parents and society and exploited by his mother. She possibly fears poverty will be her fate—there being limited supports in old age in India.[10] There would have been no need to cut contact with his parents if he had been conscious of the pressures he was under to live up to these norms. He would have taken a more considered approach early on in the marriage. Had he recognised his parents were putting him under unreasonable pressure, he could have told them he would discuss their requests with his wife and transfer funds whenever it was possible. He could have told them that his first duty was to his wife. In any case, his parents were not poor. Their demands were a ploy to maintain control over him—and he did not recognise this until he took part in therapy.

In Myma's case (we met her in chapter 9), she did better than her husband. After having made a decision to live her life of choice, she managed the situation with her parents in India and moved to

Australia to be with her husband. She made a commitment and she had enough ego-strength to go through with it. Her husband was the one who faltered.

Krishnan continued to harass her after separation with threatening text messages. He wanted her to go back to India. He stopped only after she obtained an intervention order against him. His inability to let go of her suggests that he wished to continue his control over her. He must feel powerless that she is getting on with her life. How can he be a happy man? Myma found out that he recently remarried—a woman from India with a big dowry, possibly chosen by his mother. The system in Krishnan's house perhaps is unlikely to change. Will the mother-son duo continue to dominate and control the new bride? I fear for his new wife.

In my experience, men like Krishnan often become sad and depressed after separation (possibly the reason Krishnan decided to remarry so soon). It is sad to hear of their stories of sadness and loneliness. Men's Behaviour Change Programs are there to support them, help them change, and even return to their wife if they so wish (and if their wives wish, also).

One man I know—let us call him Vishnu—attended the same program once a week for two hours for a whole year, while continuing to live with his wife. He changed to the extent that he stopped using violence, but his verbal dominance, control, and sense of entitlement continued. He demanded she work full-time, take care of their two children, and carry out domestic chores in the manner of a servant. He refused to help her. Worse still, he bullied her and stopped her from getting outside support with babysitting. Vishnu was seething with rage inside but did not express anger, only coercive control. His self-image as the 'real man' was damaged. His wife had reversed the power balance by calling the police, shamed him with an intervention order and the court-ordered Men's Behaviour Change Program. One day he just walked out, leaving her to fend for herself and care for two small children.

Vishnu needed additional support in individual counselling—reflective-insight-directed psychotherapy underpinned by a feminist framework might have been able to help him explore his irrational fear of being dominated by his wife, his childhood experiences, and other influences on his conscious and unconscious attitudes and behaviours. He might have found alternatives to use, understanding that dominance and violence was simply covering his fears, such as an underlying sense of fragility and insecure self-image.

Under patriarchy, it seems that even when men get what they want, or think they want, it may not lead to happiness for them either.

Societal level prevention programs, school-based education, and the media all need to make an effort to reveal unconscious gender norms, make them more conscious. And essentially parents, especially mothers and fathers with sons, need to learn to avoid the thousands of years of the unconscious and negative power of patriarchy, guiding them to hold on to sons as their prized possession and, in doing so, harming their son's mental health, his life, and their own lives, and helping to bring forth domestic violence and broken homes. This can be done through parenting programs when their sons are not yet born or are still small. And individual therapy will benefit those sons and mothers who have already established patterns of abuse.

Racism, contempt and oppressive practices by the British Raj on the men of India would have added enormous psychological pressures to these family expectations.[11] I wondered if my uncle let Betty go in part due to internalised feelings of inferiority—a sad result of colonialism. It is hard to imagine how the men coped with it, though a strong cultural identity, and strong family ties must certainly have helped. Despite two hundred years of British colonial deprivation, Indian men and women were able to continue their language and religion, and, in fact, strengthened these by absorbing the new influences on their culture. It is a trait that can be discerned in immigrant Indians of Australia.

There is no doubt that racist pressures exist in Australia too. Racism is an emotive word and calling someone a racist is an insult. But instances of racism happen daily. In a café, standing next to an Indian man, I noted the shopkeeper's previously smiling attitude change to one of disdain, all but sneering as she asked him what he wanted to buy. At another time, in Melbourne's Little Collins Street, I offered a peck on the cheek of a friend in the street, a dark-skinned Indian man, as I waved him goodbye. A white man walking past looked at me in utter disgust, I assume mistakenly thinking I was a white woman lowering myself and the status of white people by affectionately kissing a man of colour.

Discrimination is an abuse of human rights and has a negative impact on health and wellbeing, the World Health Organization tells us; particularly on mental health.[12] Around 24 per cent of Victorians are born overseas. Three-quarters of these are born in countries where English is not the main language spoken.[13] This leads to a sense of internalised oppression. The mind of the racially subordinated unconsciously accepts negative societal beliefs and stereotypes about themselves, internalising the racial oppression by the dominant group. Sadly, the oppressed group starts to use the methods of the oppressors against itself.[14] A VicHealth Scanlan Survey found that people who were born in a country in which the main language spoken was not English were more than twice as likely as Australian-born people to report being treated with disrespect because of their ethnicity/race (42 per cent compared with 18 per cent).[15] The Scanlan survey reported by VicHealth showed that 47 per cent had experienced discrimination because of their national or ethnic background at some point in their lives, compared with 20 per cent of the Australian-born. And Sikhs and Muslims were likely to experience racism more than Hindus and Christians.

The process happens unconsciously and can take a long time to overcome. Racism, according to the intersectional theory proposed by Kimberlé Crenshaw, leads to a complex interplay with gender, class, and other forms of oppression contributing to domestic violence. There is no typical woman. Women of colour, Dalit women, Muslim women, migrant women, Indigenous women, disabled women, and homosexual women experience their disadvantages differently; their experience of access to resources and lack of power is unique to them. The drivers of domestic violence are varied, and interact with one another. Prevention strategies need to address the intersectionality of themes to be culturally responsive, and to therefore be effective.[16]

Things are changing. Australia is a highly multicultural country, with 200 countries represented in its migrant population.[17] Indians make up the highest number of migrants since 2017, occupying more than 20 per cent of the skilled migrant visa program and contributing $16 billion in taxes to the Australian economy.[18] Close to 15 per cent of the 720 150 students enrolled in Australian universities and colleges as of September 2019 in Australia were Indian students—about 108 000.[19] COVID-19 has, however, led to many going back home to India. With more than 721 000 Indians living in Australia, making up 2.6 per cent of the entire population, we are a significant, highly educated, skilled minority, and that in itself will cause a change to the culture of the dominant group of Australia for the better. It is my hope that labelling, stereotyping, and judging will diminish because Indian and other people of colour's differences will not be perceived as unusual, deviant, or threatening. My experience, and anecdotal evidence from influential Indian business and professional people, is that the Australian and Victorian State governments are providing employment opportunities to under-employed or unemployed new migrants. It creates a level playing field. The American experience with Indian migrants reveals a sizeable minority of highly successful group of people, creating a more level playing field.[20]

This will also impact family life for the better. The burden men are under to please their mothers at the expense of their wives will no doubt be influenced to some extent by the modern era of international life.

Acculturation, or getting used to the new culture, can be a stressful process. Supporting non-English-speaking migrants with language training, social connectedness and employment can help; some Federal Government programs already offer support programs to help with these issues.[21]

How can we support a change that rejects the inequitable gender system? As I said in earlier chapters—it starts with the gendered socialisation of children. What kind of messages do society and parents give early on in life that influence gendered behaviours in boys and girls? Girls are cautioned; boys are encouraged to explore. There are things we can all do to enhance gender equality. In everyday life, for example, encouraging signs are visible. In the home more men are taking part in childcare. More men share equal responsibility for household chores; more women are gaining influential decision-making positions; organisations are promoting more women in managerial roles. The UN Women has worked tirelessly to lead change in attitudes towards gender equality, and lead policy framework, and inspired countries globally including Australia, India and beyond. Changes are occurring.[22] But more needs to be done. Hire diverse people. Reject racism and chauvinistic attitudes, and most of all, let there be no silence around signs of domestic violence.[23] The world economic forum 2020 report gives us hope. Progress is being made in economic gender pay gap. The world has achieved at least 60 per cent gender parity; Europe has progressed above 70 per cent and South Asian gender parity is at 65.8 per cent.[24]

It is hard to go against gender stereotypes and expectations, but we are seeing results.

Increasingly, results show that boys and men take a clear position against violence against women. That is a good thing. What is difficult is to show sustained attitudinal change or change at the deeper level thinking: the societal privileges given to men, their sense of entitlement, the dominant roles played by men and the subordinate roles enforced upon women.[25]

To ensure change, adequate sustained community engagement and political support for funding and scaling up successful programs is required. In Victoria, Australia our NGO, the AustralAsian Centre for Human Rights and Health runs programs such as United We Stand and Mutual Relational Respect, mentioned previously. They help facilitate community discussion and community ownership around these topics. The short-term evaluation shows there is a shift in attitude following these programs, but the impact on behaviour and levels of violence is a long term change. That is a change we all want to see within our lifetime.

# 13

# ACTIONS AGAINST DOWRY ABUSE IN AUSTRALIA

My psychiatric practice in Melbourne is largely focused on gender-based violence in South Asian migrant communities, and in 2012, as a result of treating a series of women for mental health harm caused by domestic violence, I identified a pattern of dowry abuse.

The abuse and demands were similar to those found in India: a perceived lack of dowry gifts from a bride and her family would lead to emotional abuse from her husband, and often his family. This consisted of disrespecting and diminishing the worth of the woman— for example, chastising her for ordinary daily events; criticising her abilities as a cook, homemaker, social being, job-hunter, English-speaker; criticising her appearance and clothes. This was compounded by persistent shaming and contempt for her parents and family: for being too mean or lower class, uneducated or unsophisticated, and for not giving enough or a good enough dowry. Abuse and violence occurred if she (and her family) refused to comply with constant demands for more gifts. The husband would exaggerate his own status yet blame the victim for his aggression and degrading comments. This would lead the victim to self-blame and experience a loss of self-confidence, and feelings of utter helplessness and powerlessness. Research shows that chronic repeated psychological abuse results in as much mental health trauma and illness as physical abuse.[1]

My clinical observations were confirmed by the community-based action research projects we conducted under the umbrella of the NGO I co-founded that year—the AustralAsian Centre of Human Rights and Health (ACHRH).

It became clear to me that the problem was growing with the increasing migration of Indian people to Australia. Over the past two decades, India has come to be the second-largest country of origin for permanent migrants in Australia, growing from 3000 annually in 1996 to 721 000 people in 2019 who had been born in India, constituting 2.8 per cent of the population.[2] Victoria has the largest share, followed closely by New South Wales.

Research in the Indian community showed that the patterns of migrant life in Australia are fairly similar to those in India: a supportive extended family system, with a strong sense of duty and familial responsibility and commitment to one's parents and extended family. Family needs are prioritised over individual needs, and emotional restraint is encouraged to maintain family harmony; there is a hierarchical system of respect with elders and men commanding the most; arranged marriages are common.[3] This growing community brought with them ambition, and a love of education and hard work. That Indians were the second-largest tax paying migrant group made us popular with employers and governments. Out of the $112.3 billion income generated by migrant taxpayers, Indian-born taxpayers contributed a huge $18 billion in the year 2016–17, while

British migrants added $21 billion.[4] The data also revealed that the median income for migrant taxpayers was higher than the median income of an Australian taxpayer.[5]

At the same time, worrying trends have started to appear. The practice of sex-selective abortions has become apparent in Victoria. The Indian and Chinese community has a higher preponderance of boy children than girl children. Australian mothers generally have 105 boys to 100 girls, which is the biological standard; for Indian and Chinese-born mothers, the figures were 108 and 109 boys to every 100 girls respectively, in the period from 1999 to 2015. In the five years following, if the mother had two or more subsequent births, the figure ballooned to 122 boys and 125 boys respectively. In other words, the greater the number of children, the greater the risk of distorted ratio in favour of male babies.[6] The increase in male babies was also found in the Filipino and Vietnamese communities.

Victorian legislation bans people from terminating pregnancies because of the sex of the child, other than for medical reasons, but that did not stop one couple from making this demand in 2013. The mother was nineteen weeks pregnant with a female baby and wanted the baby aborted. Her GP, Dr Mark Hobart, refused to refer her, stating conscientious objection. The couple threatened to lodge a complaint against him, but did not follow through. The Medical Board of Australia, overlooking the fact that legislation prohibits sex selection, investigated him for professional misconduct for breaking the Victorian law in not offering the woman the opportunity for abortion. He was at risk of losing his licence.[7] The Australian Doctors Fund (now called Australian Doctors Federation) hastily organised a conference in support of Dr Hobart. I was invited as guest speaker, alongside Dr Hobart and Labor MP Christine Campbell. Christine Campbell put forward a statement in the Legislative Council of the Victorian Parliament in support of Dr Hobart. The couple is said to have gone to another GP who provided the referral for a sex selective abortion.

And the problem goes on.

Patriarchal beliefs have followed Indian migrants to Australia. Parents have a responsibility to examine the deep conscious and unconscious motivations for their actions that favour sons and are biased against daughters.

Would criminalisation of the practice help?

India's laws criminalise sex-selective abortion, but this has not helped. The laws are necessary in that they give guidance, but they must be supported by community education. The Mutual Relational Respect community education workshops, funded by the Australian Government and run by ACHRH, address this question in a hypothetical case study.[8] A pregnant woman feels fear. She confides in her Maternal and Child Health Nurse that she is afraid of how her husband will react if the baby is not a boy. The community workshop participants are invited to dig deeper to understand the layers of bias against the girl child. The Indian, African, Middle Eastern, and Indonesian participants all recognise it as a familiar story and connect gender norms with this practice. One woman said, 'It is violence against women even before she is born. It cannot be allowed to occur.'

GPs, too, need to be educated to remain alert to this practice and act ethically. There is some confusion in the legislation, as demonstrated by the case again Mark Hobart. Victorian Abortion Law Reform offers women the choice whether or not to continue a pregnancy. But the sex-selective abortion ban came into force as early as 2004 in federal legislation. The federal laws can be used to prosecute the cases of sex-selective abortion.

Regardless, it is hard to police the law. On its own, it will not change attitudes.

Another trend that has become obvious is that of family violence. In the Indian community, a series of fifteen murders and suicides in the context of family violence reared their ugly heads between 2009, 2017 and again in January 2022.[9] The headlines in newspapers were startling: 'Their terrifying last moments: A decade of domestic violence deaths in Hindu and Sikh communities.'[10] Dowry was reported as a factor in some of the cases, and the role of multiple perpetrators identified.

As a result, and inspired by the strong activism of Indian women leaders and academics,[11] I led the ACHRH in a public campaign against dowry abuse, with a petition that demanded it be included as an example of financial abuse within the Victorian laws against family violence.[12] We received extensive media coverage and made a significant submission, 'Refusal to Comply with Dowry Demands Contributes to Family Violence and Death in Victoria', to the Victorian Royal Commission into Family Violence in 2015.[13] That led to recommendation number 156, that dowry abuse be included as a statutory example of financial abuse in the Family Violence Protection Act of Victoria.[14] The Commission noted that 'these forms of abuse are not readily recognised as family violence by some within these communities', and the same can be said for the service providers, the police, the judiciary and the general public. The Victorian Parliament Lower House passed the Bill 'JUSTICE LEGISLATION AMENDMENT (FAMILY VIOLENCE PROTECTION AND OTHER MATTERS) BILL 2018' unanimously on 19 June 2018 and the Upper House on 27 July 2018. It was proclaimed in March 2019.

So it was that the world's first Western nation got its first dowry abuse law. The Victorian legislation now lists as an example of the 'Meaning of family violence': '*using coercion, threats, physical abuse or emotional or psychological abuse to demand or receive dowry, either before or after a marriage*'.[15]

It needs to be stated that the majority of grooms and their families follow the custom and are respectful of the bride and her family. They have no expectations and do not make demands or use violence. But the minority is significant, and its negative effects have travelled to Australia.

Dowry is given in lieu of inheritance—reparation for a woman expected to forego her substantial property inheritance. Large sums of money and wealth are handed to a vulnerable bride's in-laws in a new household; sometimes she is isolated in a strange country. Firstly, this creates an enabling environment of abuse by many grooms and in-laws. Secondly, exorbitant gifts have produced a culture of entitlement in grooms and boys. Thirdly, dowry increases the value of sons and decreases the value of daughters. This sets out gender norms that aid and abet family violence. Finally, Australian permanent residency status is being used to extort money from brides' families overseas. Money is power, and like any power it is open to abuse in an unequal situation. Dowry is one such practice.

In her eloquent speech in the Victorian Parliament on Tuesday 19 June 2018, then MP Gabrielle Williams (now Minister for Prevention of Family Violence) explored the meaning of dowry and why the new law was justified in the face of opposition from some of her multicultural electorate, with whom she'd had numerous discussions:

> … the way this bill has been crafted will respond to many voices in my community that have been eager to highlight the cultural and often symbolic significance of the practice within certain cultural groups, a practice they claim should be permitted where it does not involve those negative behaviours, where it does not involve threats or acts of violence.

> … I have had people remind me that even within Christian marriage traditions there are practices that convey similar, sometimes uncomfortable and certainly outdated in contemporary Australia, notions of gender inequality. Examples that were put to me included a groom asking permission of a bride's father for somebody's hand in marriage, and the tradition that the bride's family pay for the wedding.

> ... there are many marriage traditions across many religious and cultural communities that might seem quaint but are actually steeped in quite archaic notions or an archaic world of gender inequality.
>
> ... It is simply not right to have women and their families living in fear because of a practice that sees them held captive to the demands of a husband and his family
>
> ... I want to thank Dr Manjula O'Connor. She is a woman who first awakened me to the issues that can surround the practice of dowry. She has been tireless in her campaigning on this issue over many, many years ... as a part of her quest both to raise awareness about dowry-related violence and inequality but also to advocate for a government response to the negative impacts of the practice.[16]

Other MPs who spoke in favour of the Bill on the same day included Liberal MP Ms Heidi Victoria, and Labour MP Ms Danielle Green. In the Upper House, a number of MPs spoke in favour of the Bill. Ms Georgie Crozier, Shadow Minister for Prevention of Family Violence, said:

> I want to place on record the work of Ted Baillieu because he ran a series of petitions on this very issue on behalf of Dr O'Connor. The former Premier was also very concerned about dowry-related abuse and what needed to be done. It is 2018, and we are finally getting some recognition of this. I am very pleased that the royal commission looked at the submission and spoke to Dr O'Connor and others about the specific issues around dowry and how it is a form of abuse.[17]

This major victory was followed by the federal government's announcement in June 2018 that it would hold a Senate Inquiry into the practice of dowry and incidence of dowry abuse in Australia.[18]

Our campaign was further strengthened by the findings of the Senate: that the problem of dowry abuse was far more extensive and complex than had been realised previously.[19] The Inquiry made a set of recommendations, the most important of which was that dowry abuse, as an example of economic abuse, be inserted into the federal *Family Law Act*. This would result in dowry gifts being returned in full to the giver in the event of marriage breakdown.

Our anti-dowry campaign, which started from my office on Collins Street in Melbourne, soon expanded to all of Victoria and resonated with the Indian migrant population across the whole of Australia. It was widely covered by Australian and international media. The campaign also met with pushback and resistance. Some said the problem did not exist. Others said the problem was too small to merit a law, and some said it was a publicity stunt. Yet, in the Australia-wide Senate Inquiry into the nature and prevalence of dowry abuse in Australia, more than eighty submissions were received from Australia and India's abandoned brides. Other submissions were made by men's groups claiming that the dowry problem was fake: that young brides marry Indian Australian men, come to Australia to get permanent residency, and start making false claims of dowry abuse and dowry confiscation.

But the Senate Hearings Report released on 14 February 2019 in the federal parliament disagreed. It further stated that dowry abuse needs to be acknowledged as an example of family violence in the federal *Family Law Act of Australia*, just as it had been in the *Family Violence Protection Act of Victoria*. Another key recommendation of the Senate Inquiry was for the Immigration Department to recognise dowry abuse as an example of family violence in the absence of physical violence, and that temporary visa holders should be allowed a pathway to permanent residency if they suffer such violence in Australia. This would include victims who are on international student visas or their partner's working visa, and imported brides on tourist visas.[20]

At the Second National Dowry Abuse Summit, held in Sydney on 22 February 2019, initiated by ACHRH and partnered by the University of NSW, we were lucky to have the Shadow Minister for Preventing Family Violence, the Hon Linda Burney, Senator Louise Pratt, chairperson of the Senate inquiry, and the Hon Julian Hill MP, all members of the Opposition party, the Australian Labour Party, give a firm undertaking that they would implement the Inquiry's recommendations if elected in 2019. With the Liberal Party winning the election, Minister for Families and Social Services Anne Ruston and her department have set about tackling this problem, listing it as a complex form of violence in the Fourth Action Plan to reduce violence against women and children.[21]

This year 2020 marked the twenty-fifth anniversary of the UN Beijing Declaration and Platform held in 1995. The platform is a blueprint to attain equality between women and men; a human right, and a necessary and fundamental prerequisite for equality, development and peace. To this end, governments, the international community and civil society, including non-governmental organisations and the private sector, are called upon to take strategic actions in what are called Sustainable Development Goals, or SDGs.[22] Thus, seventeen SDGs broadly outline the goals around poverty, inequality, health, education, biodiversity, and climate. SDGs recognise the impact of gender inequality in attaining the goals. One of the goals related to violence is SDG 5, which includes two specific targets on elimination of violence and harmful practices against women and girls, and sets out global agendas for prevention.[23] Dowry abuse is a harmful practice.

In 2017, as a result of the momentous law change in Victoria, a TV producer approached us and invited us to act in an advisory capacity on the documentary *Australia's Dowry Deaths* (produced by Al Jazeera). The film received more than 1.6 million views on YouTube and has helped to raise awareness that the practice of dowry is causing harm in Australia.

At the same time, the community participatory theatre project *Natak Vihar* and other programs have gradually increased the community's understanding of the issues.

In 2019–2020, I saw dowry abuse drop down to about 45 per cent of female clients in my practice. But some form of financial abuse was ubiquitous—controlling money, wages, transferring a wife's income to in-laws without her permission or demanding her savings, and so on.

The true incidence of dowry abuse in Australia is not known. We had a notion it was widespread, and the notion was confirmed in 2021 by the national survey conducted by ACHRH and Harmony Alliance (HA) partnership. The survey filled in largely by the South Asian community revealed 32 per cent of respondents suffered dowry abuse themselves or knew someone who had. Eighty five per cent of respondents identified associated verbal abuse as the most common behaviour connected to dowry demands, followed by humiliation (77 per cent) and controlling behaviour (77 per cent).[24]

In Australia, every domestic violence service provider is reporting an increase in dowry violence. Dowry-related deaths in India occur every ninety minutes and account for half of all homicides of Indian women. Dowry-related deaths have been recorded in Australia too.[25] This is structural violence. It needs a structural response, a societal response. The laws on their own will not change anything. It is societal education that is needed.

The ACHRH-HA 2021 survey also identified driving factors related to dowry abuse—outdated patriarchal arrangements, societal norms, long term customary expectation, and the perception of dowry as a status symbol and prestige.

The ACHRH—in partnership with HA, the peak migrant women body received funding for three years to tailor a national platform of education for South Asian communities. Training materials based on the survey data were prepared. South Asian community leaders nationally are being trained as facilitators and they are facilitating interactive community educational workshops across the country. The aim is to enhance community education around how to prevent dowry abuse in Australia.

The workshops are mostly attended by women. Why? Women want to learn how to prevent dowry abuse. Men do not find this a relevant issue. Dowry is as much men's problem as it is women's.

We are working with the government to expand the federal legislation and service provision to protect the wellbeing of victims of family violence and dowry abuse in Australia. We are advocating to include multiple perpetrators such as mothers-in-law also as primary perpetrators[26] in Family Violence Laws and the Migration Laws. so that women from India and South Asia broadly can embrace the moment 'which comes but rarely in history, when we step out from the old to the new, when an age ends, and when the soul … long suppressed, finds utterance.'[27]

# 14

# THE WAY FORWARD: MANUSMRITI REIMAGINED

*When one husband beats his wife there is a clear case of personal violence, but when one million husbands keep one million wives in ignorance there is structural violence.*

Johan Galtung[1]

One father said to me once: 'Why do you have a problem with the dowry system? It is, after all, with good intentions that parents help establish the new couple in their life together.'

I agree that dowry in the right circumstances can be a good support for the new couple. After all, that is why people bring gifts at weddings.

The question to answer is this: Why should the bride's parents bear the burden for setting up the couple's new life? The cost of dowries often exceeds the annual income of the bride's family. This causes debt in the bride's family, and the systemic giving of huge gifts and cash sets up a culture of expectation in the groom's family.

It sets up a system in which men demand to be rewarded for being men, and where a woman is valued only if she brings a good dowry.

Another question is this: Has the arranged marriage system and the idea of a daughter being *paraya dhan*—someone's else's wealth—gone too far? In the Hindu Indian marriage, the father hands the daughter over to her husband in a ceremony called Kanyadaan. Literally, this is the donation of daughter to husband—she is now his property. Elaborate ceremonies are held to welcome a new wife as daughter-in-law into a husband's family. But the system has gone wrong for millions of women—the daughter neither belongs to her parents, nor to her husband's family. She is ever a foreigner and an outsider. Does the system need an overhaul? Why have we reached the point where exorbitant dowry gifts are compulsory, bankrupting the bride's family, and there is an entitlement to demand more when the groom or his family deem the dowry to be 'insufficient'?

Why has it reached a point that society by and large discourages women from marrying for love or choosing her partner?

Ninety per cent of Indian marriages are arranged, and young people trust their relatives to find them a match. What about the young people who speak up against this tradition? What about the brides who are not subservient, who will not accept their unequal status, who are too forward, who refuse to be someone who will 'get along with his family'—the family who chooses to treat her with disrespect—at significant cost to mental health?

There is an urgent need for mothers and grandmothers to stand up for their daughters: the appallingly low female to male ratio remains unchanged since the very first census conducted by the British Government in 1871.[2] Why is there woman-to-woman violence—some older women hating their daughters-in-law, the deaths of unborn daughters?

Women who turn into perpetrators against other women perhaps do not recognise that they are supporting and encouraging

## THE WAY FORWARD: *MANUSMRITI* REIMAGINED

domestic violence and murder. In their actions, they are 'bargaining with patriarchy'.[3] For short-term rewards from the men in their lives—husband, son, or brother—such women put every other woman's life at risk. These women do not identify with other women but feel their own value is solely based on their position in relation to males. This is an insidious and particularly troubling aspect of patriarchy.

Suicide deaths in women of India are rising; their rates are higher than most women of the world, higher than the men of India, and far more than their global share.[4] As they migrate to other countries, including Australia, these high rates of suicide travel with them, making them a vulnerable group. Additional studies and larger numbers are needed to examine this further. However, the high frequency of events seen in this group of migrant women highlights the significant need for awareness of risks in these groups.[5]

After suffering violence, the women who want to divorce abusive, violent husbands are told to stay there—to disregard their anger, sadness, tears, hopelessness, their fear for their life—helpless as dowry demands, emotional and physical abuse continue.

India's modern-day women, whether in India, Australia or elsewhere, live complex lives, having to balance ancient Vedic cultural heritage endowed by *Manusmriti*, Muslim invasions, and colonisation with the demands of modern educated living. I have felt these contradictory forces myself.

But there are always options. India's women are resilient, intelligent, and capable. Every country has victim care and support programs. There is help always.

Women can go into space, fly aeroplanes, become politicians, doctors, scientists, work, and study like men, yet remain sensitive and empathic and caring. It is now time for men to do what women do—the household chores like cooking and cleaning, the emotional labour of caring for the elderly and children—for shared decision-making at every level, and for men to be empathic. Cultural and social norms that support violence need to change. It is the structural response.

*Manusmriti* is approximately two thousand years old. It may have been an enlightened and flexible guide to living. The new genomic evidence suggests that about seventy generations ago, Indian society became rigid under the conservative Gupta Empire, in 319–350 CE. This period gave rise to harmful rules around caste, marriage, and prevented free mixing of people.[6] It stilted the growth of Indian culture.[7] *Manusmriti* may have been rewritten during this period with harmful verses on caste and women. It has remained colossally influential in determining the structure and function of Indian society since then.[8] The community as a whole, home by home, person by person, needs to examine the attitudes that have shaped and influenced our culture, and recognise the need to modernise *Manusmriti*.

*Manusmriti* has been revised by writers over the past millennium. I wonder how a daughter of Durga, the Goddess of power, would rewrite the harmful verses of *Manusmriti*.

Here is my modern reimagining of *Manusmriti*.

> *Chapter 5, Verse 147*. Ancient *Manusmriti*:
> By a girl, by a young woman, or even by an aged one, nothing must be done independently, even in her own house.[9]
>
> Modern *Manusmriti* gives women agency:
> Whether a girl, a young woman, or even an aged one, a woman will have freedom to act independently, even in her own house.

*Verse 5.148.* Ancient *Manusmriti* shrinks her world:
> In childhood a female must be subject to her father, in youth to her husband, when her lord is dead to her sons; a woman must never be independent.

Modern *Manusmriti* gives women freedom:
> In childhood a child must be subject to their mother and father; in youth both a girl and her brother learn to share power and control; after marriage a woman shares power and control with her husband, and when her husband is dead, she lives independently of her sons; a woman must always be independent.

*Verse 5.150.* Ancient *Manusmriti*:
> She must always be cheerful, clever in (the management of her) household affairs, careful in cleaning her utensils, and economical in expenditure.

Modern *Manusmriti* gives women gender equality in the home:
> Man and woman must always be cheerful, clever in the management of household affairs; husband and wife together careful in cleaning the utensils, and economic expenditure.

*Verse 5.151* Ancient and outdated *Manusmriti*:
> Him to whom her father may give her, or her brother with the father's permission, she shall obey as long as he lives, and when he is dead, she must not insult (his memory).

Modern *Manusmriti* gives her sexual freedom:
> After marriage the husband and wife shall respect and attend upon each other as long as they live, and when either is dead, neither shall insult (the other's memory).

*Verse 5.154.* Ancient and outdated *Manusmriti*:
> Though destitute of virtue, or seeking pleasure (elsewhere), or devoid of good qualities, (yet) a husband must be constantly worshipped as a god by a faithful wife.

Modern *Manusmriti* gives women self-respect:
> If destitute of virtue, or seeking pleasure (elsewhere), or devoid of good qualities, a husband may be cast aside, or divorced, unless he improves his behaviour.

*Verse 5.153.* Ancient and outdated *Manusmriti*:
> There is no separate sacrificing for women, no observances, no fastings; it is by means of serving her husband that she becomes exalted in heaven.

Modern *Manusmriti* asks society to respect women:
> There is to be separate sacrificing for women, observances, fastings; a husband must serve his wife and wife serve her husband equally to be exalted in heaven.

*Verse 5.156.* Ancient *Manusmriti*:
> A faithful wife, who desires to dwell (after death) with her husband, must never do anything that might displease him who took her hand, whether he be alive or dead.

Modern *Manusmriti* allows empowerment:
> A faithful husband and wife, who desire to dwell (after death) with each other, must never do anything that might displease each other, who took each other's hand, whether they be alive or dead.

*Verse 5.160.* Ancient and outdated *Manusmriti*:
> A virtuous wife who after the death of her husband constantly remains chaste, reaches heaven, though she have no son, just like those chaste men.

Modern *Manusmriti* gives widows a new lease of life:
> A virtuous husband or wife after the death of their partner may re-marry.

*Verse 3.16.* Ancient and outdated *Manusmriti*:
> According to Atri and to (Gautama) the son of Utathya, he who weds a Sudra woman becomes an outcast, according to Saunaka on the birth of a son, and according to Bhrigu he who has (male) offspring from a (Sudra female, alone).

Modern *Manusmriti* gives permission to society to get rid of the chains of caste:
> According to Atri and to (Gautama) the son of Utathya, he or she who weds a Sudra man or woman enters the age of enlightenment, and breaks the chains of caste or varna imposed on humanity by *Manusmriti*, ushering in the modern era.

As a culture we harness the positive influences espoused by *Manusmriti*.

Chapter 3. Rules Regarding Marriage. Verse 57:
> Where the female relations live in grief, the family soon wholly perishes; but that family where they are not unhappy ever prospers.

Section VI. Verse 3.58:
> The houses on which female relations, not being duly honoured, pronounce a curse, perish completely, as if destroyed by magic.

Section VI, Verse 3.60:
> In that family, where the husband is pleased with his wife and the wife with her husband, happiness will assuredly be lasting.

Verse 59:
> In urging men to respect women he eulogises them.
> Hence men who seek (their own) welfare, should always honour women on holidays and festivals with (gifts of) ornaments, clothes, and (dainty) food.

The ancient, learned culture of India, to which I am proud to belong, remains strong and solid, unchanged over the millennia even as it travels across the seven seas. The benefit it gives us is a strong sense of self. In no small measure this is due to the Laws of Manu. It was ahead of its time, giving laws, rules and guidance on how to live a just and happy life. But it harmed as well—dividing society in rungs of caste, shrinking the world of India's women. It is time to change. We must leave behind the paralysing chains of caste system and erase the disturbing, negative sentiments against women. Let us enter modern times. Let women take their respectful, rightful equal place in the home, and in a society oblivious to caste. At the stroke of the midnight hour, when the world sleeps, let India awake to life and freedom, freedom from misogyny, freedom from women's inequality, freedom from ridiculing women.

# Acknowledgments

This book is representative of a collective effort. It would never have been possible without the wonderful women and men I met in my life, my family and friends, my patients and their families. It would never have been possible without the terrific volunteers who gave up their valuable time, too numerous to name, but young and old, men and women of Indian and South Asian and Australian communities who formed the AustralAsian Centre for Human Rights and Health (ACHRH).

I am indebted to the board of ACHRH and to the National Council of Women of Victoria for their support. I am also indebted to the Royal Australian and New Zealand College of Psychiatrists, especially the Victorian branch, its chairman Professor David Castle, and Professor Richard Newton, who provided enormous support and guidance, and allowed me to found its first Family Violence Working Group in Victoria, which became the bi-national (Australia and New Zealand) Family Violence Psychiatry Committee with the help of Dr Kym Jenkins, Past President of the (RANZCP). I was appointed the inaugural Chair. I acknowledge the contributions of Members of Bi-national Family Violence Psychiatry Network to my learning experience. The members of the first Family Violence Working Group included Dr Samir Ibrahim, who collaborated with me on the study on suicides in migrant women who were victims of family violence. My thanks also to Professor Maurice Eisenbruch, who ensured the cross-cultural analysis of the community dialogue recorded in *Natak Vihar* community participatory theatre was academically sound.

I have been a member of Clinical Psychopharmacology Group for more than thirty years. Thanks to Dr Michael Piperoglou, Professor Bruce Singh, Professor David Copolov, Professor David

Castle, Dr Samir Ibrahim, Professor Chris Davies, Professor Christos Pentalis, Associate Professor David Horgan and all the peer review group members for their support and understanding of my community-based advocacy, action research, for great collegiality and peer learning.

Thanks to Associate Professor Harry Minas, at the University of Melbourne's Centre for International Mental Health (later Global Mental Health), Dr Erminia Colucci, and Drummond Street Centre who were partners in the first action research project using community participatory theatre conducted with women of Indian community in 2011, which explored and explained the nature of family dynamics in extended families, especially when it goes wrong.

I am grateful to the Victorian Indian Psychiatrists group and the Overseas Medical Graduates Association, Australian peers from my alma mater Maulana Azad Medical College MAMCOS who have been supportive and recognised the value of the difficult work, and inherent problems I encountered when exposing the transnational nature of dowry abuse in Australia—dowry being illegal in India since 1961, and although widely understood by South Asian communities was hidden, out of view in Australia.

I enjoyed my voluntary teaching stints between 2006 and 2009 at the Dev Sanskriti Vishwavidyalaya DSVV in Haridwar India. It was wonderful to learn Hindi again from students, and to have the company of other volunteer teachers from the world. Meetings with Chancellor (Cardiologist) Prof Pranav Pandaya were always insightful; and conversations about the Vedic Indian knowledge written in ancient scriptures, the Vedas, being adapted to modern Indian education with Vice Chancellor Professor Saryu Prasad Mishra and Dean Professor Mishra were fascinating, and opened my mind to the lost treasures of ancient India.

I met some 200 delightful children of nomads, receiving education at the primary school set up by the NGO, Divya Prem Sewa Mission in Haridwar, located not far from the DSVV. The children were coming to school hungry, and attendance was irregular. I helped to set up their breakfast program. The children started coming to school regularly and they seemed much happier in the classroom and in the playground.

The Victorian Royal Commission into Family Violence recognised the harm being caused by dowry abuse in Victoria and adapted the petition commenced by ACHRH in 2013. The petition demanded that the Legislative Assembly of Victoria amend the *Family Violence Protection Act 2008*—SECT 6 as soon as possible to add the word 'Dowry or coercive demands or pressure to supply gifts or cash in the context of a new marriage (up to seven years)' under the examples cited in Section 6 titled 'Meaning of Economic Abuse'. It was to become the famed Recommendation 156—that 'the Victorian Government amend Section 6 of the Act … to expand the statutory examples of family violence to include … dowry related abuse'. The Victorian State Government led by Premier Daniel Andrews and Minister for Family Violence Prevention Gabrielle Williams withstood opposition from patriarchal forces, as the bill was read and passed unanimously by both houses of the Parliament in June 2018 and finally in August 2018. I am very grateful to the seven MPs who acknowledged my work in Parliament—Gabrielle Williams; Heidi Victoria; Danielle Green in the Lower House; and Senators in Upper House Opposition Minister for prevention of family violence Georgie Crozier, Opposition Minister for Multi-cultural Affairs Inge Peulich, Greens Senator Leader Dr Samantha Ratnam, and Greens family violence spokeswoman Nina Springle. They helped to legislate dowry abuse as a crime in Victoria's Family Violence Protection Act, in March 2019.

Former Premier Ted Baillieu has been a staunch supporter of ACHRH and the dowry abuse campaign. We are grateful to him for tabling the first ACHRH Petition in Victorian Parliament in 2014. Julian Hill MP supported us against patriarchal tirade, speaking in favour of my work in Australian Federal Parliament in 2017, helping to trigger a Senate national hearing into 'The practice of dowry and the incidence of dowry abuse in Australia' in 2018. The hearing Chaired by Senator Louise Pratt and Senator (Hon) Ian Macdonald released the Report in February 2019; its first recommendation was inclusion of dowry abuse in the Australian Federal Family Law Act.

The Second National Dowry Abuse Summit was held in February 2019, co-organised by ACHRH and University of New South Wales Department of Psychiatry's Professor Susan Rees and Professor Henry Brodaty, who were the largest donors of the event. I am very thankful to the Gender Violence Research Network, Professor Jan Breckenridge and Mailin Suchting, and Gabrielle Dunlevy and Professor Louise Edwards of School of Social Sciences, and the Australian Human Rights Institute at the University of New South Wales. It was gratifying to have key women's organisations of Australia to co-host the event— AWAVA, InTouch, Good Shepherd Foundation. The function was attended by Federal Opposition Minister for Prevention of Family Violence The Hon Linda Burney; Senator Louse Pratt; our supporter Julian Hill MP; and Former Premier Ted Baillieu. The Summit gave momentum to the formation of National Alliance against dowry abuse, giving rise to partnership with Harmony Alliance, the peak migrant women's body, in a national action research and education project around dowry education, and funded by the Federal Australian Government over three years (2020–2022).

Suicide prevention working group called Crossroads to Community Wellbeing is acknowledged. The group was convened to kickstart suicide prevention, and prevention of family violence in the South Asian Community in the Whittlesea region. I enjoyed working with the group. ACHRH will continue the work begun by Crossroads, engage the community and make an impact with a new project, Victorian Government-funded community participatory theatre project 'Sneh' ( Hindi for affection).

I value the title Hon. Clinical Associate Professor to the Department of Psychiatry, University of Melbourne. I am very grateful to the University of New South Wales for conferring me the title of Adjunct Professor in School of Social Sciences.

I am grateful to colleague and friend Professor Anne Buist for reading the first draft and giving me guidance and encouragement.

I am forever grateful to my alma mater: the Maulana Azad Medical College, New Delhi India. And my classmates—they made learning pleasurable and fun.

Nothing would have been possible without my family and friends in Australia, my first mother-in-law Beryl (deceased) who was a genuine second mother, my parents, my sister and our children, the extended family, and my Medical School friends in India who support me unconditionally, and provide me with a stabilising emotional anchor. Lastly, I thank my partner Dr Jonathan Harrison for his incisive comments and support.

# Notes

### INTRODUCTION
1   Evlin, 2020.
2   Our Watch, Quick Facts 2021.
3   Morgan, 2022
4   Smethhurst, 2019.
5   Ganguly-Scrase, pp. 544–566.
6   Menon, 2004.
7   Various authors, *Celebrate! Dussehra & Durga Puja*, 2011.
8   The Supreme Court of India in 2012 ordered the Government of India to provide adequate care and funeral rights to widowed women. See Schultz, 2019.
9   Recent Indian research shows that households that are weakly religious and removed from caste networks find it easier to be flexible, adopt modernity and shift rigid gender norms for women, compared with highly religious and caste-oriented families. See Desai, 2017.
10  Dias, 2016.
11  Australian Bureau of Statistics, 2017.
12  Pandey, 2018; Sasha R, 2019.
13  Segrave, 2017.
14  Dev Sanskriti Vishwavidyalaya.
15  'Excerpt From Jawaharlal Nehru's "A Tryst With Destiny" Speech, August 15, 1947' in Roberts, 1 August–27 October, 2017.
16  Eggeling, 1882–1900.
17  Smears, 2019.

### 1   WOMEN OF INDIA
1   Child marriage was noted as desirable in the *Manusmriti*, which was written around the second-century BC: the number of girls getting married before eighteen years of age in India was still over 50 per cent in 2007 (International Center for Research on Women, 2015); it fell to 27 per cent in 2015–2016. See also Gupta and Fletcher, p. 9.
2   Ananthaswamy and Douglas, 2018.
3   Griffith, 2012.

4   Bader, pp. 15–16.
5   Guha, 2015.
6   Bader, p. 34.
7   *The Laws of Manu* is believed to have been written somewhere between 200 BC and 200 CE, and some believe additions were made in the seventh-century CE. For the purposes of this book, we will date it as at the first century CE. The dating is significant because most of the verses were written during the period when Brahminical tradition was seriously threatened by non-Vedic movements such as Buddhism. Its harsh treatment of women in contrast to Vedic times when women were highly respected is said to be a reaction against changing times and influx of new ideas such as Buddhism. *Manusmriti* is a confusing document regarding how women should be treated. There are contradictory messages—for example, verses III–55, 56, 57, 59, 62 glorify the position of women, whereas other verses (IX–3, 17) seem to attack the position and freedom of women. Some scholars deny legitimacy to *Manusmriti* as a useful document. See Puthenveetil, 2016.
8   Denike, pp. 10–43.
9   Lal, 2018.
10  The British exercised absolute power in a cruel and oppressive way with a self-justification; see Tharoor, 2016.
11  Carroll, p. 364.
12  See Liddle and Joshi, 1985.
13  Pillai, 2016.
14  India Today, January 2019.
15  Mukhoty, p. 141.
16  Lal, 2018.
17  Hildebrand, 2016.
18  Liddle and Joshi, 1985, p. 527.
19  Nehru, 1946.
20  Liddle and Joshi, 1985, p. 527.
21  Liddle and Joshi, 1988.
22  Roy, pp. 165–173; Rojak, 2019; Datta, R., pp. 25–32.
23  The laws to ban sex selective abortions and social education campaigns such as Beti Bachao Beti Padao (Hindi for protect your daughter, educate your daughter) have produced only some signs of change. The pattern continues in India: See Sharma, January 2021.

24 Edvardsson et al, 2018.
25 World Economic Forum, 'Global Gender Gap Report 2020'.
26 World Economic Forum, 'The Global Gender Gap Report 2018'.
27 Australian Bureau of Statistics, 2019.
28 Garvan Institute of Medical Research, 2021.
29 See Chugh and Puri, pp. 535–42.
30 Times of India, 9 July 2021.
31 Sethi, 2018.
32 Ineichen, pp. 135–138.
33 Gibson et al., 2021.
34 Muralidharan et al, 2015.
35 India State-Level Disease Burden Initiative Suicide Collaborators, 2018; Lifeline Australia, 2021; Evlin, 2020; Asher, 2020.
36 Hoeffler and Fearson, 2014.
37 United Nations, 2018.
38 Chowdhury and Patnaik, pp. 455–471.
39 *The Economic Times*, 2018.

## 2  THE HAPPY FAMILY

1 Dutt, 1900.
2 Australia and other countries were labouring under similar patriarchal pressures. See Greer, pp. 140–142.
3 Han, pp. 1876–1884.
4 Thompson and Langendoerfer, p. 119.
5 Whether or not women desire to have power, dominance and engage in violence is a hotly debated question amongst modern day feminists. There is a rise in 'equal-opportunity feminists' who believe that women can be a force for more ethical use of dominance, power and violence. See Crozier-De Rosa, 2017.
6 World Bank Group, 2019.
7 Gupta, 1991.
8 Colucci et al., pp. 9–26.
9 Gupta, 1991.
10 Flood, 2020.
11 Health and Human Services, 2021.
12 Colucci et al., pp. 9–26.
13 I use my schema of culturally constructed trauma therapy when treating victims and perpetrators of family violence.

14  Kandiyoti, pp. 274–290.
15  Galtung, pp. 167–191.
16  Webster et al., 2018.

## 3  THE COSTS OF A HIERARCHICAL SOCIETY

1  Modern young tech savvy Indian women are defying societal controls and discussing the issues of premarital sex on the internet. See Saini, 2021.
2  Jaffrelot, 2019.
3  Allendorf, pp. 453–469.
4  Dholakia, 2015.
5  Australian Government, 2017.
6  See for example Wilcox, 2020.
7  According to data, in the year 2013 around 5740 divorce cases were filed in the Family Court of Mumbai, a jump of 48.58 per cent from those filed four years earlier. See Vyas, 2015.
8  Anderson, pp. 151–174.
9  Sharma et al., pp 243–249.
10  Anukriti et al., 2018.
11  Chiplunkar and Weaver, 2019; New Delhi TV, 2018.
12  White, pp. 247–272.
13  Srinivasan, pp. 593–615.
14  Chiplunkar and Weaver, 2019.
15  Abraham, pp. 56–65; Anderson, pp. 151–174.
16  Chiplunkar and Weaver, 2019; Maertens and Chari, 2020.
17  A 1948 study of a village by sociologist MN Srinivas noted that while villagers maintained the caste system by segregation—for example, by denying inter-caste marriage and eating together—there was a lot of inter-dependence and 'cheating', whereby a 'low' Hindu caste or tribal or other group, would change its customs, rituals, ideology, and way of life to imitate a higher caste. He coined the term 'Sanskritization' to denote this process. See Srinivas, 1976; see also Abraham, pp. 56–65.
18  Devi, pp. 01–09.
19  Young people increasingly participate in spouse selection, with a rising trend of parents consulting their children more and giving sons (more than daughters) veto power. Allendorf, pp. 453–469.
20  Rao, 2016.

21  Paul, 1986.
22  Devi, pp. 01–09.
23  Rao, 2019.
24  Statista, 2019; Statista Research Department, 2016.
25  McClelland, 2018; Australian Bureau of Statistics, 2018.
26  Bloch et al., 2004.
27  Bīrūnī, pp. 154 and 164.
28  Oldenburg, 2002.
29  See Singh and Sidhu, pp. 35–50.
30  Mitchell and Soni, pp. 1026–1042.
31  Increasing women's rights gives them more bargaining power and it increases conflict within household and suicide rates. This is a global phenomenon and observed in most countries, that is until the countrywide institutions adapt to greater gender equality. See Anderson and Genicot, 2012.
32  Bhalotra et al., 2018.

## 4   A DAUGHTER IS ONLY EVER A GUEST IN THE FATHER'S HOME

1  Hanifie, 2018.
2  O'Connor, 2017; Chowdhary and Patel, 2008.
3  In recognition of the vulnerability suffered by thousands of immigrant women like Yesha, my NGO, the Australasian Centre for Human Rights and Health, joined with a national alliance of many women's organisations to advocate for such women under the umbrella of national body AWAVA. We helped write the Blueprint for Reform, which charts pathways to permanent residency without a husband's sponsorship. We are very hopeful that Australian Government will take note. See AWAVA, 2019.
4  O'Connor, 2017.
5  National Commission of Women, India.
6  Natak Vihar Community Participatory Theatre, AustralAsian Centre. https://www.achrh.org/natak-vihar/
7  'Duties of Women: verse 5.152': *Manusmriti*, Wisdom Library.
8  In India, the median age at first marriage was 19.7 years for women in the richest quintile of their sample, compared to 15.4 years for the poorest women: Singh and Vennam, p. 7.
9  White, pp. 247–272.

10 On 8 March 2016, the students at Jawaharlal Nehru University protested against derisory verses against women in the *Manusmriti* on International Women's Day. (The university asked them to 'explain their position'.) See The Economic Times, 2016.
11 Modern research, however, is uncovering a version of Sita's story where she was a warrior, a feminist. In the Indic way, the Sacred Feminine has always been respected in traditional India. Perhaps this message is needed today. See Damodaran, 2017.
12 Horney, 1967.
13 Bejanyan et al., 2015.
14 Anitha et al., pp. 67–75.
15 Arora, 2019.
16 Ministry of External Affairs, 2019.
17 Ctol News desk, 2019.
18 Singh, 2017.
19 Jain, 2018.
20 Datta, A., 2019.
21 Deccan Herald, 2020.
22 Two women in India whose rogue husbands live in Australia recently obtained extradition orders, but six months later neither man has been repatriated back (Email correspondence, 6 May 2020).
23 Family Court of Australia, 2016.
24 The Australian National Senate Hearing into dowry abuse report strongly recommended this inclusion in 2019. Senate Legal and Constitutional Affairs References Committee, Parliament of Australia, 2019.
25 The All India Survey on Higher Education 2018–19 shows that women's enrolment in higher education rose from 47.6 per cent in 2017–18 to 48.6 per cent in 2018–19 (Ministry of Human Resource Development, 2019); The Telegraph India Editorial Board, 2019.
26 AustralAsian Center for Human Rights and Health, 2020.
27 Chatterjee, 2019. The number of complainants increased to 515 000 cases by the end of 2016, an increase of more than 150 per cent in 11 years: National Crime Records Bureau, p. 4.
28 Ghosh, 2013.
29 Rautray, 2018.

## 5 THE MALADY (DOWRY DEATHS)

1. Kumari, 1989.
2. Jacobson, 2004.
3. Migrating family loses support of their extended family in bringing up children, making decisions, and economic arrangements. The families can break down under the strain of being a nuclear family. The positives include greater gender equality, more economic empowerment for women, and more decision-making power, but may be followed by patriarchal backlash and greater degree of family violence: Ayika et al., 2018.
4. Assari, 2019.
5. Dang et al., 2018.
6. United Nations Office on Drugs and Crime, pp. 10 and 32.
7. Anderson, 2000.
8. United Nations Office on Drugs and Crime, 2018.
9. 101 East, 2017.
10. Acharya, 2016.
11. AustralAsian Centre for Human Rights and Health, 2021; Acharya, 2018.
12. Royal Commission into Family Violence, 2015.
13. O'Connor and Asthana, 2015.
14. O'Connor and Ibrahim, pp. 224–225.
15. Our Watch, Evidence Paper 2021.
16. Karmakar, 2019.

## 6 SOCIETAL FEAR PARALYSES SOCIAL CHANGE

1. Squarcini, p. 125.
2. 'Duties of Women: verse 5.152', *Manusmriti*, Wisdom Library.
3. While at only half that of Australian rates (around 40 per cent), the current trends suggest India may catch up in the not-too-distant future: Biswas, 2016.
4. Some brave women are breaking barriers. The contemporary Indian culture is changing rapidly and is affecting various regions and socio-economic groups in disparate ways. Indian women are taking decisions to seek divorce when in abusive marriage in spite of many barriers: see Afroz, 2021.

5 'Duties of Husband and Wife: verse 14, chapter 9', *The Laws of Manu*, 1886.
6 The inconsistent verses regarding women and verses that appear to have been added later by unknown authors have undermined its legitimacy. See Olivelle, pp. 353–354, 356–382.
7 'Verse 154, Chapter 10', *The Law Code of Manu*, p. 157.
8 Sacred Texts of the East, *The Laws of Manu*, 1886.
9 Erminia Colluci et al., pp. 9–26.
10 Jack and Ali, 2010.
11 Ibid.
12 After multiple action research projects with the Indian and broader South Asian immigrant communities of Australia, I devised a culturally responsive trauma therapy. Paper submitted to the BMC Women's Health Open. Awaiting result.
13 Jack and Ali, p 5.
14 Banerjee, 2014.
15 Postmus et al, 2012.
16 Monani, 1–13.
17 Singh and Sidhu, pp. 35–50.
18 Hill, 2019.
19 Kutin et al., 2017.
20 In Australian law, slavery is defined as the condition of a person over whom any or all of the powers attaching to the right of ownership are exercised, including where such a condition results from a debt or contract made by the person. See Burn, 2019.

## 7 WISH YOU WERE A SON

1 World Health Organization, 2002.
2 Moylan et al, 2010.
3 Qu, 2020.
4 TNN, 2017.
5 Victorian State Government, 2018.
6 Ugargol and Bailey, 2018.
7 World Economic Forum, 2019.
8 AustralAsian Centre for Human Rights and Health, 2020.
9 Census 2011.

## 8  CASTE AND HONOUR KILLINGS

1. Recent scientific evidence from a genomic study puts the age of the caste system as 1,575 years old. The practice of endogamy, or preference for marrying within the caste was established, possibly by decree of the rulers, probably during the reign of the ardent Hindu Gupta rulers (319–550 CE): the Gupta dynasty. See Basu et al., pp. 1594–1599.
2. 'Introduction', Manu Samhita, *The Laws of Manu*.
3. Chakravorty, 2019.
4. 'Chapter 3, Verse 43 and 44', *The Laws of Manu*.
5. Bīrūnī, 2012, pp. 101–104.
6. de Zwart, 2000.
7. A thousand years later, in the newly independent India in 1948, M. N. Srinivas conducted a field study for nine months in a village in Karnataka. He confirmed the hierarchical nature of caste and segregation, but he also found crucial interdependence of various castes that would cause mixing up of hierarchies. The villagers would play with the hierarchy, and even cheat the system—adopting the eating habits of upper caste by becoming vegetarian, for example. The tendency to emulate the upper caste he labelled 'Sanskritization': see Srinivas, pp. 1870–1878.
8. Banerjee et al., 2013.
9. Pew Research Centre, 2021.
10. Singh, pp. 276–283.
11. Times of India, 2018.
12. Banerjee et al, 2013.
13. TNN, 2020.
14. de Zwart, 2000.
15. Chakravorty, 2019.
16. Fongay and Target, 1997.
17. John et al., 2017.
18. De Maio et al., 2017.
19. Banulescu-Bogden, 2020.
20. Borker, 2016.

## 9 HUGE COST OF MENTAL ILLNESS

1. O'Connor and Ibrahim, 2018.
2. American Psychiatric Association, 2013.
3. Ford, 2009.
4. Fortunately, there are methods women can use to protect themselves. See eSafety Commissioner, 2021.
5. Short et al., 2014.
6. O'Connor and Asthana, 2015.
7. 'Modern slavery' is an umbrella term that is often used to describe human trafficking, slavery, and slavery-like practices such as servitude, forced labour and forced marriage. Essentially, slavery in this context is when a person is exploited for personal gain and married by deception. Many cases of dowry abuse occur in situations where the marriage was never intended to be genuine and was undertaken for obtaining dowry.
8. International Labour Organization, 2021.
9. AWAVA Secretariat, 2018.
10. Australian Government, 2019.
11. We have demonstrated the effectiveness of mental health treatments in victims of domestic violence in a small observational study published in 2018 in the *Australasian Journal of Psychiatry*: see O'Connor and Ibrahim, 2018.
12. Australian Bureau of Statistics, National Health Survey 2018.
13. Remes, 2016.
14. Alonso et al., pp. 195–208; Patel and Kleinman, 2003.
15. Lomborg, 2014.
16. VicHealth, 2004.
17. Victims of domestic violence had double the rate (58%) of developing a common mental disorder, including depression, anxiety disorder, post-traumatic stress disorder (PTSD), substance abuse or attempted suicide, compared with a rate of 27% among women who had not experienced DV: Rees et al., pp. 513–521.
18. O'Connor and Ibrahim, 2018.
19. Since March 2020's COVID lockdown, two Middle Eastern women locked up with their perpetrators, presented back for treatment, with suicidal thoughts, agitation, insomnia, deep depression, breathlessness, tremors, nightmares, poor self-esteem, crying most of the time, no interest in domestic duties: ibid.

20 Significant numbers of the Middle Eastern women continued to receive ongoing mental health treatments for years. See O'Connor, 2018.
21 O'Connor and Kirtley, 2018.
22 Eye Movement Desensitization and Reprocessing Institute, Inc., 2020.

## 10 MIGRATION, FAMILY, AND SUICIDE

1 Fleischmanm, 2016.
2 Orygen News and Events, 2019.
3 Snowdon, 2019.
4 Evlin, 2020.
5 India State-Level Disease Burden Initiative Suicide Collaborators, 2018.
6 Jamieson, 2019.
7 Dyal and Dyal, pp. 301–328.
8 The AustralAsian Centre for Human Rights and Health, 2020.
9 Programs are available in Australia. For example, the Brotherhood of St Lawrence Help for refugees and migrants is funded by the Victorian Government Department of Premier and Cabinet. But the demand is great, and many migrant women and men are not receiving the support and education needed. See Brotherhood of St Lawrence, 2021.
10 World Health Organisation, 2014.
11 Weiyuan, pp. 888–9.
12 Hill et al., 2021.
13 Shivji, 2021.
14 Nair, 2020.
15 Recent research from India finds that the authoritative parenting style is the most common parenting style. The authors note that proper counselling of parents on the appropriate parenting style in early childhood will optimize development in children: Rangarajan et al., 2020.
16 Ng et al., 2010.
17 Huang et al., 2019.
18 Han and Ma, 2014.
19 Snowdon, 2019.
20 Australian Bureau of Statistics, Research Paper, 2017.
21 Fu and Markus, pp. 739–749.

22  Rangarajan et al., 2020.
23  Parikh, 2019.
24  World Health Organization, 2005; Victorian State Government, 2021.
25  Shinde et al, 2017.
26  Øien-Ødegaard et al., 2021.
27  Vijayakumar, 2015.
28  O'Connor and Portzky, pp. 12–17.
29  Mateos-Aparicio and Rodríguez-Moreno, p. 66.

## 11  EDUCATION IS THE KEY TO EQUALITY

1  World Economic Forum, December 2019.
2  Our Watch. Quick Facts 2021.
3  Brown and Adetunji, 2013.
4  Kalokhe et al., 2015.
5  Parker and Stepler, 2017.
6  UN Women, 2021.
7  Australian Bureau of Statistics, 2017.
8  World Bank Group, 2019.
9  Kandiyoti, pp. 274–290.
10  Lakra, 2017.
11  Daruwalla et al., 2019.
12  MacNaughton and Davis, pp. 83–93.
13  Blum, Mmari and Moreau, 2017.
14  Stott-Despoja, 2017.
15  Das, 2012.
16  Shinde et al., 2017.
17  Lee, 2021.
18  Cunningham, 2001.
19  UN Women, 2018.
20  AustralAsian Centre for Human Rights and Health, 2019.
21  Easthope, 2009.
22  Klostermaier, 2014.
23  Dev Sanskriti Vishwavidyalaya.
24  Sivakumar and Manimekalai, K, pp. 427-436.
25  Yu, 2016.

## 12 THE BURDEN ON MEN OF INDIAN SOCIETY

1. Irvine et al., 2018.
2. Australian Institute of Health and Welfare, 2019.
3. Chowdhry, 2019.
4. Venkatraman, 2016.
5. Kedia, 2019.
6. Pearlman, 2015.
7. Kakar, 1978.
8. Younger, 2018.
9. Bejanyan et al., 2015.
10. Down to Earth, 2021.
11. Ashis Nandy writes about the dominance of western culture and its effect on non-western people. See Nandy, pp. 142-9.
12. World Health Organization, 2001.
13. Australian Bureau of Statistics, Media Release, 2019.
14. Bhatia, 2017.
15. VicHealth, 2008.
16. Crenshaw, pp. 1241–99.
17. Australian Bureau of Statistics, Media Release, 2017.
18. Australian Bureau of Statistics, Media Release, 2019.
19. ICEF, 2019.
20. Chakravorty et al., 2016.
21. AMES in Australia is a leading provider of humanitarian settlement, education, training and employment services to refugees, asylum seekers and newly arrived migrants in Australia. See AMES https://www.ames.net.au/csp/victoria/about-ames-australia.
22. United Nations, 2021.
23. Sanchez, 2018.
24. World Economic Forum, 2019, p. 10.
25. World Health Organization, 2009.

## 13 ACTIONS AGAINST DOWRY ABUSE IN AUSTRALIA

1. International Classification of Diseases 2019 has identified a new category of mental health condition arising from prolonged psychological or physical abuse called Complex Post Traumatic Stress Disorder. This leads to emotional dysregulation, anger, depression, suicidal feelings, low confidence and negative self-image, difficulty

making relationships and loss of meaning, in addition to usual features of Post-Traumatic Stress Disorder.
2. Australian Bureau of Statistics, 2020.
3. O'Connor Colucci, 2015.
4. Acharya, 2019.
5. Australian Bureau of Statistics, Media Release, 2019.
6. Studies have identified sex selection in other high-income Western countries such as the US, Canada, and the UK: Latrobe University, 2018.
7. Victorian Numbered Acts 2008; Gye, 2013.
8. Effective Change, 2019.
9. Kleinman, 2015.
10. Jopson, 2017.
11. The action against dowry abuse began in early 1980s, spurred on by frequent news reports of brides being burnt alive. They all had one common element—newly married young women. Dowry death was finally recognised as a reality. New laws were written, including Section 498A which made dowry abuse a non bailable criminal offence. See Kishwar, 2005.
12. Indira Jaising helped draft the Protection of Women from Domestic Violence Act 2005 in India. Implementation has been the most important hurdle, as Shalu Nigam's work shows. See Nigram, 2015.
13. O'Connor and Asthana, 2015.
14. Victorian Royal Commission into Family Violence, 2016, p.22.
15. Family Violence Protection Act 2008, Section 5.
16. Williams, 2018.
17. Crozier, 2018.
18. Parliament of Australia, 2021.
19. Parliament of Australia, 2019.
20. Department of Social Services, 2019.
21. Ibid, pp. 29-30. The action listed as number 12. 'Better equip the service system and communities to address complex forms of violence and harmful cultural practices including dowry abuse.'
22. United Nations, 2020.
23. García-Moreno and Amin, pp. 396–397.
24. O'Connor and Lee, 2022.
25. Argoon, 2015.

26  AustralAsian Centre for Human Rights & Health and Harmony Alliance, 2020.
27  'Jawaharlal Nehru's "A Tryst With Destiny" Speech, August 15, 1947' in Roberts, 2017.

## 14 THE WAY FORWARD: *MANUSMRITI* REIMAGINED

1  Galtung, pp. 167-191.
2  Mayer, p. 323.
3  Kandiyoti, 1988.
4  India State-Level Disease Burden Initiative Suicide Collaborators, 2018.
5  Evlin, 2020.
6  Basu et al., pp. 1594–1599.
7  Sanyal, 2008.
8  Ghosh, 2018.
9  Sacred Texts of the East, *The Laws of Manu*, 1886.

# Bibliography

Abraham, Janaki, 'Contingent Caste Endogamy and Patriarchy: lessons for our understanding of caste', *Economic and Political Weekly*, vol. 49, no. 2, 11 January 2014, pp. 56–65. www.jstor.org/stable/24479015.

Acharya, Mosiqi, 'New court documents reveal how Sunil Beniwal killed his wife Deepshikha', *SBS Hindi News [online]*, 15 August 2016. https://www.sbs.com.au/language/english/new-court-documents-reveal-how-sunil-beniwal-killed-his-wife-deepshikha-godara-after-years-of-torturing-her.

—'Victorian parliament passes legislation banning dowry abuse', *SBS Hindi News [online]*, 9 August 2018. https://www.sbs.com.au/language/english/victorian-parliament-passes-legislation-banning-dowry-abuse.

—'Indian Migrants Generate billions for Australian economy', *SBS News [online]*, 2 December 2019. https://www.sbs.com.au/language/english/indian-migrants-generate-billions-for-australian-economy

Afroz, Shamima, 'Facing divorce stigma in South Asian communities', *ABC Everyday News*, 4 April 2021. https://www.abc.net.au/everyday/facing-divorce-stigma-in-south-asian-communities/100026742.

Allendorf, Keera, 'Schemas of Marital Change: from arranged marriages to eloping for love', *Journal of Marriage and the Family*, vol. 75, no. 2, 14 March 2013, pp. 453–469. https://doi.org/10.1111/jomf.12003.

Alonso, J., Z. Liu, S. Evans-Lacko, E. Sadikova, N. Sampson, S. Chatterji, J. Abdulmalik, S. Aguilar-Gaxiola, A. Al-Hamzawi, L. H. Andrade, R. Bruffaerts, G. Cardoso, A. Cia, S. Florescu, G. de Girolamo, O. Gureje, J. M. Haro, Y. He, P. de Jonge, E. G. Karam, N. Kawakami, V. Kovess-Masfety, S. Lee, D. Levinson, M. E. Medina-Mora, F. Navarro-Mateu, B. E. Pennell, M. Piazza, J. Posada-Villa, M. Ten Have, Z. Zarkov, R. C. Kessler, G. Thornicroft and WHO World Mental Health Survey Collaborators, 'Treatment gap for anxiety disorders is global: Results of the World Mental Health Surveys in 21 countries', *Depress Anxiety*, 35(3), 2018, pp. 195–208. https://pubmed.ncbi.nlm.nih.gov/29356216/.

American Psychiatric Association, *Diagnostic and Statistical Manual of Mental Disorders, 5th ed.*, Washington, DC., American Psychiatric Association, 2013.

Ananthaswamy, Anil and Kate Douglas, 'The origins of sexism: how men came to rule 12 000 years ago', *New Scientist*, 18 April 2018. https://www.newscientist.com/article/mg23831740-400-the-origins-of-sexism-how-men-came-to-rule-12000-years-ago/.

Anderson, K. S., 'The Economics of Dowry Payments in Pakistan', CentER Discussion Paper, 2000-82, *Macroeconomics*, Tilburg University, 2000. https://research.tilburguniversity.edu/en/publications/the-economics-of-dowry-payments-in-pakistan.

Anderson, Siwan, 'The Economics of Dowry and Brideprice', *Journal of Economic Perspectives*, vol. 21, no. 4, Fall 2007, pp. 151–174. https://www.jstor.org/stable/30033756?seq=1.

Anderson, Siwan and Garance Genicot, 'Suicide and Property Rights in India', *University of British Columbia and Georgetown University*, July 2012. https://economics.yale.edu/sites/default/files/genicot-121001.pdf.

Anitha, Sundari, Harshita Yalamarty & Anupama Roy, 'Changing nature and emerging patterns of domestic violence in global contexts: dowry abuse and the transnational abandonment of wives in India', *Women's Studies International Forum* 69, 2018, pp. 67–75.

Anukriti, S., Sungoh Kwon, Nishith Prakash, 'Household Savings and Marriage Payments: evidence from dowry in India', *IZA Institute of Economics Discussion Paper Series*, April 2018. http://ftp.iza.org/dp11464.pdf.

Argoon, Ashley, 'Dowry link to murders and family violence in Victoria', *Herald Sun*, 23 April 2015. https://www.heraldsun.com.au/news/law-order/dowry-link-to-murders-and-family-violence-in-victoria/news-story/65da7055d98a3eece3435076fbacff70.

Arora, Avneet, '80 per cent of all dowry cases in India end in acquittal', *SBS News Punjabi [online]*, 27 February 2019. https://www.sbs.com.au/language/english/80-per-cent-of-all-dowry-cases-in-india-end-in-acquittal.

Asher, Nicole, 'Suicide cluster highlights dangerous combination of social isolation and family violence for some migrant women'. *ABC News [online]*, 20 September 2020. https://www.abc.net.au/news/2020-09-20/priya-survived-abuse-isolation-suicide-clusters-coroner/12678298.

Assari, Shervin, 'How unjust social structures help some but harm others', *The Conversation,* April 4, 2019. https://theconversation.com/how-unjust-social-structures-help-some-but-harm-others-113622.

AustralAsian Center for Human Rights and Health, 'Mutual Relational Respect (MRR) Workshop', February 2020. https://www.achrh.org/mutual-relational-respect-mrr%E2%80%8B/.

—'Anti-Dowry Legislation: How we achieved the legislation', ACHRH, 2021. https://www.achrh.org/anti-dowry-legislation/.

—'Second National Dowry Abuse Summit', ACHRH, 2019. https://www.achrh.org/national-dowry-abuse-summits/.

AustralAsian Centre for Human Rights & Health and Harmony Alliance: Migrant & Refugee Women for Change, *Dowry Abuse in Australia: Issues Paper,* May 2020. https://www.achrh.org/wp-content/uploads/2020/05/ISSUES-PAPER.pdf.

Australian Bureau of Statistics, '4906.0 – Personal Safety, Australia, 2016'. ABS, Canberra.

—'4125.0 – Gender Indicators, Australia, Sep 2018', ABS, Canberra, 25 September 2019. https://www.abs.gov.au/ausstats/abs@.nsf/Lookup/by%20Subject/4125.0~Sep%202018~Main%20Features~Education~5.

—'Personal Safety, Australia: statistics for family, domestic, sexual violence, physical assault, partner emotional abuse, child abuse, sexual harassment, stalking and safety, 2016', Canberra, 2019. https://www.abs.gov.au/ausstats/abs@.nsf/mf/4906.0.

—'Characteristics of Employment, Australia, August 2018', ABS, Canberra, 29 November 2018. https://www.abs.gov.au/ausstats/abs@.nsf/lookup/6333.0main+features1august%202018?opendocument.

—*National Health Survey: First results 2017-18 financial year,* 12 December 2018. https://www.abs.gov.au/statistics/health/health-conditions-and-risks/national-health-survey-first-results/latest-release.

—'Research Paper: Psychosocial risk factors as they relate to coroner-referred deaths in Australia 2017', ABS, Canberra, 2017.

—'Personal Income of Migrants, Australia: statistics on personal income of migrants including employee income, own unincorporated business income, investment income and other income 2016–17', Media Release, 29 November 2019. https://www.abs.gov.au/statistics/people/population/migration-australia/latest-release.

—'2024.0–Census of Population and Housing: Australia Revealed, 2016', Media Release, ABS, Canberra, 27 June 2017. https://www.abs.gov.au/ausstats/abs@.nsf/Latestproducts/2024.0Main%20Features22016.

—'Migration, Australia: statistics on Australia's international migration, internal migration (interstate and intrastate) and the population by country of birth 2018-19', Canberra, 28 April 2020. https://www.abs.gov.au/ausstats/abs%40.nsf/mediareleasesbyCatalogue/35A203AB6DD3CA0BCA257600002314F7?OpenDocument.

Australian Government, 'Divorce rates in Australia', Australian Institute of Family Studies, *Family Facts*, 2017. https://aifs.gov.au/facts-and-figures/divorce-rates-australia.

—'Blueprint for Reform: removing barriers to safety for victims/survivors of domestic and family violence who are on temporary visas', *Australian Institute of Family Studies*, Canberra, 29 October 2019. https://aifs.gov.au/cfca/2019/10/29/blueprint-reform-removing-barriers-safety-victims-survivors-domestic-and-family-violence.

—'Chapter 18. An India Economic Strategy to 2035: the role of the diaspora', *Department of Foreign Affairs and Trade*, Canberra.

Australian Institute of Health and Welfare, 'The Health of Australia's males', web report, Australian Government, Canberra, 10 Dec 2019. https://www.aihw.gov.au/reports/men-women/male-health/contents/how-healthy/burden-of-disease.

Australian Women Against Violence Alliance, 'Blueprint for Reform: removing barriers to safety for victims/survivors of domestic and family violence who are on temporary visas', AWAVA, 2019. https://awava.org.au/2019/10/02/research-and-reports/blueprint-for-reform.

AWAVA Secretariat, 'Path to Nowhere Report: women on temporary visas experiencing violence and their children', AWAVA, 11 December 2018. https://awava.org.au/2018/12/11/research-and-reports/path-to-nowhere-report-women-on-temporary-visas-experiencing-violence-and-their-children?doing_wp_cron=1556344203.6392560005187988281250.

Ayika, David, Tinashe Dune, Rubab Firdaus and Virginia Mapedzahama, 'A Qualitative Exploration of Post-Migration Family Dynamics and Intergenerational Relationships', *SAGE Open*, October 2018. https://journals.sagepub.com/doi/full/10.1177/2158244018811752.

Bader, Clarisse, *Women in Ancient India: moral and literary studies*, Mary E. R. Martin (trans.), Routledge, London, 1925.

Banerjee, Abhijit, Esther Duflo, Maitreesh Ghatak and Jeanne Lafortune, 'Marry for What? Caste and mate selection in modern India', *American Economic Journal, Microeconomics*, vol 5, no. 2 May 2013. https://economics.mit.edu/files/8979.

Banerjee, Pallavi, Soulit Chacko and Bhumika Piya, 'Paradoxes of Being and Becoming South Asian Single Mothers: The Enclave Economy, Patriarchy, and Migration', *Women Gender and Families of Color*, 8(1), 2020, pp. 5–39.

Banerjee, Priya R., 'Dowry in 21st-Century India: the sociocultural face of exploitation', *Trauma Violence Abuse*, vol. 15, no. 1, 2014. https://journals.sagepub.com/doi/10.1177/1524838013496334.

Banulescu-Bogden, Natalia, *Beyond work: Reducing Social Isolation for Refugee Women and Other Marginalised Newcomers*, Washington, DC, Migration Policy Institute, 2020.

Basu, Analabha, Neeta Sarkar-Roy, Partha P. Majumder, 'Genetic history of ethnic populations of India', *Proceedings of the National Academy of Sciences,* vol. 113, no. 6, Feb 2016, pp. 1594–1599.

Bejanyan, Kathrine, Tara C Marshall and Nelli Ferenczi, 'Associations of collectivism with relationship commitment, passion, and mate preferences: opposing roles of parental influence and family allocentrism', *PLoS One*, 10(2), 26 Feb 2015. https://journals.plos.org/plosone/article?id=10.1371/journal.pone.0117374.

Bhalotra, Sonia, Rachel Brulé and Sanchari Roy, 'Women's Inheritance Rights Reform and the Preference For Sons in India', *Journal of Development Economics*, 10 August 2018. https://www.researchgate.net/publication/326962325_Women%27s_inheritance_rights_reform_and_the_preference_for_sons_in_India.

Bhatia, Sunil, *Decolonizing Psychology: Globalization, Social Justice, and Indian Youth Identities,* Oxford Scholarship Online, 2017.

Bīrūnī, Muḥammad ibn Aḥmad, *Alberuni's India, vol. 1*, trans. Edward Sachau, Cambridge University Press, 2012.

—*Alberuni's India: an account of the religion, philosophy, literature, geography, chronology, astronomy, customs, laws and astrology of India about AD 1030*, vol. 2, Edward Sachau and Paul Kegan (eds), Trench, Trübner & Co, 1910.

Biswas, Soutik, 'What divorce and separation tell us about modern India', *BBC News [online]*, 29 September 2016. https://www.bbc.com/news/world-asia-india-37481054.

Bloch, Francis, Vijayendra Rao and Sonalde Desai, 'Wedding Celebrations as Conspicuous Consumption: signaling social status in rural India', *The Journal of Human Resources*, vol. 39, no. 3, 2004. https://www.researchgate.net/publication/46552543_Wedding_Celebrations_as_Conspicuous_Consumption_Signaling_Social_Status_in_Rural_India.

Blum, Robert W., Kristin Mmari and Caroline Moreau, 'It Begins at 10: how gender expectations shape early adolescence around the world', *Journal of Adolescent Health*, vol. 61, 2017. https://www.ncbi.nlm.nih.gov/pmc/articles/PMC5612023/.

Borker, Suhas, 'How to be free of caste', *The Hindu*, 13 April 2016. https://www.thehindu.com/opinion/op-ed/how-to-be-free-of-caste-in-india/article8467518.ece.

Brotherhood of St Lawrence, 'Help for refugees and migrants', *BSL*, 2021. https://www.bsl.org.au/services/refugees-immigration/.

Brown, Emily Lindsay and Jo Adetunji, 'One in three women worldwide is a victim of partner violence', *The Conversation*, 21 June 2013. https://theconversation.com/one-in-three-women-worldwide-is-a-victim-of-partner-violence-15389.

Burn, Jennifer, 'Human trafficking and slavery still happen in Australia: this comic explains how', *The Conversation*, June 12, 2019. https://theconversation.com/human-trafficking-and-slavery-still-happen-in-australia-this-comic-explains-how-112294.

Carroll, Lucy, 'Law, Custom, and Statutory Social Reform: the Hindu widows' remarriage act of 1856', *The Indian Economic and Social History Review*, 20(4), 1983, p. 364.

Census 2011, 'Delhi Population 2011–2020 Census: corona virus, covid 19 data', *Census 2011*, Delhi. https://www.census2011.co.in/census/state/delhi.html.

Chakravorty, Sanjoy, *The Truth About Us: the Politics of Information from Manu to Modi*, Hachette India, 2019.

Chakravorty, Sanjoy, Devesh Kapur and Mirvikar Singh, *The Other One Percent: Indians in America*, Oxford University Press, 2016.

Chatterjee, Kaushiki, 'Dowry—the shame lives on', *Deccan Herald*, 22 June 2019. https://www.deccanherald.com/specials/dowry-the-shame-lives-on-742126.html.

Chiplunkar, Gaurav and Jeffrey Weaver, 'Marriage Markets and the Rise of Dowry in India', University of Virginia and University of Southern California, 23 June 2019. https://gauravchiplunkar.com/wp-content/uploads/2019/06/Chiplunkar-Weaver-Dowry_public-draft.pdf.

Chowdhary, N. and V. Patel, 'The Effect of Spousal Violence On Women's Health: findings from the Stree Arogya Shodh in Goa, India', *Journal of Postgraduate Medicine*, vol. 54, no. 4, Oct–Dec 2008. https://pubmed.ncbi.nlm.nih.gov/18953151/.

Chowdhry, Prem, *Gender, Power and Identity: Essays on Masculinities in Rural North India*, New Delhi, Orient Black Swan, 2019.

Chowdhury, Aparajita, and Manoj Manjari Patnaik, 'Empowering Boys and Men to Achieve Gender Equality in India', *Journal of Developing Societies*, 26(4), 2010, pp. 455–471.

Chugh R. and S. Puri, 'Affluent adolescent girls of Delhi: Eating and weight concerns', *Br J Nutr*, 86, 2001, pp. 535–42.

Colucci, Erminia, M. O'Connor, K. Field, A. Baroni, R. Pryor and H. Minas, 'Nature of domestic/family violence and barriers to using services among Indian immigrant women', *Alterstice*, vol. 3, no. 2, 2013, pp. 9–26.

Crenshaw, Kimberlé, 'Mapping the Margins: Intersectionality, Identity Politics, and Violence Against Women of Color', *Stanford Law Review*, vol. 43, no. 6, 1991, pp. 1241–99. https://doi.org/10.2307/1229039.

Crozier, Georgie, 'Speech by Ms. Georgie Crozier MLC', Parliamentary Debates, (Hansard), Legislative Council. Fifty-Eighth Parliament. First Session. Book 10. 24, 25, 26 and 27, July 2018, Justice Legislation Amendment (Family Violence Protection and Other Matters) Bill 2018. Friday, 27 July 2018 Council, p. 3433. https://www.parliament.vic.gov.au/images/stories/daily-hansard/Council_2018/Council_Weekly_Jul-Sep_2018_Book_10.pdf.

Crozier-De Rosa, Sharon, 'As a peace loving warrior, might Wonder Woman unite feminists?', *The Conversation*, 7 June 2017. https://theconversation.com/as-a-peace-loving-warrior-might-wonder-woman-unite-feminists-78905.

Ctol News desk, 'Indian Government receives over 4,700 complaints from spouses abandoned by NRIs', *Connected to India*, 27 September 2019. https://www.connectedtoindia.com/indian-government-receives-over-4700-complaints-from-spouses-abandoned-by-nris-6279.html.

Cunningham, Mick, 'The Influence of Parental Attitudes and Behaviors on Children's Attitudes toward Gender and Household Labor in Early Adulthood', *Journal of Marriage and Family*, vol. 63, no. 1, February 2001. https://www.researchgate.net/publication/249405994_The_Influence_of_Parental_Attitudes_and_Behaviors_on_Children%27s_Attitudes_Toward_Gender_and_Household_Labor_in_Early_Adulthood.

Damodaran, Akhila, 'Sita not submissive but a strong-willed woman', *The New Indian Express,* 5 April 2017. https://www.newindianexpress.com/cities/chennai/2017/apr/05/sita-not-submissive-but-a-strong-willed-woman-1590321.html.

Dang, Geetika, Vani S. Kulkarni and Raghav Gaiha, 'Dowry Death or Murder', *The Sunday Guardian [online]*, 18 March 2018. https://www.pressreader.com/india/the-sunday-guardian/20180318/281870118968063.

Daruwalla, Nayreen, Surinder Jaswal, Prakash Fernandes, Preethi Pinto, Ketaki Hate, Gauri Ambavkar, Bhaskar Kakad, Lu Gram and David Osrin, 'A theory of change for community interventions to prevent domestic violence against women and girls in Mumbai, India', *Wellcome Open Research* vol. 4, no. 54, 21 August 2019. doi:10.12688/wellcomeopenres.15128.2.

Das, Sushi, *Deranged Marriage: A Memoir,* Random House Australia, 2012.

Datta, Archana, 'Abandoned by husband, not backed by law either', *The Tribune*, 24 March 2019. https://www.tribuneindia.com/news/archive/features/abandoned-by-husband-not-backed-by-law-either-746773

Datta, Runi, 'Emancipating and Strengthening Indian Women: An Analysis of B. R. Ambedkar's Contribution', *Contemporary Voice of Dalit*, 11(1), 2019, pp. 25–32.

Deccan Herald, 'Parliamentary standing committee approves bill on compulsory registration of NRI marriages', *Deccan Herald*, 13 March 2020. https://www.deccanherald.com/national/

parliamentary-standing-committee-approves-bill-on-compulsory-registration-of-nri-marriages-813485.html.

De Maio, John, Michelle Silbert, Mary Stathopoulos, Pilar Rioseco, Rebecca Jenkinson and Ben Edwards, 'Empowering migrant and refugee women: Supporting and empowering women beyond five-year post-settlement', Australian Institute of Family Studies, Research Report September 2017. https://aifs.gov.au/publications/empowering-migrant-and-refugee-women.

Denike, Margaret, 'The Devil's Insatiable Sex: A Genealogy of Evil Incarnate', *Hypatia*, 18(1), 2020, pp. 10–43. https://www.cambridge.org/core/journals/hypatia/article/abs/devils-insatiable-sex-a-genealogy-of-evil-incarnate/993E22AE84A47CDEAA91F17407EE2FFA.

Department of Social Services, *Fourth Action Plan: national plan to reduce violence against women and their children 2010–2022*, Canberra, 2019. https://www.dss.gov.au/sites/default/files/documents/08_2019/fourth_action-plan.pdf.

Desai, Sonalde, 'Doing Gender Vs. Doing Modernity', in M. Bhatia (ed.), *Locating Gender in the New Middle Class in India*, Shimla: Indian Institute of Advanced Study, 2017.

Dev Sanskriti Vishwavidyalaya, http://www.dsvv.ac.in.

Devi, Rajni, 'Marriage among Hindus with Special reference to Dowry', *IOSR Journal Of Humanities And Social Science*, vol. 20, no. 7, July 2015, pp. 01–09. http://www.iosrjournals.org/iosr-jhss/papers/Vol20-issue7/Version-6/A020760109.pdf.

de Zwart, Frank, 'The Logic of Affirmative Action: caste, class and quotas in India', *Acta Sociologica*, vol. 43 no. 3, September 2000. https://www.researchgate.net/publication/249770427_The_Logic_of_Affirmative_Action_Caste_Class_and_Quotas_in_India.

Dholakia, Utpal, 'Why Are So Many Indian Arranged Marriages Successful?', *Psychology Today*, 24 November 2015. https://www.psychologytoday.com/us/blog/the-science-behind-behavior/201511/why-are-so-many-indian-arranged-marriages-successful?page=1.

Dias, Avani, 'Activist captured "original" 1975 photo of Whitlam pouring sand into Lingiari's hand', *ABC News*, 3 September 2016. https://www.abc.net.au/news/2016-09-03/activist-took-original-gough-whitlam-vincent-lingiari-sand-photo/7805880.

Down To Earth, 'Less than a third BPL senior citizens benefit from old age pension scheme: Health ministry survey', *Down To Earth*, 8 January 2021. https://www.downtoearth.org.in/news/economy/less-than-a-third-bpl-senior-citizens-benefit-from-old-age-pension-scheme-health-ministry-survey-74962.

Dutt, Romesh C., *The Civilisation of India*, J.M. Dent, London, 1900. Available at Internet Archive, https://archive.org/details/civilizationofin00dutt/page/n5/mode/2up.

Dyal, J. and R. Y., 'Acculturation, stress and coping: Some implications for research and education', *International Journal of Intercultural Relations*, vol. 5, no. 4, 1981, pp. 301–328.

Easthope, Hazel, 'Fixed Identities in a Mobile World?: the relationship between mobility, place and identity', *Identities: Global Studies in Power and Culture*, vol. 16, no. 1, 8 January 2009. https://www.tandfonline.com/doi/abs/10.1080/10702890802605810.

Edvardsson, Kristina, Anna Axmon, Rhonda Powell, and Mary-Anne Davey, 'Male-biased Sex Ratios in Australian Migrant Populations: a population-based study of 1 191 250 births 1999–2015', *International Journal of Epidemiology*, 47(6), 2018. https://doi.org/10.1093/ije/dyy148.

Effective Change, *Evaluation of the Mutual Relational Respect Training Project*, Prepared for the Australasian Centre for Human Rights & Health, December 2019. https://www.achrh.org/wp-content/uploads/2020/06/Final-ACHRH-MRR-Training-Project-Report.pdf.

Eggeling, Julius (trans.), *The Satapatha Brahmana: sacred books of the East*, (vols. 12, 26, 24, 37, 47), published 1882–1900.

Email correspondence between author and anonymous person, 6 May 2020.

eSafety Commissioner, 'What is technology-facilitated abuse?', Australian Government, 2021. https://www.esafety.gov.au/key-issues/domestic-family-violence/technology-facilitated-abuse.

Evlin, Lin, 'Why did seven women die of suicide within months of each other?', *SBS News*, 2 June 2020. https://www.sbs.com.au/news/why-did-seven-women-from-one-area-of-melbourne-die-by-suicide-within-months-of-each-other.

Eye Movement Desensitization and Reprocessing Institute, Inc., 'What Is EMDR?', EMDR Inc., 2020. https://www.emdr.com/what-is-emdr/.

Family Court of Australia, 'Property and Finances After Separation', Family Court Australia, 3 May 2016. http://www.familycourt.gov.au/wps/wcm/connect/fcoaweb/family-law-matters/property-and-finance/property-and-money-after-separation/property-and-finances-after-separation.

Family Violence Protection Act 2008, 'Section 5, meaning of family violence', Victorian Current Acts. http://www5.austlii.edu.au/au/legis/vic/consol_act/fvpa2008283/s5.html.

Fleischmanm, Alexandra, 'Suicide Prevention from a Global Perspective', Department of Mental Health and Substance Abuse, World Health Organization, May 2016. https://www.paho.org/hq/dmdocuments/2016/1-WHO-global-perspective-of-suicide.pdf.

Flood, Michael, 'Inside the "man box": how rigid ideas of "manning up" harm young men and those around them', *The Conversation*, 20 July 2020. https://theconversation.com/inside-the-man-box-how-rigid-ideas-of-manning-up-harm-young-men-and-those-around-them-143081.

Fongay, Peter and Mary Target, 'Attachment and Reflective Function: their role in self-organization', *Development and Psychopathology*, vol. 9, no. 4, 1997. https://www.researchgate.net/publication/13781713_Attachment_and_reflective_function_Their_role_in_self-organization.

Ford, Julian D., 'Neurobiology of Stress Disorders and Their Impact on Physical Health', *Posttraumatic Stress Disorder*, Academic Press, 2009. https://www.sciencedirect.com/topics/psychology/stress-response-system.

Fu, Alyssa S. and Hazel Rose Markus, 'My Mother and Me: Why Tiger Mothers Motivate Asian Americans But Not European Americans', *Personality and Social Psychology Bulletin*, vol. 40, no. 6, 2014, pp. 739–749.

Galtung, Johan, 'Violence, Peace, and Peace Research', *Journal of Peace Research*, vol. 6, no. 3, 1969, pp. 167–191. https://www.jstor.org/stable/422690.

Ganguly-Scrase, Ruchira, 'Paradoxes of Globalization, Liberalization, and Gender Equality: The Worldviews of the Lower Middle Class in West Bengal, India', *Gender & Society*, 17(4), 2003, pp. 544–566.

García-Moreno, Claudia and Avni Amin, 'Perspectives: the sustainable development goals, violence and women's and children's health',

*Bulletin of the World Health Organization,* vol. 94, no. 5, 2016, pp. 396–397. https://doi.org/10.2471/BLT.16.172205

Garvan Institute of Medical Research, 'Anorexia Nervosa', 2021. https://www.garvan.org.au/research/diseases/anorexia.

Ghosh, Biswajit, 'How Does the Legal Framework Protect Victims of Dowry and Domestic Violence in India? A Critical Review', *Aggression and Violent Behaviour,* vol. 18, no. 4, July 2013. https://www.sciencedirect.com/science/article/abs/pii/S135917891300027X.

Ghosh, Sreyashi, 'Manusmriti: the ultimate guide to becoming a "good woman"', *Feminism in India* (FII), 11 January 2018. https://feminisminindia.com/2018/01/11/manusmriti-ultimate-guide-good-woman/.

Gibson, Mandy, J Stuart, S Leske, R Ward, and R Tanton. 'Suicide rates for young Aboriginal and Torres Strait Islander people: the influence of community level cultural connectedness', *Med J Aust* vol. 214, no. 11, 2021. https://doi.org/10.5694/mja2.51084.

Greer, Germaine, *The Female Eunuch,* HarperCollins, 1970.

Griffith, Ralph T.H. (trans.), *The Rig Veda: Book 2,* Classic Century Works, 2012.

Guha, Brishti, 'Ancient India's liberated women: in classical times India was more egalitarian than the West – at least in women's education', *The Times of India,* 13 July 2015.

Gupta, Bina, 'Modernity and the Hindu Extended Family System: a problematic interaction', [conference presentation], Unity of the Sciences 18th Annual Conference, Seoul Korea, 23–26 August 1991. https://icus.org/wp-content/uploads/2017/04/Gupta-Bina-Modernity-and-the-Hindu-Extended-Family-System-A-Problematic-Interaction.pdf.

Gupta, Taveeshi and Erin K. Fletcher, *Child Marriage in South Asia: An Evidence Review,* UNFPA and UNICEF, 2019. https://www.unicef.org/rosa/media/4251/file/Child%20Marriage%20Evidence%20Review_Web.pdf.

Gye, Hugo, 'Australian doctor could be struck off after refusing to carry out abortion on woman who didn't want to have a girl', *Daily Mail,* 9 October 2013. https://www.dailymail.co.uk/news/article-2449568/Doctor-Mark-Hobart-struck-refusing-abortion.html.

Han, Shihui and Yina Ma, 'Cultural Differences in Human Brain Activity: a quantitative meta-analysis', *NeuroImage*, 29 May 2014.

Han, Yuchen, 'The politics of kitchen work: Co-production of a retired man's "hegemonic masculinity" during the COVID-19 quarantine', *Gender, Work & Organization,* 28(5), 2021, pp. 1876–1884.

Hanifie, Sowaibah, 'Domestic Violence Support Services Want More Protection For Women On Temporary Visas', *ABC News (Australia)*, 5 October 2018. https://www.abc.net.au/news/2018-10-03/domestic-violence-groups-groups-want-update-to-legislation/10324338.

Health and Human Services, 'Men's Behaviour Change Program Resources', Children, Youth, and Families, Victoria State Government, Melbourne, 2021. https://providers.dhhs.vic.gov.au/mens-behaviour-change-program.

Hildebrand, Vera, '"They Became Soldiers For…Their Own Liberty": why women joined Subhas Chandra Bose's Rani of Jhansi Regiment', *Caravan*, 26 December 2016. https://caravanmagazine.in/vantage/women-bose-rani-jhansi-regiment.

Hill, Jess. *See What You Made Me Do: Power, Control and Domestic Abuse.* Black Inc., 2019.

Hill, Nicole T. M., Katrina Witt, Gowri Rajaram, Patrick D. McGorry and Jo Robinson, 'Suicide by young Australians, 2006–2015: a cross-sectional analysis of national coronial data', *The Medical Journal of Australia,* vol 214, no. 3, 2021, pp.133–139. https://www.mja.com.au/journal/2021/214/3/suicide-young-australians-2006-2015-cross-sectional-analysis-national-coronial.

Hoeffler, Anke, and James Fearson, 'Conflict and Violence Assessment Paper: benefits and costs of the conflict and violence targets for the post-2015 development agenda', *Copenhagen Conesus Centre*, 22 August, 2014. https://www.copenhagenconsensus.com/sites/default/files/conflict_assessment_-_hoeffler_and_fearon.pdf.

Horney, Karen, *Feminine Psychology,* W.W. Norton & Company, Inc., New York, 1967.

Huang, Chih-Mao, Robert Doole, Changwei W. Wu, Hsu-Wen Huang and Yi-Ping Chao, 'Culture-Related and Individual Differences in Regional Brain Volumes: a cross-cultural voxel-based morphometry study', *Frontiers In Human Neuroscience*, 10 September 2019. https://www.frontiersin.org/articles/10.3389/fnhum.2019.00313/full.

ICEF (International Consultants for Education and Fairs) Monitor, 'Australian international student enrolments up 11% through September 2019', ICEF, 18 Nov 2019. https://monitor.icef.com/2019/11/australian-international-student-enrolments-up-11-through-september-2019/

India State-Level Disease Burden Initiative Suicide Collaborators, 'Gender differentials and state variations in suicide deaths in India: The Global Burden of Disease Study 1990–2016', *The Lancet,* 3(10), 2018. https://doi.org/10.1016/S2468-2667(18)30138-5.

India Today, 'All about Rani Lakshmibai of Jhansi, the young queen who became an icon against the British Raj', *India Today*, 10 January 2019. https://www.indiatoday.in/education-today/gk-current-affairs/story/know-all-about-rani-lakshmibai-of-jhansi-born-as-manikarnika-tambe-1316804-2018-08-17.

Ineichen, Bernard, 'Suicide and attempted suicide among South Asians in England: who is at risk?', *Mental Health in Family Medicine*, 5(3), 2008, pp. 135–138.

International Center for Research on Women, and United Nations Children's Fund India, *District-Level Study on Child Marriage in India,* New Delhi, 2015.

International Labour Organization, 'What is Forced Labour, Modern Slavery and Human Tracking', International Labour Organization, 2021. https://www.ilo.org/global/topics/forced-labour/definition/lang--en/index.htm.

Irvine, Hannah, Michael Livingstone, Dr Michael Flood, John Armytage and Andrew Bunn, 'The Man Box: a study on being a young man in Australia', *The Men's Project,* Jesuit Social Services, Melbourne, 2018. https://jss.org.au/wp-content/uploads/2018/10/The-Man-Box-A-study-on-being-a-young-man-in-Australia.pdf.

Jack, Dana C. and Alisha Ali (eds.), *Silencing the Self Across Cultures: Depression and Gender in the Social World*, Oxford University Press, Oxford, 2010.

Jacobson, Doranne, 'Indian Society and Ways of Living. Organization of Social Life in India', *Asia Society Centre for Global Education*, 2004. https://asiasociety.org/education/indian-society-and-ways-living.

Jaffrelot, Christophe, 'The Fate of Secularism in India', *Carnegie Endowment for International Peace*, 4 April 2019. https://carnegieendowment.org/2019/04/04/fate-of-secularism-in-india-pub-78689.

Jain, Ritika, 'Abandoned by NRI Husbands, women move SC to restore strict anti-dowry law provisions', *The Print*, 22 November 2018. https://theprint.in/india/governance/abandoned-by-nri-husbands-women-move-sc-to-restore-strict-anti-dowry-law-provisions/152961/.

Jamieson, Audrey, 'Finding Into Death Without Inquest. Ms MH. Court reference COR 2019 3839', Coroner's Court of Victoria, Melbourne, 2019. https://www.coronerscourt.vic.gov.au/sites/default/files/2020-09/19%203839%20Redacted%20finding%20-%20Ms%20MH.pdf.

John, Neetu A., Kirsten Stoebenau, Samantha Ritter, Jeffrey Edmeades and Nikola Balvin, 'Gender Socialization during Adolescence in Low- and Middle-Income Countries: conceptualization, influences and outcomes', *Innocenti Discussion Paper 2017*, UNICEF Office of Research, Florence, March 2017. https://www.unicef-irc.org/publications/pdf/IDP_2017_01.pdf.

Jopson, Debra, 'Their terrifying last moments: a decade of domestic violence deaths in Hindu and Sikh communities', *ABC News [online]*, 19 December 2017. https://www.abc.net.au/news/2017-12-19/terrifying-last-moments-hindu-sikh-domestic-violence/9257808?nw=0

Kakar, Sudhir, *The Inner World: A Psychoanalytical Study of Childhood and Society in India*, New York–New Delhi, Oxford University Press, 1978.

Kalokhe, Ameeta, Carlos del Del Rio, Kristin Dunkle, Rob Stephenson, Nicholas Metheny, Anuradha Paranjape and Seema Sahay, 'Domestic Violence Against Women in India: a systematic review of a decade of quantitative studies', *Global Public Health*, vol. 12 no. 4, 15 July 2015. https://doi.org/10.1080/17441692.2015.1119293.

Kandiyoti, Deniz, 'Bargaining with Patriarchy', *Gender and Society*, vol. 2, no. 3, 1988, pp. 274–290. https://www.jstor.org/stable/190357.

Karmakar, Debashish, 'Bihar second in dowry deaths and murders: NCRB report', *The Times of India*, 23 October 2019. https://timesofindia.indiatimes.com/city/patna/bihar-second-in-dowry-deaths-and-murders-ncrb-report/articleshow/71710851.cms?utm_source=contentofinterest&utm_.

Kedia, Sapna, 'Case Study: men as key stakeholders in gender equity', *ALiGN: Advanced Learning and Innovation on Gender Norms,* 13 June 2019. https://www.alignplatform.org/resources/case-study-men-key-stakeholders-gender-equity#main-body.

Kishwar, Madhu Purnima, *Strategies for Combating the Culture of Dowry and Domestic Violence in India,* UN Division for the Advancement of Women, 2005. https://www.un.org/womenwatch/daw/egm/vaw-gp-2005/docs/experts/kishwar.dowry.pdf.

Kleinman, Rachel, 'Advocate Documents Family Violence Deaths in Victoria's Indian Community. *Sydney Morning Herald*, March 5, 2015. https://www.smh.com.au/national/advocate-documents-family-violence-deaths-in-victorias-indian-community-20150305-13w4vv.html.

Klostermaier, Klaus K., *Hinduism: A Short History*, Oneworld Publications, London, 2014.

Kumari, Ranjana, *Brides Are Not for Burning: Dowry Victims in India*, Radiant Publishers, New Delhi, 1989.

Kutin, Jozica, Mike Reid and Roslyn Russell, 'Revealed: the hidden problem of economic abuse in Australia, *The Conversation,* 2 March 2017. https://theconversation.com/revealed-the-hidden-problem-of-economic-abuse-in-australia-73764.

Lakra, Vinay, at the *United We Stand* filming on 8 October 2017. www.achrh.org.

Lal, Ruby, *Empress: the Astonishing Reign of Nur Jahan,* W. W. Norton & Company, New York, 2018.

Latrobe University, 'Gender Bias Leads to More Male Births', Latrobe University website, 12 August 2018. https://www.latrobe.edu.au/news/articles/2018/release/gender-bias-leads-to-more-male-births.

*The Law Code of Manu,* Patrick Olivelle (ed. and trans.), New York, Oxford University Press, 2004.

*The Laws of Manu,* Georg Bühler (ed. and trans.), Oxford, Clarendon Press, 1886. Available via Internet Archive, https://archive.org/details/lawsofmanu00bh/page/330/mode/2up.

Lee, Ruhi, *Good Indian Daughter,* Affirm Press, 2021.

Liddle, Joanna and Rama Joshi, 'Gender and Colonialism: women's organisation under the Raj', *Women's Studies International Forum*, 8(5), 1985.

—*Daughters of Independence: Gender, Caste and Class in India*, Zed Books, London, 1988.

Lifeline Australia, 'Suicide Statistics', 2021. https://www.lifeline.org.au/about-lifeline/lifeline-information/statistics-on-suicide-in-australia.

Lomborg, Bjørn, 'Why Domestic Violence Costs More Than War', *World Economic Forum,* 19 September 2014. https://www.weforum.org/agenda/2014/09/domestic-violence-cost-war-development-goals/.

MacNaughton, Glenda and Karina Davis, 'Beyond "Othering": Rethinking Approaches to Teaching Young Anglo-Australian Children about Indigenous Australians', *Contemporary Issues in Early Childhood,* vol. 2, no. 1, 2001, pp. 83–93. https://doi.org/10.2304%2Fciec.2001.2.1.10.

Maertens, Annemie and Amalavoyal Chari, 'What's Your Child Worth?: an analysis of expected dowry payments in rural India', *World Development,* vol. 130, June 2020. https://www.sciencedirect.com/science/article/abs/pii/S0305750X2030053X.

*Manusmriti with the Commentary of Medhatithi,* Ganganatha Jha, (trans.), Wisdom Library. https://www.wisdomlib.org/hinduism/book/manusmriti-with-the-commentary-of-medhatithi/d/doc200538.html.

Mateos-Aparicio, Pedro and Antonio Rodríguez-Moreno, 'The Impact of Studying Brain Plasticity', *Frontiers in Cellular Neuroscience,* vol. 13, 2019. https://doi.org/10.3389/fncel.2019.00066.

Mayer, Peter, 'India's falling sex ratios', *Population and Development Review,* vol. 25 no. 2, 1999. https://www.adelaide.edu.au/directory/peter.mayer?dsn=directory.file;field=data;id=37236;m=view.

McClelland, Anna, 'Just how much the average Australian wedding costs in 2018 will shock you', *Marie Claire,* 23 February 2018. https://www.marieclaire.com.au/average-australian-wedding-cost-2018.

Menon, Ramesh. *The Ramayana: A Modern Retelling of the Great Indian Epic,* McMillan, USA, 2004.

Ministry of External Affairs, Media Center, 'Question No. 575: Complaints by NRI brides', Government of India, New Delhi, 6 February 2019. https://www.mea.gov.in/lok-sabha.htm?dtl/30995/QUESTION+NO575+COMPLAINTS+BY+NRI+BRIDES.

Ministry of Human Resource Development, 'All India Survey on Higher Education 2018-19', Government of India, Department of Higher Education, New Delhi, 2019. https://ruralindiaonline.org/en/library/resource/all-india-survey-on-higher-education-2018-19/.

Mitchell, Austin M. & Suparna Soni, 'Institutional development and the dowry death curve across states in India', *Journal of International*

*Development, John Wiley & Sons, Ltd.,* vol. 33(6), August 2021, pp. 1026–1042.

Mohandoss, Anusa Arunachalam, 'A Study of Burden of Anorexia Nervosa in India – 2016', *Journal of Mental Health and Human Behaviour,* 23(1), 2018, pp. 25–32.

Monani, Devaki and Felicity Gerry, 'Dowry and its link to violence against women in India', *Issues in Legal Scholarship* 15(1), 2017, 1–13.

Morgan, Cassandra, 'Husband charged with murdering wife, six-year-old daughter in stabbing attack', *The Age,* 25 January 2022. https://www.theage.com.au/national/victoria/husband-charged-with-murdering-wife-six-year-old-daughter-in-stabbing-attack-20220119-p59pjw.html

Moylan, Carrie A., Todd I. Herrenkohl, Cindy Sousa, Emiko A. Tajima, Roy C. Herrenkohl and M. Jean Russo, 'The Effects of Child Abuse and Exposure to Domestic Violence on Adolescent Internalizing and Externalizing Behavior Problems', *Journal of Family Violence,* 25, no. 1, 2010. https://www.ncbi.nlm.nih.gov/pmc/articles/PMC2872483/.

Mukhoty, Ira, *Heroines: Powerful Indian Women of Myth and History,* Aleph Book Company, New Delhi, 2017.

Muralidharan, Arundhati, Jessica Fehringer, Sara Pappa, Elisabeth Rottach, Madhumita Das, and Mahua Mandal, 'Transforming Gender Norms, Roles, and Power Dynamics for Better Health: evidence from a systematic review of gender-integrated health programs in low- and middle-income countries', Public Health Foundation of India, Measure Evaluation, Futures Group, International Center for Research on Women, Health Policy Project, Washington DC, 2015.

Nair, Sunil, 'In India suicide peaks in young people', *Times of India,* 10 September 2020. http://timesofindia.indiatimes.com/articleshow/78033732.cms?utm_source=contentofinterest&utm_medium=text&utm_campaign=cppst.

Nandy, Ashis, 'Defining a New Cosmopolitanism: Towards a Dialogue of Asian Civilisations', in Kuan-Hsing Chen (ed) *Trajectories: Inter-Asia Cultural Studies,* London, Routledge, 1998, pp.142–9.

Natak Vihar Community Participatory Theatre, AustralAsian Centre. https://www.achrh.org/natak-vihar/.

National Commission of Women, India, 'How to address issues related to Marriages of Indian Women to NRI/PIOs'. 22 December 2021. https://mea.gov.in/images/pdf/faq-marraiges-of-indianwomen.pdf.

National Crime Records Bureau, Ministry of Home Affairs, 'Crime in India 2016 Statistics'. http://ncrb.gov.in/StatPublications/CII/CII2016/pdfs/Crime%20Statistics%20-%202016.pdf.

Nayar, Sushila, and Kamla Mankekar (eds), *Women Pioneers in India's Renaissance, as I Remember Her: Contributions from Eminent Women of Present-day India*, National Book Trust India, New Delhi, 2002.

Nehru, Jawaharlal, *The Discovery of India,* The John Day Company, New York, 1946.

New Delhi TV, 'Dowry deaths make significant share of female killings in India', 27 November 2018. https://www.ndtv.com/india-news/dowry-deaths-make-significant-share-of-female-killings-in-india-report-1954056.

Ng, Sik Hung, Shihui Han, Lihua Mao and Julian C. L. Lai, 'Dynamic Bicultural Brains: fMRI study of their flexible neural representation of self and significant others in response to culture primes', *Asian Journal of Social Psychology,* 20 May 2010. https://onlinelibrary.wiley.com/doi/full/10.1111/j.1467-839X.2010.01303.x.

Nigram, Shalu, 'The Right to Information Act: Ten Years of Transparency or a Decade of Ambiguity', 31 August, 2015. Available at SSRN: https://ssrn.com/abstract=2653596 or http://dx.doi.org/10.2139/ssrn.2653596.

O'Connor, Manjula, 'Dowry-related Domestic Violence and Complex Posttraumatic Stress Disorder: a case study', *Australasian Journal of Psychiatry,* 28 March 2017. https://journals.sagepub.com/doi/abs/10.1177/1039856217700464.

—'Culturally Constructed Trauma Therapy for South Asian Family Violence Victim-survivors', Conference presentation, Break-out session, *International Domestic Violence and Health Conference 2018, University of Melbourne,* Tuesday 20 November 2018. https://www.saferfamilies.org.au/breakout-migrant

O'Connor, Manjula and Molina Asthana, 'Refusal to comply with dowry demands leads to dometic violence and death', Submission to VRCFV, 2015. http://rcfv.archive.royalcommission.vic.gov.au/getattachment/43B1945E-83EC-490D-B1F9-73B44B79CC2E/Australasian-Centre-for%C2%A0Human-Rights-and-Health.pdf.

O'Connor, Manjula and Samir Ibrahim, 'Suicidality and Family Violence in Australian Immigrant Women Presenting to Out-patient

Mental Health Settings', *Australasian Psychiatry*, vol. 26, no. 2, 2018, pp. 224–225.

O'Connor, Manjula and Erminia Colucci, 'Exploring domestic violence and social distress in Australian-Indian migrants through community theater', *Transcultural Psychiatry*, 4 September 2015. https://journals.sagepub.com/doi/10.1177/1363461515599327.

O'Connor M, Lee A. 'The health impacts of dowry abuse on South Asian communities in Australia', *Med J Aust* vol. 216 no. 1, 2022. doi: 10.5694/mja2.51358.

O'Connor, Rory C. and Olivia J. Kirtley, 'The Integrated Motivational–Volitional Model of Suicidal Behaviour', *Philosophical Transactions of the Royal Society*, 16 July 2018. https://royalsocietypublishing.org/doi/10.1098/rstb.2017.0268

O'Connor, Rory C. and Gwendolyn Portzky, 'The relationship between entrapment and suicidal behavior through the lens of the integrated motivational-volitional model of suicidal behaviour', *Current Opinion in Psychology,* vol 22, August 2018, pp. 12–17.

Øien-Ødegaard, C., L. J. Hauge and A. Reneflot, 'Marital status, educational attainment, and suicide risk: a Norwegian register-based population study', *Population Health Metrics,* vol. 19, no. 33, 2021. https://pophealthmetrics.biomedcentral.com/articles/10.1186/s12963-021-00263-2.

Oldenburg, Veena Talwar, *Dowry Murders: The Imperial Origins of a Cultural Crime*, Oxford University Press, Oxford, 2002.

Olivelle, Patrick, *Manu's Code of Law,* Oxford University Press, 2005.

Orygen News and Events, 'Rates of suicide continue to increase for young Australians', *Orygen*, 26 September 2019. https://www.orygen.org.au/About/News-And-Events/2019/Rates-of-suicide-continue-to-increase-for-young-Au

Our Watch, 'Quick Facts' https://www.ourwatch.org.au/quick-facts/ (viewed 19 December 2021).

Our Watch, 'Respectful relationships education in schools', Evidence Paper, 2021. https://media-cdn.ourwatch.org.au/wp-content/uploads/sites/2/2021/03/29130252/RRE-Evidence-paper-accessible-100321.pdf.

Pandey, Rekha, 'The History of Feminism and Doing Gender in India', *Revista Estudos Feministas,* 26(3), 2018. https://doi.org/10.1590/1806-9584-2018v26n358567.

Parikh, Samir, 'Relationship Stress and More: what's troubling our kids', *The Health Collective India*, 18 February, 2019. http://www.healthcollective.in/2019/02/relationship-stress-troubling-our-kids/.

Parker, Kim and Renee Stepler, 'Americans see men as the financial providers, even as women's contributions grow', *Pew Research Center*, 20 September 2017. https://www.pewresearch.org/fact-tank/2017/09/20/americans-see-men-as-the-financial-providers-even-as-womens-contributions-grow/.

Parliament of Australia, 'The practice of dowry and the incidence of dowry abuse in Australia', Parliamentary Business, Parliament House, Canberra. https://www.aph.gov.au/Parliamentary_Business/Committees/Senate/Legal_and_Constitutional_Affairs/DowryAbuse. Accessed 2021.

—'Report: the practice of dowry and the incidence of dowry abuse in Australia', Parliament House, Canberra, 14 February 2019. https://www.aph.gov.au/Parliamentary_Business/Committees/Senate/Legal_and_Constitutional_Affairs/DowryAbuse/Report.

Patel, Vikram and Arthur Kleinman, 'Poverty and Common Mental Disorders in Developing Countries', *Bulletin of the World Health Organization: the International Journal of Public Health*, vol. 81, no. 8, 2003. https://apps.who.int/iris/handle/10665/72028.

Paul, Madan C., *Dowry and Position of Women in India: A Study of Delhi Metropolis*, Inter-India Publications, New Delhi, 1986.

Pearlman, Jonathan, 'Australian man accused of stalking escapes conviction after blaming Bollywood', *The Telegraph*, London, 29 January 2015. https://www.telegraph.co.uk/news/worldnews/australiaandthepacific/australia/11377511/Australian-man-accused-of-stalking-escapes-conviction-after-blaming-Bollywood.html.

Pew Research Centre, 'Attitudes about caste', *Religion in India: Tolerance and Segregation*, 29 June 2021. https://www.pewforum.org/2021/06/29/attitudes-about-caste/.

Pillai, Manu, *The Ivory Throne: Chronicles of the House of Travancore*, HarperCollins, India, 2016.

Postmus, Judy L., Sara-Beth Plummer, Sarah McMahon and N. Shaanta Murshid, 'Understanding Economic Abuse in the Lives of Survivors', *Journal of Interpersonal Violence*, 2012.

Puthenveetil, Radhakrishnan, 'A deeper look at manusmriti to understand why students at JNU burned it in protest', *Society*, 24 March 2016. https://www.researchgate.net/

publication/314230861_A_Deeper_Look_At_Manusmriti_To_Understand_Why_Students_At_JNU_Burned_It_In_Protest.

Qu, Lixia, 'Families Then & Now: Households and families', Research Report, Australian Government, Australian Institute of Family Studies, July 2020. https://aifs.gov.au/publications/households-and-families.

Rahman, Shaikh Azizur, '"We decided to take a stand": why some Indian families are returning dowries', *The Guardian*, 5 June 2017. https://www.theguardian.com/global-development/2017/jun/05/take-a-stand-indian-families-returning-dowries-dahez-roko-abhiyan-campaign.

Rangarajan, Janani, Udayakumar Narasimhan, Abhinayaa Janakiraman, Prajitha Sasidharan and Pavithraa Chandrasekaran, 'Parenting Styles of Parents Who Had Children With and Without High Risk at Birth: A Cross-sectional Comparative Study', *Cureus,* vol. 12, no.2, 23 February 2020.

Rao, Priya, 'Who pays for the wedding?: a guide to cost splitting in 2019', *Vogue*, 23 October 2019. https://www.vogue.com/article/who-pays-for-the-wedding-etiquette-rules.

Rao, Vijayendra, 'The Economics of Dowries in India', Development Research Group, World Bank, 2016. http://vijayendrarao.org/papers/dowryecon.pdf.

Rautray, Samanwaya, 'Supreme Court Modifies Its Order On Dowry Harassment', *The Economic Times*, 15 September 2018. https://economictimes.indiatimes.com/news/politics-and-/supreme-court-modifies-its-order-on-dowry-harassment/articleshow/65806068.cms?from=mdr.

Rees, Susan, Derrick Silove, Tien Chey, Lorraine Ivancic, Zachary Steel, Mark Creamer, Maree Teesson, Richard Bryant, Alexander C McFarlane, Katherine L Mills, Tim Slade, Natacha Carragher, Meaghan O'Donnell and David Forbes, 'Lifetime prevalence of gender-based violence in women and the relationship with mental disorders and psychosocial function', *JAMA* 306, 2011, pp. 513–521.

Remes, Olivia, 'Women are far more anxious than men – here's the science', *The Conversation*, 10 June 2016. https://theconversation.com/women-are-far-more-anxious-than-men-heres-the-science-60458.

Roberts, Stuart, *Freedom and Fragmentation: images of independence, decolonization and partition at Cambridge University*, Cambridge Museums

Unboxed Exhibition, 1 August–27 October, 2017. https://www.cam.ac.uk/tryst_with_destiny#a-tryst-with-destiny-NkEaWAsnXj.

Rojak, Komal, 'The Hindu Code Bill—Babasaheb Ambedkar and his Contribution to Women's Rights in India', *Dalit History Month*, 17 April 2019. https://dalithistorymonth.medium.com/the-hindu-code-bill-babasaheb-ambedkar-and-his-contribution-to-womens-rights-in-india-872387c53758.

Roy, Arundhati, 'All the World's a Half-Built Dam', *Economic and Political Weekly*, 20(25), 2015, pp. 165–173.

Royal Australian and New Zealand College of Obstetricians and Gynaecologists, 'Gender Equity and Diversity Report', 2019. https://ranzcog.edu.au/RANZCOG_SITE/media/RANZCOG-MEDIA/Our%20College/Gender%20Equity%20and%20Diversity/Gender-Equity-and-Diversity-Report.pdf.

Royal Commission into Family Violence, 'Australasian Centre for Human Rights and Health Submission: refusal to comply with dowry leads to domestic violence and death', Royal Commission into Family Violence, 2015. http://rcfv.archive.royalcommission.vic.gov.au/getattachment/43B1945E-83EC-490D-B1F9-73B44B79CC2E/Australasian-Centre-for%C2%A0Human-Rights-and-Health.pdf.

Saini, Bhavya, 'Why do Indian women lie to their parents?', *She The People*, 20 June 2021. https://www.shethepeople.tv/point-toh-hai/indian-women-lie-to-parents/.

Sanchez, Giovana Romano, '10 ways to promote gender equality in daily life', *Believe Earth*, 20 December 2018. https://believe.earth/en/10-ways-to-promote-gender-equality-in-daily-life/.

Sanyal, Sanjeev, *The Indian Renaissance: India's Rise After A Thousand Years Of Decline*, Penguin Books, 2008.

Sasha R, 'Six Indian women who dedicated their lives to advancing feminism', HERSTORY, 23 March 2019. https://yourstory.com/herstory/2019/03/indian-feminist-icons-history/amp.

Schultz, Kai, 'India's widows, abused at home, have sought refuge in this holy city for centuries', *New York Times*, 27 August 2019. https://www.nytimes.com/2019/08/27/world/asia/india-women-widows.html.

Segrave, Marie, *Temporary Migration and Family Violence: An Analysis of Victimisation, Vulnerability and Support*, Monash University, 2017.

Sen, Amartya, *The Argumentative Indian: Writings on Indian History, Culture and Identity*, Allen Lane, 2005.
Senate Legal and Constitutional Affairs References Committee, Parliament of Australia, 'The Practice of Dowry and Incidence of Dowry Abuse in Australia', *Australian Government*, Canberra, 2019. https://www.aph.gov.au/Parliamentary_Business/Committees/Senate/Legal_and_Constitutional_Affairs/DowryAbuse.
Sethi, Parizaad Khad, 'These women showcase the true diversity of Indian beauty', *Vogue India*, 2 November 2018. https://www.vogue.in/content/these-women-showcase-the-true-diversity-of-indian-beauty.
Sharma, Indira, Balram Pandit, Abhishek Pathak and Reet Sharma, 'Hinduism, Marriage and Mental Illness', *Indian Journal of Psychiatry*, vol. 55, no. 6, 2013, pp 243–249. doi: 10.4103/0019-5545.105544.
Sharma, Neetu Chandra, 'Sex ratio at birth improved by 16 points during the last six years', *Mint*, 24 January 2021. https://www.livemint.com/news/india/sex-ratio-at-birth-improved-by-16-points-during-the-last-six-years-govt-11611510090707.html.
Shinde, Sachin, Bernadette Pereira, Prachi Khandeparkar, Amit Sharma, George Patton, David A. Ross, Helen A. Weiss and Vikram Patel, 'The Development and Pilot Testing of a Multicomponent Health Promotion Intervention (SEHER) For Secondary Schools in Bihar, India', *Global Health Action*, vol. 10, no. 1, 8 November 2017. https://doi.org/10.1080/16549716.2017.1385284.
Shivji, Salimah, 'Burdened by debt and unable to eke out a living, many farmers in India turn to suicide', *CBC News*, 30 Mar 2021. https://www.cbc.ca/news/world/india-farmers-suicide-1.5968086.
Short, Emma, Sarah Linford, Jacqueline M. Wheatcroft and Carsten Maple, 'The Impact of Cyberstalking: the lived experience – a thematic analysis', *Studies in Health Technology and Informatics*, vol. 199, 2014. https://pubmed.ncbi.nlm.nih.gov/24875706/.
Singh, Manpreet K., 'Indian women are the largest migrant group in Australia to call family violence helpline', *SBS News Punjabi [online]*, 10 February 2017. https://www.sbs.com.au/language/english/indian-women-are-the-largest-migrant-group-in-australia-to-call-family-violence-helpline.
Singh, Renu and Uma Vennam, 'Factors Shaping Trajectories to Child and Early Marriage: evidence from young lives in India', *Young Lives*

*Working Paper 149*, 2016, p. 7. https://www.younglives.org.uk/sites/www.younglives.org.uk/files/YL-WP149-Trajectories%20to%20early%20Marriage.pdf.

Singh, Sneha, 'Honour Killings in India: Need For a Composite and Strict Legal Framework', *International Journal of Interdisciplinary and Multidisciplinary Studies* (IJIMS), vol. 4, no.3, 2017, pp. 276–283.

Singh, Supriya & Jasvinder Sidhu, 'Coercive control of money, dowry and remittances among Indian migrant women in Australia', *South Asian Diaspora* 12:1, 2020, pp. 35–50.

Sivakumar, I. and K. Manimekalai, 'Masculinity and Challenges for Women in Indian Culture', *Journal of International Women's Studies*, 22(5), 2021, pp. 427–436.

Smears, Ali, 'Mobilizing Shakti: Hindu goddesses and campaigns against gender-based violence', *Religions*, 10(6), 2019. https://doi.org/10.3390/rel10060381.

Smethhurst, Sue. 'Till death do us part', *Weekend Australian Magazine*, 2019. https://www.theaustralian.com.au/weekend-australian-magazine/dowry-death-and-despair-in-australias-indian-community/news-story/b49666d96ac623af5147d6d4edcce09e.

Snowdon, John, 'Indian Suicide Data: what do they mean?', *The Indian Journal of Medical Research*, vol. 150, no. 4, 29 November 2019. https://doi.org/10.4103/ijmr.IJMR_1367_19.

Squarcini, Federico, *Tradition, Veda and Law: Studies on South Asian Classical Intellectual Traditions*, Anthem Press, London, 2011.

Srinivas, M. N., *The Remembered Village*, Delhi, Oxford University Press, 1976.

Srinivasan, Sharda, 'Daughters or Dowries? The Changing Nature of Dowry Practice in South India', *World Bank,* April 2005, 33(4):593–615.

Statista, 'Median age of first time marriages in Australia from 1997–2018, by gender (in years)', November 2019. https://www.statista.com/statistics/610905/australia-first-time-marriage-median-age/.

Statista Research Department. 'Mean age at marriage in rural and urban India—by gender 2014', 20 June 2016. https://www.statista.com/statistics/678453/mean-age-at-marriage-by-gender-and-region-india/#:~:text=As%20per%20the%20results%20of,22%20years%20in%20rural%20areas.

Stott-Despoja, Natasha, 'Gender stereotypes that children absorb can shape attitudes and expectations into adulthood', *Our Watch*, 19 June 2017. https://www.ourwatch.org.au/resource/gender-stereotypes-that-children-absorb-can-shape-attitudes-and-expectations-into-adulthood/.

Tharoor, Shashi, *The British Empire in India*, Aleph Book Company, New Delhi, 2016; published in Australia as *Inglorious Empire: What the British Did to India*, Scribe, Melbourne, 2017.

The Economic Times, 'What is wrong in Manusmriti burning? JNU students to varsity', *The Economic Times*, 20 March 2016. https://economictimes.indiatimes.com/news/politics-and-nation/what-is-wrong-in-manusmriti-burning-jnu-students-to-varsity/articleshow/51499704.cms?from=mdr.

The Economist, 'Why dowries persist in South Asia', *The Economist, Asia Edition*, 16 May 2019. https://www.economist.com/asia/2019/05/16/why-dowries-persist-in-south-asia.

The Telegraph India Editorial Board, 'Educated women are a positive force in a nation', *The Telegraph [online]*, 27 September 2019. https://www.telegraphindia.com/opinion/educated-women-are-a-positive-force-in-a-nation/cid/1707754.

Thompson, E.H. and K. B. Langendoerfer, 'Older Men's Blueprint for "Being a Man"', *Men and Masculinities*, 19(2), 2015, p. 119.

Times of India, 'Women's most absurd beauty standards around the world', *Times of India*, 9 July 2021. https://timesofindia.indiatimes.com/life-style/beauty/womens-most-absurd-beauty-standards-around-the-world/articleshow/84133179.cms.

—'Supreme Court Declares It Illegal For Khap Panchayats to Stall Marriage Between Consenting Adults', *The Times of India*, 27 March 2018. https://timesofindia.indiatimes.com/india/supreme-court-declares-it-illegal-for-khap-panchayats-to-stall-marriage-between-consenting-adults/articleshow/63476839.cms.

TNN, 'Pranay Murder Case: Amrutha's dad, prime accused, kills himself', *Times of India*, 9 March 2020. https://timesofindia.indiatimes.com/city/hyderabad/pranay-murder-case-amruthas-dad-prime-accused-kills-himself/articleshow/74543825.cms?utm_source=contentofinterest&utm_medium=text&utm_campaign=cppst.

—'Why Joint Families Are Back in Urban India', *Times of India*, Jul 16, 2017. https://timesofindia.indiatimes.com/home/sunday-times/why-joint-families-are-back-in-urban-india/articleshow/59614752.cms.

Ugargol, Allen Prabhaker and Ajay Bailey, 'Family Caregiving for Older Adults: gendered roles and caregiver burden in emigrant households of Kerala, India', *Asian Population Studies*, vol. 14, no. 2, 2018. https://www.tandfonline.com/doi/full/10.1080/17441730.2017.1412593

United Nations, 'Gender Equality: women's economic empowerment', *UN India Business Forum*, 2018. https://in.one.un.org/unibf/gender-equality/.

—'Take Action for the Sustainable Development Goals', *UN Sustainable Development Goals*, New York, 2020. https://www.un.org/sustainabledevelopment/sustainable-development-goals/.

—'Goal 5: Achieve gender equality and empower all women and girls', *UN Sustainable Development Goals*, 2021. https://www.un.org/sustainabledevelopment/gender-equality/.

United Nations Office on Drugs and Crime, 'Global Study On Homicide: gender-related killing of women and girls', United Nations Office of Drugs and Crime, Vienna, 2018, pp. 10 and 32. https://www.unodc.org/documents/data-and-analysis/GSH2018/GSH18_Gender-related_killing_of_women_and_girls.pdf.

UN Women, 'Facts and Figures: Economic Empowerment', *UN Women*, 2021. https://www.unwomen.org/en/what-we-do/economic-empowerment/facts-and-figures.

—'New UN Women report uncovers significant gaps for women's empowerment and puts forth robust agenda to shift gears', *UN Women*, 15 February 2018. https://unwomen.org.au/new-un-women-report-uncovers-significant-gaps-for-womens-empowerment-and-puts-forth-robust-agenda-to-shift-gears/.

Various authors, *Celebrate! Dussehra & Durga Puja*, Hachette, India, 2011.

Venkatraman, Shai, 'Every Life Counts: how young boys bear the burden of patriarchy in India', *New Delhi TV Limited (NDTV)*, 4 November 2016. https://everylifecounts.ndtv.com/how-young-boys-bear-the-burden-of-patriarchy-in-india-6556.

VicHealth, 'The Health Costs of Violence: measuring the burden of disease caused by intimate partner violence', Victorian Health

Promotion Foundation, 6 January 2004. https://www.vichealth.vic. gov.au/media-and-resources/publications/the-health-costs-of-violence.
—'Ethnic and Race-based Discrimination: as a determinant of mental health and wellbeing', *VicHealth Research Summary 3*, August 2008. https://www.vichealth.vic.gov.au/-/media/ProgramsandProjects/ Publications/Attachments/ResearchSummary_Discrimination.pdf?la= en&hash=BD183D8A923712D3205C7A77ACBCFAB160639DF3
Victorian Numbered Acts, 'Assisted Reproductive Treatment Act 2008 (no. 76 of 2008)', Australian Legal Information Institute, UTS and UNSW. http://classic.austlii.edu.au/au/legis/vic/num_act/ arta200876o2008406/.
Victorian Royal Commission into Family Violence, *Report 2016*, Volume 5, Melbourne. http://www.rcfv.com.au/MediaLibraries/ RCFamilyViolence/Reports/Final/RCFV-Vol-V.pdf.
Victorian State Government, 'Funded Projects to Prevent Elder Abuse', Health Victoria, Melbourne, 18 June 2018. https://www2.health. vic.gov.au/ageing-and-aged-care/wellbeing-and-participation/ preventing-elder-abuse/funded-projects-to-prevent-elder-abuse.
—'Promoting mental health and wellbeing in your school', Department of Education and Training, 7 October 2021. https://www.education. vic.gov.au/school/teachers/health/mentalhealth/Pages/promoting-mental-health.aspx.
Vijayakumar, Lakshmi, 'Suicide in Women', *Indian Journal of Psychiatry*, vol. 57, no. 6, 27 July 2015. https://doi.org/10.4103/0019-5545. 161484
Vyas, Maulik, 'What is leading to the growing number of divorces in Mumbai', *The Economic Times/Panache*, 4 July 2015. https:// economictimes.indiatimes.com/articleshow/47937469.cms?utm_ source=contentofinterest&utm_medium=text&utm_campaign=cppst.
Webster, K, K. Diemer, N. Honey, S. Mannix, J. Mickle, J. Morgan, A. Parkes, V. Politoff, A. Powell, J. Stubbs, and A. Ward, *'Australians' Attitudes to Violence Against Women and Gender Equality: findings from the 2017 national community attitudes towards violence against women survey (NCAS)*, Sydney, 2018. https://ncas.anrows.org.au/wp-content/ uploads/2018/11/NCAS-report-2018.pdf.
Weiyuan, Cui, 'Women and suicide in rural China', *Bulletin of the World Health Organization*, vol. 87, no.12, 2009, pp. 888–9.

White, Sarah C., 'Patriarchal Investments: marriage, dowry and the political economy of development in Bangladesh', *Journal of Contemporary Asia*, vol. 47, no. 2, 18 October 2016, pp. 247–272. https://www.tandfonline.com/doi/full/10.1080/00472336.2016.1239271.
Wilcox, W. Bradford, 'The Evolution of Divorce', *National Affairs*, no. 45, Fall 2020. https://www.nationalaffairs.com/publications/detail/the-evolution-of-divorce.
Williams, Gabrielle, 'Speech by Ms. Gabrielle Williams MP', Parliament of Victoria, Parliamentary Debates (Hansard), Legislative Assembly, Fifty-eighth Parliament, First Session, Extract from Book 8, 20 June 2018, p. 2116. https://www.parliament.vic.gov.au/images/stories/daily-hansard/Assembly_2018/Assembly_Daily_Extract_Wednesday_20_June_2018_from_Book_8.pdf.
World Bank Group, 'Working for Women in India', 19 March 2019. https://www.worldbank.org/en/news/feature/2019/03/08/working-for-women-in-india.
World Economic Forum, 'The Global Gender Gap Report 2018', Switzerland, 2018. http://www3.weforum.org/docs/WEF_GGGR_2018.pdf.
—'Global Gender Gap Report 2020', Switzerland, 2019. http://www3.weforum.org/docs/WEF_GGGR_2020.pdf.
—'Mind the Hundred Year Gap', *World Economic Forum Report*, 16 December 2019. https://www.weforum.org/reports/gender-gap-2020-report-100-years-pay-equality.
World Health Organization, 'Summary', *Global Campaign for Violence Prevention: world report on violence and health*, World Health Organization, Geneva, 2002. https://www.who.int/violenceprevention/approach/ecology/en/.
—*Preventing Suicide: A global imperative,* World Health Organization, Geneva, 17 August 2014. https://www.who.int/publications/i/item/9789241564779.
—*Promoting Mental Health: Concepts Emerging Evidence Practice,* World Health Organization, Department of Mental Health and Substance Abuse in collaboration with the Victorian Health Promotion Foundation and The University of Melbourne, 2005. https://www.who.int/mental_health/evidence/MH_Promotion_Book.pdf.

—*WHO's contribution to the World Conference against Racism, Racial Discrimination, Xenophobia and Related Intolerance: Health and freedom from discrimination,* World Health Organization, 2001. https://apps.who.int/iris/handle/10665/66891.

—'Promoting Gender Equality to Prevent Violence Against Women', *World Health Organization,* 2009. https://www.who.int/violence_injury_prevention/violence/gender.pdf.

Younger, Emma, 'When police misjudge domestic violence, victims are slapped with intervention order applications', *ABC Digital News,* 15 August 2018. https://www.abc.net.au/news/2018-08-15/domestic-violence-victims-mistaken-for-perpetrators/10120240.

Yu, Rongjun, 'Stress Potentiates Decision Biases: a stress induced deliberation-to-intuition (SIDI) model', *Neurobiology of Stress,* vol 3, June 2016.

101 East, 'Australia's Dowry Deaths', *Aljazeera News [online],* 20 June 2017. https://www.aljazeera.com/program/101-east/2017/6/30/australias-dowry-deaths.

# Index

1800RESPECT call centre 79

abortion, sex selection via 214–15
acculturation 210
adolescence, development in 135
Akbar (king) 15
Alberuni 129
Alka (client), enslaved by husband 150–1
Ambedkar, BR 19
*ardhangini* 9, 107–8, 200
*The Argumentative Indian* 2, 8
arranged marriages
 advertising for 133
 lack of disclosure in 69–70
 prevalence of 44, 48, 223–4
Arti (client), post-traumatic stress disorder 158–60
Aruna (client), traumatised by abuse 151–4
AustralAsian Centre for Human Rights and Health
 Mutual Relational Respect workshops 163, 187, 191, 211
 national survey of dowry abuse 221–2
 petition to recognise dowry abuse in law 89
 research projects 213
 United We Stand project 98, 211
 working for Federal government to protect victims 153
Australia
 allows permanent residency for abuse victims 160
 countering dowry abuse 212–22
 eating disorders in 22
 elderly parents migrating to 123–4
 failing victims of domestic abuse 153
 family violence in 5–6, 21
 immigration system 69–70, 77
 literacy rates 180
 migrant brides abandoned after arrival 63–7

migrant support services 143
 patriarchal culture in 42
 political representation of women 21
 racism in 208
 rising divorce rate 44–5
 South Asian women travelling to 3–4
 suicide rates 164
 women's age at marriage 54
 women's rights in 6–7
*Australian Women's Weekly* 42
*Australia's Dowry Deaths* 88–9, 220
autonomy for young women 175–6
Ayesha (client) 102–4, 106–7, 116

Bader, Clarisse 14
Baillieu, Ted 191, 218
Balia, Sandeep 200–1
'Baraat' procession 51–2
Barlow, Dr 184
behavioural paralysis 148
Beijing Declaration and Platform 220
Beti Bachao Beti Padao campaign 20
Bihar
 Buddhist University Nalanda 174
 dowry deaths in 57–8
Bīrūnī, Muḥammad ibn Aḥmad 56
Bose, Subhas Chandra 18
Brahmin caste
 as desirable husbands 46
 dowry customs begin in 47
 original status 129
 writings by 16–17
brain structure, influenced by upbringing 170
Britain
 codifies caste system 129
 colonial rule over India 16–18, 207
Buddhism, women practitioners 13
Buhler, George 127–8
Burney, Linda 220

Campbell, Christine 214
caste system *see also* Brahmin caste
  interaction with patriarchy 199–200
  marriages within 48
  significance of 129–44
Champions of Change Coalition 185–6
Chattopadhyay, Kamala Devi 6
children
  inculcating gender norms 186–8
  learning to eat 169–70
China, declining suicide rates 164
Chinese families in Australia, sex-selective abortions 214
Christianity, attitudes to women 14
*The Civilization of India* 25
Convention on the Elimination of All Forms of Discrimination Against Women 109
Cowan, Edith 6
Crenshaw, Kimberlé 208–9
Crozier, Georgie 218
cybercrime, domestic abuse via 149–50

Dalits 12
Das, Sushi 186–7
Datta O'Connor, Manjula (author)
  at DSVV University 7–9, 168–9, 193–4
  college entrance interview 38–9
  early education 184–5
  early married life 61
  family background 130–1, 136–7
  family history 11–12
  family life 27–31
  family pressures on 165–7
  first wedding 58
  migrates to Australia 42–3
  move to Australia 3–4
  parents' and aunts' weddings 55
  relations with father 38–42, 118–19
  relations with grandmother 202–3
  relations with mother 30–1, 42
  uncle's visitor 196–8
Delhi, cost of dowries in 46–7
Department of Home Affairs (Australia), extradition policy 80

Dera Ismail Khan province 11–12
Dev Sanskriti Vishwavidyalaya 7–8, 168–9
*Devdas* (film) 143
discrimination *see* gender equality; racism
divorce *see* separation and divorce
Divya Prem Sewa Mission 8
domestic violence *see* family violence
dowries
  ceremonial transfer 51
  cost of providing 45–6
  economic consequences 52
  'faked' claims for 83–4
  history of 46–7
  increasing demands for 94
  reasons for paying 91–4
  repayment of 80–1
  used to enrich husbands 71
dowry abuse *see also* honour killings
  countering 212–22
  dowry deaths 46–7, 57–8, 87–91
  financial abuse 110, 112–13
  not recognised in *Family Law Act* 81–2
  psychological effects 148–9, 159
  surveillance and confinement 149–50
DSVV University 193–4
Durga (client), abused after marriage and migration 68
Durga (goddess) 2
Dutt, RD 25

East India Company 16
economic abuse *see* dowries; financial abuse
education
  as key to equality 177
  marital disparities in 67
  role in preventing domestic violence 95
engagement ceremony 50
Epping (Vic), suicide cluster in 163
Erikson, Erik 135
extended household living arrangements, South Asian families 122

Eye Movement Desensitization and
    Reprocessing  160

*Family Law Act 1975* (Cth)  44–5
Family Law system
    policy on dowry payments  80
    proposed reforms  219
family violence
    after marriage and migration  63,
        67–9, 74
    dowry demands not recognised as
        81
    economic costs of  23
    effect on mental health  145–56
    financial abuse as  113–15
    from other family members  131–2
    global cost of  154
    in Australia  5–6, 21
    incidence of  178
    men not interested in learning about
        94
    migrant families in Australia  32–4,
        134–5
    murders and suicides  215–16
    *Natak Vihar* project  72, 107–8, 221
    secretiveness and  76–7
    victims misidentified as perpetrators
        204
fathers
    abusive towards daughters  172–3
    estrangement due to inter-caste
        marriage  139–42
    role modelling by  120–1
*The Female Eunuch*  43
financial abuse
    as domestic violence  113–15
    dowry abuse  110, 112–13

Galtung, Johan  37, 223
Gandhi, Mahatma  12, 18
Gargi (philosopher)  13
gender equality
    cultural opposition to  83
    education key to  177
    failure of laws in India  59
    tertiary education in  193–4
    United Nations on  124
Gender Equity Movement in Schools
    200
gender norms
    development of  186–7
    role modelling for  120–1
gender pay gap, closure of  21, 177, 210
*ghar jawaii*  73
Godara, Ashok Kumar  89–91, 115–16
Godara, Deepshikha, murdered for
    dowry  88–90
Goldstein, Vida  6
government support for migrants
    209–10
Green, Danielle  218
Greer, Germaine  43
Griha Pravesh ritual  62
Gupta, Bina  29
Gupta Empire  226
Guterres, António  109

Harmony Alliance  221–2
Hill, Julian  220
Hindu Code  19
Hobart, Mark  214–15
honour killings  131–3, 136, 140–1
house painter, dowry obligations  45–6,
    58–60
hybrid identity  193
hyper masculinity  200
hypergamy  44 *see also* arranged
    marriages

*Identity: Youth and Crisis*  135
immigration law, proposed reforms  219
Ina E (client)  62–3, 65
Independence Day (India), speeches at
    12–13
India
    Australian students from  209
    economic position of women  23
    gender equity in  179–80
    gender imbalance in  224
    historical development  16

migration to Australia from 209, 213
  suicide rates in 162–5
Indian culture
  attempts to change behaviour 34–5
  child raising methods 171–4
  enabling change 174–5
  family's role in suicide 171
  gender norms in 186–91
  incidence of domestic violence 178
  male self-images 25–8, 31–2
  masculinity in 194–211
  women stalked 201
Indian National Army 18
Indian National Commission for Women 71–2, 78
Indian Penal Code, on dowry deaths 87
Indian women *see also* South Asian women
  abandoned by husbands 78–9
  age at marriage 54
  arranged marriages for 44
  arrival at husband's home 62
  child raising by 183
  cosmetic pressures on 22–3
  early equality 13
  eating disorders 22
  education of undervalued 184–5
  family pressure to remain in unhappy marriages 99–103
  ideals of family 29–30
  increasing financial independence 82–3
  legal status codified 17
  modern status 25–6, 29–30
  preference for male children 19–20
  prevented from contacting families 20
  seen as inferior to men 118–21
  sex-selective abortions 214
  single status seen as disadvantaged 101–2
  social identity process 136
  struggle against colonial rule 17–19
  telecommunicate with migrant children 201–3
International Labour Organization, on slavery 150

Jahangir (emperor) 14–15
*Jati see* caste system
Jats sub-caste 129
jewellery taken by mothers-in-law 53, 70–1
Jhansi, Rani of 17
John and Mary (clients) 34, 37
June (author's mother-in-law) 42–3, 61
*Justice Legislation Amendment (Family Violence Protection and Other Matters) Act 2018* (Vic) 216–18

Kakkar, Sudhir 203
Kamla (maid) 178–80, 183
Kandiyoti, Deniz 3, 73, 180–1
Kangna Kholna ceremony 52–3
Kanyadaan ceremony 224
Kaur, Amrit 6
Kerala 17
Khan, Mr 200
Khap Panchayat councils 131
Krishnan (client's husband) 134–7, 206
*kshatriya see* Brahmin caste
Kumari, Ranjana 85–6

Lakra, Vinay 183
Laushika (client), abandoned by husband 63–4
*Laws of Manu see* Manusmriti laws
Lee, Mary 6
Lehmann, Damian 163

'man box' or 'man prison' 31, 199
Manavdhramashtra, quote from 97
Manusmriti laws
  caste system in 127–8
  creation of 14
  on control over women 72
  on marital relations 97, 104–5, 108
  on patrilocation of wives 74
  positive aspects 109
  reimagining of 223–30
  unmarried women obliged to live with parents 21

written by and for Brahmins 16–17
marriage *see also* dowries; separation and divorce; weddings
  across caste system 129–44
  attempts by family to prevent 131–3
  Australian vs South Asian expectations 77
  perceived as permanent 35–6
  protective factor against suicide 175
masculinity, in Indian culture 25–8, 31–2, 194–211
Maulana Azad Medical College, author studies at 39
Maya (client) 131–3
medication for depression and anxiety 152–3, 157
Melbourne, dowry deaths in 87–8
men, bias in favour of 118–20
Men's Behaviour Change Programs 34–5, 172–3, 206
mental health
  effect of racism on 208
  prevalence of illness 153–4
  role ideals and 145
  role in suicide 171
Middle Eastern women, suicidal thoughts after suffering violence 155–7
migrant families in Australia *see also* non-resident Indian men
  communication with parents 201–3
  cultural changes in 193
  government support for 209–10
Mills, James 25
'Milni' ceremony 52
Ministry of External Affairs (India), response to desertion cases 79–80
Minni (client), abused by husband and mother-in-law 192
Mira (client), marries across caste boundaries 134–6
Mishra, Surya Prasad 8
Mohan (student), suicidal feelings 167–8, 174
mothers-in-law
  bride's jewellery taken by 53, 70–1
  critical of daughter-in-law 73–4
  death threats from 147
  dowry abuse by 86, 137, 158–9, 181–2
  husbands dependent on 203–4
MRI studies, cultural influences on brain structure 170–1
Mughal Empire 14–15
murders *see also* dowry abuse; honour killings
  by marital partners 1, 5–6, 85–6
  family violence 215–16
  for dowries 88–90
  of Indian student 5, 10
Mutual Cultural Respect 193
Mutual Relational Respect workshops
  educational role of 163
  insights from 191
  shifts in attitudes due to 211
  stories discussed at 125, 187, 215
Myma (client) 145–7, 205–6

Naidu, Sarojini 6, 18–19
narrative therapy 160–1
*Natak Vihar* project 72, 107–8, 221
National Crime Records Bureau (India), on dowry deaths 87
National Dowry Abuse Summit 191, 220
Nayar communities 17
Negar, Patel (author's uncle) 196–8
Nehru, Jawaharlal 8–9, 12–13, 18–19
Nehru, Kamla 18
Neru (client), abused by mother-in-law 203–5
neuroplasticity 176
Nina (client's daughter) 112–14, 116
Nirbhaya (student), rape and murder of 5, 10
NK, Dr (colleague) 133–4
non-resident Indian men
  bride's assets stolen by 113
  dependence on mothers 201–3
  risks in marrying 71–4
  seen as desirable husbands 47–8, 63–70
  spouses abandoned by 78–9

spouses of institutionally disadvantaged 77–8
wives abused by 181–2
wives murdered for dowries 87–90
Nur Jahan 15
Nutan (client) 99–100

Oldenburg, Veena Talwar 56–7
'othering' 186
Our Watch, on family violence 1
Over-Eye theory 106–7

Pakistan
  dowry customs 87–8
  life in disrupted by Partition 184–5, 196–8
  literacy rates 180
Pandit, Kamaladevi Vijaya Lakshmi 19
Pani vaarna ritual 62
Parvati (goddess) 9, 18
Patel, Vikram 164–5, 174
patriarchal culture
  awareness of 98
  disrupted by migration 86
  effect on men 198–9, 207
  in Australia 42
  in India 194
  sex-selective abortions in 215
  women's education disregarded 185
patrilocal customs
  abuse related to 33–4, 74
  effect on birth rates 59
  impact of 20–1
Phule, Savitribai 6
pornography, influence of 201
post-traumatic stress disorder *see* mental health
Pratt, Louise 220
*praya dhan* 125–6
Preeti (client) 32, 36
Pundits, training 194
Punjab
  desertion cases pending in 79
  early dowry customs 57
'purdah' system 15–16

racism
  in Australia 208
  in childhood 186
Radha (client), abused by husband and mother-in-law 181–2
Rakesh, Dr, marries across caste boundaries 140–2
Rama (god) 2
*Ramayana* 2
Ranade, Ramabai 6
Rani (client), abused by husband and mother-in-law 70–1, 75–6
Rani Jhansi Regiment 18
Rao, Damodar 17
rape *see also* sexual harassment and abuse
  of Indian student 5, 10
Reception ceremony 53
Reddy, Muthulakshmi 6
Reena (client) 99–100, 110–11, 116
'Refusal to Comply with Dowry Demands Contributes to Family Violence and Death in Victoria' 216
Rekha (client), abandoned by husband 78
resilience, teaching 173
Rig-Veda period 13, 49
Rima (second-generation migrant), attitude to dowry customs 93–5
Rokka ceremony 49–50
Roy, Raja Ram Mohan 16
Ruston, Anne 220

Samaj, Arya 12
Samya (student) 169
Sangeet ceremony 51
Sangeeta (neighbour), marries across caste boundaries 138–40
Sarasvati, Swami Dayananda 12
Saraswati (client) 148–9
Saraswati (goddess) 13
Sash (Indian man) 183–4
Satapatha Brahmana text 9
Satyagraha 12
Scott, Rose 6
secretiveness, related to domestic violence 76–7

self-perception, as part of family 170
Sen, Amartya 2
Senate Inquiry into the practice of dowry and incidence of dowry abuse 218–19
separation and divorce
 Australian divorce rate 44–5, 54
 difficulties with 35–6
 parents traumatised by 97–8
 stigma attached to 35–6, 77–8, 98–9
sex-selective abortions 214–15
sexual harassment and abuse
 by in-laws 104
 in Indian diaspora 18
 of boys 200
 of women in India 4–5, 10
sexuality, discussion of suppressed 40
Sharma, Poonam, murder of by husband 1
Sharma, Rekha 78
Sheela (neighbour) 85
Sheena (client), post-traumatic stress disorder 147–8
Shinde, Tarabai 6
Shiva (god) 9
Shivani (client), marries non-resident Indian 65–7
Shyam (client), abusive towards daughter 172–3
Singh, Ramsewak 96
Sinha, Purnima 6
Sita (client) 119–20
Sita (goddess) 2
slavery, domestic abuse via 150
sons see also men, bias in favour of
 family reliance on 121–3
South Asian cultures see also Indian culture
 child raising methods 173
 cultural uniqueness 1–3
 dowry-related abuse 91–3
 extended household living arrangements 122
 ideal self-images 25–6, 170
 strong male ties to mothers 205
 training in dowry abuse prevention 221–2

South Asian women see also Indian women
 as independent immigrants 107–8
 financial abuse of 113–15
 murdered for dowries 87–90
 parental restrictions on 186–7
 recovery from trauma 155–8
 suicide rates 162
spousal visas see non-resident Indian men
Status of Women Commission (India) 19–20
stigma attached to marital separation 98
Su Zhonghua 164
suicides
 conditions leading up to 162–76
 family's role in 171
 First Nations peoples in Australia 23
 Indian women in India 23
 of Indian women 1, 225
 regional rates of 162–4
 victims of domestic violence 155–6, 215–16
Sujatha (client), abused by mother-in-law 73–5
Supreme Court of India
 bans interference with consenting marriages 132–3
 petition by abandoned wives 79
 supports prohibition of dowries 84
Suri, Swati 125–6
Sustainable Development Goals 220

tertiary students, gender equality education 193–4
Therigatha 13
trauma therapy 152–3
Truth Still Alive group 80

UN Women 179, 188, 210
United Nations, on gender equality 124
United We Stand project 98, 189–92, 211
Universal Declaration of Human Rights 109

Upanishads 13
Uttar Pradesh, dowry deaths in 57–8

Valmiki 2
*vansh* 59
Vedas 12–13
VicHealth Scanlan Survey of racism 208
VicHealth study of domestic violence 154
Victoria
  Indian immigration to 213
  residents born overseas 208
Victoria, Heidi 218
Victorian Abortion Law Reform 215
Victorian Royal Commission Into Family Violence 216
Vidyasagar, Pandit 16
Vijay, Dr, marries across caste boundaries 141–2
violence against women *see* dowry abuse; family violence; murders
Vishnu (client), verbal abuse of wife 206–7

weddings *see also* dowries; marriage
  comparative costs of 54
  cost of borne by bride's parents 49–56
  traditional stages in 49–53
White, Sarah 47
Williams, Gabrielle 217–18
women *see also* Indian women; South Asian women
  labour force participation 177–8
World Bank projects 180
World Economic Forum Global Gender Gap Index 21, 177–9, 210
World Health Organization, on racism 208


Yesha (client), marries non-resident Indian 67–8
Yuchen Han 28